GRECO-ROMAN CITIES
OF AEGEAN TURKEY
HISTORY, ARCHAEOLOGY, ARCHITECTURE

YAYINLARI

GRECO-ROMAN CITIES OF AEGEAN TURKEY

HISTORY, ARCHAEOLOGY, ARCHITECTURE

Henry Matthews

YAYINLARI

EGE YAYINLARI

GRECO-ROMAN CITIES OF AEGEAN TURKEY
HISTORY, ARCHAEOLOGY, ARCHITECTURE
Henry Matthews

© 2014 Ege Yayınları & Henry Matthews
ISBN 978-605-4701-41-4
Publisher Certificate No: 14641

Copyediting
İnci Türkoğlu

Cover and Graphic Design
Aydın Tibet

Front Cover: Athena Temple, Priene
Back Cover: Trajan Temple, Pergamon

Printing
Oksijen Basım ve Matbaacılık San. Tic. Ltd. Şti.
100. Yıl Mah. Matbaacılar Sit. 2. Cad. No: 202/A Bağcılar - İstanbul/Türkiye
Tel: +90 (212) 325 71 25 Fax: +90 (212) 325 61 99
Certificate No: 29487

Production and Distribution
Zero Prodüksiyon
Kitap-Yayın-Dağıtım San. Ltd. Şti.
Abdullah Sokak, No: 17, Taksim, 34433 İstanbul/Türkiye
Tel: +90 (212) 244 7521 Fax: +90 (212) 244 3209
E.mail: info@zerobooksonline.com
www.zerobooksonline.com

www.egeyayinlari.com

TABLE OF CONTENTS

Author's Note

I first became fascinated by the Greek cities of Turkey as an architecture student at Cambridge. I studied and lectured on Greek and Roman architecture for many years before I travelled to Aegean Turkey. Then, standing among the ruins, I found that I needed a much fuller understanding of the history of the region and the details of the sites. George Bean's pioneering guide *Aegean Turkey* (1966) and Ekrem Agurgal's *Ancient Civilizations and Ruins of Turkey* (1970) were valuable companions as I toured the cities. When I returned home, I studied many volumes produced by archaeologists and read articles on the most recent discoveries, but I felt compelled to write the guide I wished I had had with me on my first trips.

My goal is to clarify the complex political and social history of the region and bring the architecture of twenty cities to life in as much detail as the reader can absorb while visiting. I could not have done so without the help of the authors mentioned above or the archaeologists whose years of expert work revealed the essential knowledge. They are too numerous to mention here but their works are listed in the Further Reading page at the end of this book. I thank many of them for permission to reproduce their drawings.

I am grateful to Brian Johnson who first suggested that I write this guide as well as İnci Türkoğlu who introduced me to Ege Publishers, gave me valuable advice and edited the book. Finally I express gratitude to my wife Susan Noyes Platt for her patience during my absences in Turkey, her participation in some of my trips there, and for valuable editorial suggestions.

Names of places and individuals in the classical world have been spelled in various ways by English speaking people; many Greek names ending in –os changed to –us in Latin. I have chosen the version that appears to be the most common.

Henry Matthews, Seattle 2014

Arches supporting vaults, built to level the space under the Temple of Trajan at Pergamon

INTRODUCTION

A journey down the Aegean coast of Turkey, through barren mountains and lush plains, invites us to broaden our perspective of the classical world. We can experience the surprisingly complete remains of Greek cities, largely undisturbed by modern intrusions, and see the striking contributions made by the Romans. In this book, I aim to provide travelers with sufficient historical and cultural background to bring these ancient places to life. The architecture and sculpture are still potent enough to evoke the brilliant civilizations that evolved there.

What does Greek and Roman culture mean to us?

Western civilization is deeply rooted in the worlds of ancient and classical Greece. The belief systems, mythology, philosophy, science, literature, art and architecture created in the Hellenic world are fundamental to our own culture. Greek scientists paved the way for our knowledge of astronomy, mathematics, physics, botany and medicine. Their texts, many of them preserved and translated by Arabs and Christians working together in the early middle ages, survived for centuries to provide the basis of modern science. Above all, the Greeks resonate with us today because they were deeply engaged in intellectual inquiry.

The Romans absorbed Greek mythology into their own traditions; they renamed the Greek gods and goddesses but accepted the essence of their original character. They believed that Aeneas, their legendary founder, came not from the Italian Peninsula, but from the region of Troy, as the grandson of the Greek goddess Aphrodite. The Romans admired Greek culture, emulating Greek art and architecture, but they added significantly to the architectural vocabulary, creating forms never envisioned before. While the Greeks invented the concept of democracy – they even gave us the word – the Romans codified laws that form the basis of modern western law. We may think of the Romans as cruel conquerors, but they actually inherited the Greek cities of Anatolia from a king of Pergamon, who ruled over them. They brought stability to the region and, on the whole, governed wisely. The Pax Romana, i.e. "Roman Peace", initiated by the Emperor Augustus, brought two hundred years of peace to the region.

The extent and character of the Hellenic world

Although people generally think of Athens as the principal source of Greek achievement, the creators of Greek poetry, art, science and scholarship lived throughout the Mediterranean from the shores of Spain in the west to the coast of Anatolia in the east. Aeolis and Ionia, areas of western Anatolia, as well as nearby islands such as Samos, Lesbos and Rhodes, thrived for centuries with a Greek ethos and way of life. It might surprise people to learn that Homer probably came from the Aeolian city of Smyrna (now Izmir), or that Thales, who has been called the founder of natural philosophy, and Pythagoras, famous for his mathematical theorem, were Ionian Greeks. Few of us realize that Aristotle lived for a while in Assos and married there. Galen of Pergamon advanced medical science far beyond any of his predecessors. Sculptors and architects excelled in the region; we can even find the origins of city planning and patent law there. Much of our knowledge of Hellenic history comes to us from Herodotus, a native of Halikarnassos, present-day Bodrum. Indeed the contributions to Hellenic civilization from the cities in the eastern Aegean are equal in significance to those from mainland Greece.

Such dispersal occurred because Greeks were a seafaring people with remarkable skills in shipbuilding and navigation. They traded adventurously with distant cities, both in luxury goods and staples. By the seventh century BCE Greek mariners were transporting grain from Sicily, Egypt and Black Sea ports, metals from Italy and Syria and delivering wine, oil and pottery to many destinations; they also transported slaves. Many city-states founded colonies with the aim of strengthening their trading opportunities, but also to settle in places, where their citizens could prosper. Athletes travelled long distances to compete in the Olympic Games; cities from Massalia in southern France to Miletus in Ionia sent delegations to the Oracle at Delphi seeking answers to burning questions. In the course of their travels Greeks with an interest in science or philosophy absorbed new ideas and principles. Speaking several dialects of the same language, they transcended vast distances over treacherous seas and mountainous terrain to participate in a common culture. A rich and inspiring mythology, with local variants, and devotion to the Olympian gods gave Greeks their panhellenic identity. They were, however, never unified into a single nation; their political unit, the polis or city-state, remained fiercely independent. Each polis, whether ruled by a tyrant, an oligarchy or by a democratic assembly of citizens, consisted of a single city that controlled and defended adjacent territory. When they formed political alliances, they were joining together in defense against enemies that threatened them, such as the mighty Persian Empire.

Architecture and Townscape

Greek architecture can be studied in several Mediterranean countries. The Acropolis of Athens shows classical Greek architecture at its peak; nearby Aegina and Sounion possess inspiring Doric temples. Delphi and Olympia, dedicated respectively to Apollo and Zeus, and built for unique purposes, celebrated the panhellenic world with fine buildings and sculpture. At Paestum, in Southern Italy, and Agrigento and Segesta in Sicily we can see some of the best-preserved Greek temples. But an exploration of the Greek world is incomplete without including Turkey.

Roman architecture can be seen in the heart of modern Rome, and isolated examples survive throughout the former empire, in Europe, the Middle East and North Africa, but the cities of the Roman Province of Asia, particularly Ephesus, are almost unparalleled in their ability to convey Roman urban character.

On my journeys through Aegean Turkey, I have always felt intense links with the life of the region in ancient times. Troy in the north, the largest and richest city in the Aegean during the Bronze Age, powerfully evokes the Trojan War and the *Iliad* of Homer. We can see the very walls that kept out the Myceneans during their long siege. In Pergamon, Ephesus, Priene, Didyma and Aphrodisias, enough physical evidence remains for us to experience a sense of the elegant and sophisticated life in the classical and Hellenistic eras. A journey through this region will also expose us to architecture built by Romans, as they became inheritors of their civilization. Many of the cities include Roman buildings and show the transformations and the increased scale of their architecture; some, like Ephesus and Aphrodisias, are primarily Roman.

Responding to unique topography each city in Aegean Turkey conveys its own character. The builders of Pergamon adapted the townscape to a dramatic site, high on a hill, placing their monumental architecture in a dynamic manner. The ruins of Priene occupy a broad ledge above a plain that was originally covered by the sea, and behind it rises a cliff on the face of a mountain once sacred to ancient gods. Ephesus, in contrast to the two hill towns, lies in a narrow valley leading down to a coastal plain. Miletus, built on a low-lying peninsula that also rises to higher ground, was served by four harbours. It was famous as an early example of urban planning on a grid. Aphrodisias lies peacefully on almost flat ground overlooked by the sacred Mount Salbakos. The Doric Temple of Athena at Assos, with five of its columns standing today, expresses beautifully the Greek relationship between temples and high places. The view over the Aegean and the island of Lesbos evokes the age-old bond between the Greeks and their sea.

These Greek cities occupied a pristine territory between a sea teeming with fish and fertile land, where crops, cattle and horses thrived, where sheep and goats grazed on mountain slopes. The first Minoans and Myceneans to arrive in the second millennium BCE must have seen it as a paradise when they eagerly settled here. It is no wonder that Greeks from Athens, Thebes and other city-states set out later to form colonies in the most favourable sites with safe harbours. They came with political ideals and a desire to create beautiful cities. Over the years they built some of the most elegant and sustainable urban environments that have ever existed. They developed progressive political systems and institutions. They honoured their gods, making sacrifices to them and erecting great altars and temples, but they also searched for truth as they delved into natural philosophy. Maritime trade and agriculture sustained them; philosophy, art, architecture, music and literature flourished. Tragically, their success created envy. So, again and again, powerful and greedy neighbors, the Hittites, Galatians, Cimmerians, Lydians, Persians, Macedonians and Romans invaded. Sometimes the cities were almost completely destroyed, the men slaughtered and the women enslaved. In other cases new tyrants, who took power after a city-state had surrendered, grasped the economic rewards as well as prestige. Some conquering rulers allowed their new subjects a measure of independence; others displayed their power, subjugating them brutally. All of them levied taxes on the citizens and demanded soldiers for their armies.

The Greek experiment of the polis found expression in fine architecture and civic institutions. There were periods when the citizens could live in peace for a few decades or even centuries, but inevitably their dreams and everyday lives were cut short by the actions of powerful, arrogant, pitiless rulers desiring only their own aggrandizement. All the ancient cities of Aegean Turkey now lie in ruins. To add insult to injury, the fortifications and buildings have served as stone quarries exploited for new construction elsewhere. Nature has also played a part. Rivers changed their courses, inundating settlements; they have also silted up their estuaries, leaving cities that depended on maritime trade miles from the sea. With devastating suddenness earthquakes took their toll, toppling tall columns and reducing ancient homes and civic buildings to ruins.

Such a pattern of creation and destruction has recurred worldwide throughout history and continues today. While farmers, traders, artisans, philosophers and artists have done their best to continue their work, aggressive warriors have often been elevated to the status of heroes. Empires have risen and fallen; great cities have faced disasters. I hope, as you read the historical narratives in this book and experience the physical remains of the places you see, that the spirit of the people who lived in them, from slaves to artists, philosophers and civic leaders, will come to life in your minds.

HISTORY

In the first part of this section, before the end of the first millennium BCE, dates for events before the first century are assumed to be BCE, unless marked CE

The history of Aegean Turkey is complicated. Our knowledge of the people who lived, fought, traded and built in the Bronze Age is limited. The later power struggles between independent Greek cities and the Persian Empire as well as the occasional warfare between city-states present a complex, confusing picture. On the other hand there were periods of stability and high cultural achievement that left their rich legacy in the cities. I will try to clarify the broad sweep of history and give an account of the most relevant events to bring what you are seeing alive.

The history of Greek and Roman cities in Aegean Turkey cannot be fully understood without knowledge of certain key events in Athens, Sparta, Macedonia or even Sicily. Many historical events in Hellenic history sent shock waves through the Greek-speaking world that caused dramatic changes in far-away places.

THE BRONZE AGE (ca. 3000-1100 BCE)

Archaeological evidence has revealed a lot of information about the Aegean world in the Bronze Age. A rich civilization, that we call Minoan, flourished on the Island of Crete between 2700 and 1375. The Minoans, named after the legendary king Minos, were great mariners. They engaged in long distance trade and founded several colonies, including one at Miletus, on the coast of Anatolia. The warlike Greeks we identify as Myceneans, also known as Achaeans, probably contributed to the collapse of Minoan culture. Between 1600 and 1100 they built and defended citadels at Athens, Mycenae and Tiryns. We know them best through the story of the Trojan War told in the epic *Iliad* of Homer, but today. It is clear that the Myceneans, attacked and defeated Troy after a long siege, though not exactly as Homer and other bards have related. Prior to the siege of Troy the Myceneans founded settlements and trading posts on the Aegean shore of Anatolia. The largest of these, founded in the second half of the 15th century, was at Miletus, where an earlier Minoan settlement had declined.

THE DARK AGE (ca. 1100-800 BCE)

The Dark Age, a period from which little evidence survives, followed the destruction of the Mycenean civilization. Drained of manpower, perhaps by the Trojan War, and ravaged by attacks from "sea people," the Myceneans fell to the Dorians in about 1200. It is not clear whether a ruthless, full-scale Dorian invasion occurred, as many historians believe, or whether these people infiltrated into the area after the Mycenean culture had already collapsed. The Dorians came from the north, speaking a dialect of Greek, but did not share the artistic skills of the Myceneans.

The Greeks of this time were illiterate and thus left no written records. Because they were poor, lived simply and built little of substance, we know very little about them. It is clear, however, that the unsettled life of this time caused many groups of Greeks to take refuge on the Anatolian coast. After 1200, Greeks known as Aeolians, from Thessaly and

Euboea, migrated to the region south of Troy; others from Attica, identified as Ionians, chose to settle on the central part of the coast. They founded the city-states of Aeolis and Ionia that concern us in this book. At about the same time many Dorians migrated from the Peloponnese to Crete and from there to Rhodes and Caria on the southern coast of Anatolia. The indigenous population of this region was probably an amalgam of Carians and people of Anatolian descent. Halikarnassos, present day Bodrum, remained the principal Dorian city in the region, which continued to be known as Caria.

THE ARCHAIC ERA (ca. 800-500 BCE)

Colonization *(See the migration map in the folded endpaper)*

Further waves of colonization followed from mainland Greece to the eastern Aegean coast, many of them prompted by reasons other than flight from invaders. Greece is mountainous and lacked enough good agricultural land to sustain large populations. Even green-looking valleys only offered thin, stony soil. So when populations increased, it was natural for enterprising Greeks to set off in search of new fertile, lightly populated land. Overland travel was extremely difficult, because of the precipitous terrain, but boat building and seafaring was part of their tradition. So the eastern coast of the Aegean with lush river valleys and plains between sea and mountain beckoned to colonists. It was not long before cities began to flourish in this region. Although historians refer to such cities as colonies, they were never possessions of a colonial power, but free communities with cultural and commercial links to their mother cities.

The development of literacy in the archaic era instigated major transformation in Greek life. By the middle of the eighth century, the Greek alphabet was widely used. While Homer belongs to the pre-literate era, when the prodigious memories of storytellers and an oral tradition overcame the lack of writing, it was not long before this refined and subtle alphabet served literature, philosophy and science as well as trade and affairs of state.

The Aeolian and Ionian Leagues

In the eighth century BCE, seeking mutual protection against invaders, twelve Greek cities, including Smyrna and Assos, formed the Aeolian League. In the mid-seventh century BCE twelve cities in Ionia further south joined together in the Ionian League. They soon lured Pergamon away from the Aeolian League. The Ionian League, also known as the Dodecapolis, consisted of the islands Samos and Chios and, from north to south on the mainland, Phocaea, Clazomenae, Erythrae, Teos, Lebedos, Colophon, Ephesus, Priene, Myus and Miletus. Leaders of the cities met regularly at Panionion, near Priene, and they also met annually on the island of Delos, sacred as the birthplace of Apollo. Miletus was the oldest and most powerful member of the Ionian League. This city is distinguished in Greek history as the source, in the sixth century, of the scientific and philosophical tradition, in which scholars sought rational rather than supernatural explanations for natural phenomena. The Milesians spread their influence by founding many colonies, including several on the Black Sea, and developing a strong trading presence in Egypt.

Although war and heroism appear to dominate Greek mythology and history, most notably in the cases of the Trojan War and the Persian wars, the Greeks did not engage constantly in warfare. There were rivalries between cities that sometimes became violent, but, according to Thucydides, the Greeks remained essentially peaceful during the six centuries between those two devastating wars. However, in the late fifth century the Peloponnesian War between Athens and Sparta initiated a period of inter-city hostilities that continued until the time of Alexander the Great almost a century later.

Government and politics

According to oral traditions, Greek cities in the Dark Age were mostly ruled by chieftains or kings, often referred to as "tyrants." While today the word tyrant implies a cruel and ruthless leader, in classical times it referred to rulers, whether benevolent or brutal, who had grasped power without the benefit of heredity. Homer used the term boule to describe councils of noblemen appointed to advise the ruler. By the eighth century most city-states were ruled by oligarchies, councils of the wealthiest and most powerful citizens, who met to make laws and administer their polis. Only citizens could participate, which ruled out women, slaves and foreigners. In some city-states, membership of the boule or ruling council was limited to a few powerful people, but in others hundreds or thousands participated.

Under such a quasi-democratic system, most city-states remained independent. They developed rivalries, but generally kept the peace. So, the archaic era was an age of growing prosperity and cultural flowering. New architecture rose to meet the needs of expanding populations; the manufacture of goods stimulated trade; philosophy and science thrived.

Lydian and Persian rule (585-466 BCE)

In 585 King Croesus of Lydia, whose kingdom, just east of Ionia, was militarily strong and rich in gold, annexed the Greek cities on the Aegean coast. He was supportive of Hellenic culture and his rule was not particularly oppressive. Indeed he was seen as a strong bulwark between the Greeks and the Persians, whose empire was rapidly expanding. But in 547, after consulting the Oracle at Delphi and receiving a reply that appeared favourable, Croesus attacked the Persians. He was defeated by Darius I, captured and burned with his family on a pyre. Ironically, the oracle's pronouncement that if he attacked the Persians a great empire would fall, referred not to the Persian Empire but to his own.

Thus, in 546, the Greek cities of Aeolis and Ionia fell under Persian rule. Darius did not attempt to govern their entire empire directly from his distant capital at Susa, near the Persian Gulf; he appointed governors, known as satraps, to rule over them. The Persians admired the Greeks and, following the demands of the monotheistic Zoroastrian religion, Darius believed that justice was the duty of rulers. He allowed the Aeolians and Ionians to maintain their own language, religion and culture. Some Greeks welcomed opportunities for further trade and wider cultural influences; the majority felt bitter about the loss of the autonomy but they chafed under the tyranny of the satraps. Resentment grew as the Persians demanded heavy taxes as well as soldiers to swell their army. The Greeks remained so faithful to their own culture that Persian customs made little impact on them.

THE CLASSICAL PERIOD (500-333 BCE)

The Ionian Revolt

The first two decades of the fifth century BCE proved to be as momentous for Ionia and Aeolis as they were for mainland Greece. Miletus became a pivotal source of opposition to Persian rule and suffered the consequences. In 499 Aristagoras, an independent minded Greek who served as Satrap of Miletus, led a revolt of discontented Ionian cities against

Persian domination. He sought help from Athens, which sent twenty-five triremes, and from Eritrea, the capital of Euboea, which contributed five, but the Spartans and some other city-states refused to help. In 498, after attacking the Persian controlled Lydian capital Sardis and setting the city on fire, the joint force was defeated by the Persians and Lydians near Ephesus. Discouraged, the Athenians and Eritreans returned to Greece, and the Ionians continued their campaign in the north with diminished strength. They took the city of Byzantium (Istanbul today) and some surrounding towns. In 494/3 after the naval battle of Lade off the coast near Miletus, which destroyed most of the Greek fleet, the Persians attacked and defeated Miletus. Enraged by Milesian perfidy, they razed the city, slaughtered the men and sold the women and children into slavery. They reduced to rubble and ashes the beautiful city that had contributed so much to Hellenic culture. It was not long before the other Ionian cities had surrendered, but Darius seems to have learned that the imposition of autocratic satraps on the Ionian citizens failed to create order and loyalty. In 492 Darius's son-in-law Mardonius initiated reforms in Ionia. Herodotus claims that Mardonius began to allow increased democracy.

For the Athenians and their allies, participation in the Ionian Revolt was only the beginning of conflict with the Persians: They had incurred the wrath of Darius for daring to support rebels within his own empire. In retaliation the Persians launched the Greco-Persian Wars and made Athens their main target. Darius was determined to ensure that they would never humiliate him again. According to Herodotus, he ordered a servant to call out three times a day "Master, remember the Athenians."

His first expedition against them was foiled by a storm off Cape Athos, which wrecked many ships in his fleet. In 490 BCE he sent a naval force across the Aegean, overpowered the Cyclades and destroyed Eretreia. However, while marching overland towards Athens he suffered a crushing defeat at the Battle of Marathon. In 483 BCE Darius died unavenged, but three years later, his son Xerxes I led a vast army to invade Greece. This force was at first victorious, decisively winning the battle of Thermopylae and ravaging much of Greece. But his fortunes changed when his fleet was trapped by adverse winds in the narrow Straits of Salamis, just west of Athens, and utterly destroyed by the Greek navy. After that, the Greeks attacked the Persian army on land, defeating them decisively at the battle of Plataea. In 479, the following year, they vanquished the remains of the

Persian fleet at the fateful battle of Mycale not far from Miletus. Continued Greek campaigns against the Persians contributed to the weakening of the Persian Empire and brought independence to the Greek cities in Anatolia.

The Delian League

Ionians played a significant role in the formation in 478 of the Delian League, which consisted of cities all around the Aegean and the Black Sea that banded together, under the leadership of Athens, to keep Persia at bay. In exchange for providing naval power, the Athenians levied dues from the members and built up a rich treasury on the island of Delos. Soon, however, the power they held went to the heads of the Athenians. In 454 they transferred their treasury from Delos to Athens and embarked on the building of the new temples on the Acropolis. They also began to act as imperialists, exerting more and more control over Ionian cities. It is not surprising that the Delian League became known as the Athenian Empire, or that members began to rebel. The Athenians, with their naval and military superiority, used their might to subdue subject cities, dismantle their fortifications and take control of their fleets. In some cases the Athenians crushed oligarchies that ruled them and installed democracies on the Athenian model. (see note on the Bouleuterion and Prytaneum p.34)

The Peloponnesian War (431-404, BCE)

The Spartans, chafing against the determination of Athens to dominate the whole Greek world, joined with Argos and other Peloponnesian cities to put an end to Athenian imperialism. The devastating conflict that followed, known as the Peloponnesian War, launched shock waves that reached the Eastern Aegean and changed the course of history there. At first, the land-locked kingdom of Sparta, with no navy and little wealth, seemed to be doomed to failure. Since the walls of Athens were impenetrable, and the road from the port of Piraeus to Athens was also protected by walls, they could only raid the surrounding farmland. This strategy resulted in a flight of rural people to the city. The influx was probably the cause of a plague that killed 30,000 citizens including the Athenian statesman Pericles. However, the Athenian navy was able to make several attacks on the Peloponnesian coast. This inconclusive phase of the war ended in 421 with the Peace of Nicias, but hostilities soon broke out again.

The Athenian dependence on imported grain led to two naval debacles that sealed their fate. In 415 the Athenians, seeking to dominate the island of Sicily and benefit from its abundant grain supplies, sent a navy under Alcibiades to attack Syracuse. The expedition ended in absolute disaster from which they would never recover. They lost two hundred ships and a thousand men. To make matters worse, Alcibiades, whom the Athenians accused of destroying sacred statues, before he sailed to Sicily, defected to the Spartans. In the final stage of the war, Sparta joined with Persia to foment revolt in the Ionian cities against Athens. By this time Sparta had built up a navy and based many of its ships at Miletus. Athens bought vast quantities of timber from Macedon to rebuild her fleet but would never again be a great naval power.

In 405 the Spartan general Lysander commanded the naval force that aimed to cut off Athenian grain supplies from the Black Sea region. In the battle of Aegospotami on the Hellespont, he utterly destroyed the Athenian fleet. Only twelve out of a hundred and eighty ships survived. Athens surrendered to Sparta the next year. Fortunately, the Spartans took the past role of the Athenians into account and decided on a course of clemency. But the golden age of Athens, that had lasted only a few decades, was over.

Meanwhile Lysander made alliances with the Persian king Cyrus, who appointed him satrap of Asia Minor. The Spartans did not possess the ability to rule Ionia and Aeolis from the Peloponnese, so the Greek cities that had formerly regained their independence with Athenian help fell once more under Persian domination. They remained in that state for about seventy-five years until after the invasion by Alexander the Great in 334. The Persian Empire finally collapsed in 331.

Alexander the Great and the rise of Macedon

Macedon had lain dormant for centuries while other Greek city-states rose to fame. However, during the fifth century it gained significant power. In 480 the Macedonian King Alexander I incurred the enmity of all Greeks when he joined with the Persians in their invasion of Greece. The Athenians, agreeing with denunciations by Demosthenes, called the Macedonians barbarians; many in the Hellenic world refused to accept them as Greeks. While Greek states with the exception of Sparta practiced some form of democracy, hereditary monarchs still ruled the Macedonians. In the 470s the kings of lower Macedon conquered the forested, mountainous territory of Upper Macedon and also took possession of silver mines there. Later in the century King Archelaus (413-399) took decisive actions that transformed his kingdom. He had sold vast quantities of timber to the Athenians to rebuild their fleet after their naval defeat in Sicily and used revenues from his silver mines to attract Greek artists, writers and musicians to his capital at Pella. Their cultural influence gave Macedon a new Hellenic identity.

Alexander the Great, Istanbul Archaeological Museums

Alexander, born in Pella in 356, was the first child of Philip II and his queen Olympias, a princess of Epirus, a kingdom to the west. Alexander's childhood prepared him for his extraordinary life. He was influenced by a father, who believed passionately in restoring the greatness of Greece by vanquishing the Persians, and by a powerful mother given to ecstatic rituals, and occult practices. Simultaneous dreams convinced his parents that Zeus had played a role in Alexander's conception; legend proclaimed his descent from Achilles through his mother's ancestors; prophecies left no doubt as to his future greatness. As a youth, endowed with physical strength and a sharp intellect, he showed extraordinary promise. Alexander not only tamed the wild horse Bucephalas that no other man could break, and led a decisive cavalry charge, he also flourished among scholars. His father put him in the care of Leonidas, a strict disciplinarian, and the pedagogue Lysimachus, who nicknamed him Achilles. From the age of fourteen the Athenian philosopher Aristotle tutored him in ethics, politics and formal disputation.

In 336, when he was twenty, Alexander was catapulted into kingship by the assassination of his father as he entered a theatre during the celebration of his daughter's wedding. Acclaimed by the army and endowed with supreme power, Alexander proved ready to complete what Philip II had begun. By this time, Philip had virtually become overlord of Greece, and was already embarking on the conquest of Asia. Before Alexander could invade Anatolia, he marched his army south to quell rebellions, but used diplomacy as his chief weapon. At a meeting in Corinth, he persuaded representatives from Athens and other cities to rally behind him as the leader of all Greece in the invasion of Persia. When the Thebans revolted, and rejected his demands, he retaliated with devastating and cruel force, slaughtering six thousand of them, selling thirty thousand into slavery and destroying the city. This prelude to his conquests in Asia showed the two poles of his character, the charming, magnanimous sovereign and the ruthless despot. Claiming descent from Zeus, he demanded the honour accorded to gods; on the other hand he possessed emotions and failings that were all too human. Cities that resisted his conquests paid dearly for their belligerence; others that opened their gates welcomed a generous benefactor.

Before leaving Macedon, Alexander, following Greek tradition, sacrificed to the gods and held dramatic contests in honour of Zeus. On his campaign, he carried with him his most precious possession, a copy of Homer's *Iliad* annotated and given to him by Aristotle. He regarded it as his military manual as well as his source of inspiration. In the spring of 334, less than two years after Alexander became king he assembled an army of 32,000 foot soldiers and 5,100 cavalry at Sestos on the north side of the Hellespont, ready to be ferried to Asia to join thousands of troops already there.

Alexander made sacrifices and conducted symbolic rituals at Troy before engaging the Persians at the River Granicus. There, standing out in shining armor, and executing his brilliant strategy, he defeated them decisively and with dreadful carnage. Without delay, he pressed on to the Persians' provincial capital Sardis, which quickly surrendered. As he progressed south, some of the Ionian cities welcomed him, but at Miletus he overcame Persian resistance only after a siege and a fierce naval battle. Many Greeks fought with him, but others, unable to forgive his brutality at Thebes, joined the Persian side as mercenaries. Alexander's overarching purpose was to take revenge on the Persians and to loot the riches of their empire. His victorious progress also brought about the liberation of the Greek cities and the establishment of democracy. His series of rapid conquests enabled him to establish a great empire stretching far to the east.

THE HELLENISTIC AGE (333-33 BCE)

In the course of only eleven years, Alexander the Great created an empire that extended from Greece and Egypt in the West to the Indus in the East. After his sudden death 323, his generals known as the Diadochi ("successors") struggled against each other to gain control of his empire. Their bitter wars lasted over fifty years until 280 when the empire was divided into three parts. Ptolemy, with his capital in Alexandria, ruled Egypt; Seleucus inherited most of Asia and Antigonus took Macedonia as his domain. Western Anatolia, the area that concerns us, remained volatile; various powers fought over it. At first Antigonus ruled there, but he was defeated by another rival Lysimachus in 301 at the battle of Ipsus in western Asia Minor, a conflict renowned for the hundreds of elephants on both sides. Soon this region passed to Seleucus, who attempted to dominate a territory from Syria to the Aegean in the west and India in the East.

Lysimachus took possession of a new wealthy city, the hilltop fortress at Pergamon; he concealed his vast collection of war booty there, and installed his general Philetairus as governor. But Lysimachus soon died, enabling Philetairus to take possession of a rich treasury. Philetairus founded the Attalid dynasty of kings, which wielded significant power for more than a century, and built spectacular architecture. His successor, Attalos I, defeated the Galatians, a Celtic tribe from Thrace, in Northern Greece, that had attacked and demanded tribute from Greek cities in Anatolia. The Attalids then succeeded in gaining control over the Aeolian and Ionian cities, from Assos in the north to Miletus and beyond it to the Mediterranean shore. They possessed absolute power, but seeing the economic benefits of flourishing urban life and far reaching trade, they did not impose an oppressive yoke on their subjects.

During the Hellenistic period, despite the intense struggle for political control, the warring powers did not threaten the Greek cities with destruction. On the whole, this was an era of peace, prosperity and democratic government. In most cities during this time, the ecclesia, an assembly of all eligible male citizens, made the political decisions. Many cities built bouleuteria where members of the Boule, a council chosen from the ecclesia met to met to deliberate on issues to be brought to the larger assembly. Well-organized systems of taxation, and the labor of many slaves made it possible for successive leaders to build splendid architecture, both for civic and religious purposes. Wealthy traders and ordinary citizens built fine houses and the arts flourished. Young men received education as well as athletic training in gymnasiums, though women acquired few rights or opportunities. Visitors to Aegean Turkey will be able to see far more Hellenistic architecture than that of the classical or archaic eras. Although Alexander's empire was short lived, it made a prodigious cultural impact. Vast regions became Hellenized with Greek as the lingua franca.

THE ROMAN EMPIRE (33 BCE - 395 CE)

At the end of the third century BCE the Romans lived under a republic. However, they made significant conquests around the Mediterranean. In the three Punic wars against Carthage (264-146) they gained Sardinia, Corsica, Spain and the tip of North Africa near Sicily. Early in the second century they conquered southern France, Greece and Macedonia, but they showed little interest in expanding into Asia. That reluctance ended when Attalos III of Pergamon, dying without an heir in 133, bequeathed his empire to the Romans, whom he greatly admired. This astonishing bequest, probably intended to give a stable future to the Pergamene legacy, changed the course of history.

The sudden acquisition of thriving metropolitan areas in western Anatolia, and new sources of wine, oil, grain and luxury goods, spurred the Romans' imperial ambitions. They conquered Syria in 64 and the next year took Jerusalem and created the Roman province of Judea. By the end of the first century CE the Roman Empire completely encircled the Mediterranean and reached as far north as Britain. Furthermore, the opening of new trade routes into the Black Sea introduced Romans to the potential of Byzantium. Educated Romans tended to admire Greek culture and many could read and speak Greek. Several Roman emperors took a strong interest in their Asian domains; Augustus visited Pergamon twice; Hadrian and Trajan also traveled there and were honoured by grand architecture that reflected their glory. While Hellenistic buildings generally conveyed a restrained elegance, Roman additions to the townscape tended to be monumental and sometimes exuberant. The simple Doric order and the more refined and decorative Ionic orders employed by the Greeks often gave way to the more triumphant Corinthian order. The Romans also transformed the very nature of architecture by moving beyond the post and lintel system of the Greeks. They opened new possibilities by spanning openings in walls with arches and stately interior spaces with vaults. They also introduced new building types, most notably thermae (public baths), which they built on a grand scale.

During two centuries that followed, from 27 BCE to 180 CE, the Roman territories remained relatively peaceful, enjoying the Pax Romana. During this time, administration was fairly efficient and there was little desire to expand the empire. Despite political domination by Roman imperial power, Greek continued to be the principal language of western Anatolia. Roman emperors expected to be honoured as gods in imperial temples, but the traditional worship of Olympian gods continued. Roman emperors and their high officials sometimes consulted the oracle of Apollo at Didyma in southern Ionia. However, the days of the ancient pagan religions were numbered.

Judaism and Christianity

The harshness of Roman Rule in Judea caused many Jews to migrate to Egypt, Syria, Anatolia and Greece. They joined others who had been part of a diaspora since the fourth century BCE. Wherever they settled, they kept a Jewish identity, and centred their lives on their synagogues. At the same time they adapted to their circumstances. Jews living in the cities of Anatolia received criticism for their exclusiveness but they gradually became Hellenized and spoke Greek. The Jewish community at Sardis was especially strong; both Julius Caesar and Augustus issued decrees guaranteeing their religious freedom. Early in the third century CE they built a splendid synagogue in Sardis, the largest in Anatolia. The remains of a synagogue have also been found in Priene.

The conversion of St. Paul of Tarsus, which occurred between 33 and 36 CE, proved to be a major catalyst for the spread of Christianity. Originally a Pharisee in Jerusalem, who devoted himself to the persecution of Christians, Paul experienced a dramatic conversion on the road to Damascus, and became a leading voice for Christianity. He was both a well-educated Jew and a Roman citizen. He disagreed with apostles, James the Just and Peter, who believed that they should only convert Jews to Christianity. Convinced by the idea of a universal faith, Paul and other apostles preached the gospel eloquently and founded churches in many cities in the Roman province of Asia. Beginning in 53 or 54 CE, he appears to have lived for three years in Ephesus, where he probably wrote his famous Epistle to the Corinthians. With his intellectual and spiritual leadership the numbers of the faithful grew rapidly. St. John, who wrote the *Book of Revelations* on the nearby island of Patmos is believed to have spent his last years at Ephesus; many people believed that the Virgin Mary lived for a while and died in Ephesus.

Although Christians often endured prejudice there was little official persecution by the Roman state until the reign of Nero. Many religions were tolerated in the Roman Empire, but, like Jews, Christians were monotheistic and attracted occasional wrath from authorities for refusing to worship the Olympian gods or the emperor. In 64 CE, perhaps to draw suspicion away from himself, Nero accused Christians of starting the fire that destroyed much of Rome. Four years of brutality and carnage followed. The worst persecutions, early in the fourth century CE under the Emperor Diocletian had a devastating effect on the churches and their members in Anatolia. Diocletian had consulted the Oracle of Apollo at Didyma in 302 CE and received a judgment that appeared to favour persecution. Since the Christians were attempting to triumph over the ancient religions, the pronouncement of the Oracle is hardly surprising. It can be seen as a strike by the priests of the pagan gods against a rival religion, perhaps even as Zeus's last thunderbolt. Early the next year Diocletian, in Asia at the time, issued his 'Edict against Christians.' He intended to suppress Christianity without bloodshed, but since many refused to sacrifice at the imperial temples, thousands were burnt alive. Churches were also destroyed

Only nine years later, in 313 CE, the emperor Constantine issued the Edict of Milan that legalized Christianity. In 325 CE he convened the Council of Nicaea to establish a unity of belief for the whole of Christendom. Bishops from many of the cities on the west coast of Anatolia attended. When Constantine visited Byzantium he was inspired by its superb site overlooking the Bosphorus. In 324 CE, weary of Rome, and concerned about the governance of domains spreading so far to the east, he renamed this city Constantinople and soon made it the eastern capital of the Roman Empire.

THE BYZANTINE EMPIRE (395-1453 CE)

The Byzantine Empire, formed as the eastern half of the Roman Empire, was Christian from its founding. In the Anatolian cities where Greeks had worshipped Apollo, Athena and other Olympian deities, Christian communities began to build fine churches. In 395 CE the Emperor Theodosius, divided the empire in two, with a western capital at Rome and an eastern one at Constantinople. In the fifth century, after Rome had fallen to barbarians, Constantinople survived as the sole inheritor of Roman power. Its people, although they spoke Greek, called themselves Romans. The term Byzantine was not coined until the 18th century. The succession of Byzantine emperors need not concern us much as we travel through the Greco-Roman cities of Aegean Turkey, but we should be aware of the reign of Justinian (527-65 CE), a period of military success and, above all, of glorious architecture. He built the Church of St. John in Ephesus; after reconquering Ravenna in Northern Italy, he built splendid churches there, including the quintessentially Byzantine San Vitale. Most significantly, Justinian commissioned two Ionian architects, Isidorus of Miletus and Anthemius of Tralles, to design his great church of Hagia Sophia in Constantinople.

In the centuries after the death of Justinian, Byzantine power gradually weakened. Muslim invaders, first the Seljuks and then the Ottomans, gradually conquered territories until only the walled city of Constantinople remained. The imposing fortress, built partly on top of the highest seats in the theatre at Miletus, symbolizes the doomed effort to defend a city and an empire.

GREEK RELIGION AND MYTHOLOGY

The Greeks were a deeply religious people whose worship of the Olympian gods dominated many aspects of their lives. While Egyptian and Mesopotamian gods often combined the attributes of humans and animals, the Greek gods were anthropomorphic: Sculptors represented them as exquisite human beings. Like the Greek people who had migrated to the Aegean from a variety of regions, their origins were diverse; several major gods originated in Anatolia. Hades, lord of the underworld, Poseidon, the sea god, and Hera, a fertility goddess, were indigenous to the Aegean. Zeus, the sky god, and Demeter, the earth mother, came with Indo-Europeans who moved into the area in the second millennium BCE. Athena, who became the patron goddess of Athens, was Mycenean; Aphrodite, the goddess of love, came from Cyprus and Dionysus, the god of wine and revelry, from Thrace in Northern Greece. Apollo, the god of wisdom and music, had his roots in Ionia; the traditional Anatolian fertility goddess Cybele was transformed by the Greeks into Apollo's twin sister Artemis. Another example of the Greeks embracing a potent local cult, as they migrated into western Anatolia, is their adoption of the Assyrian goddess of love, Nin (Ishtar) at the inland site that was to become Aphrodisias. They soon identified her as their own goddess of love.

Long before Homer composed his epic poems the *Iliad* and the *Odyssey*, in which the gods play active roles, the Greeks had brought these deities together as a divine family, with Zeus, the "father of the gods," as its head and Hera as his wife. Each god or goddess oversaw certain aspects of human life. In the stories that Greek poets wove into a complex mythology, the gods possessed both superhuman and human attributes; they interfered with human actions and took sides in their conflicts; however, they could not overcome the forces of fate. As many stories in Greek Mythology show, the gods were not only supremely powerful, creative or virtuous, but they also possessed desires, indulged in envy, lust and deviousness. The male gods even seduced mortals, whose offspring, for example Helen of Troy, lived among mortals.

The Greeks gave women no role in public affairs and virtually relegated them to a passive domestic role, but they venerated their goddesses and placed trust in them. Athena, the patron goddess of many Ionian cities is depicted, in vibrant works of sculpture, as a warrior goddess. Artemis is the huntress who, according to the Homeric hymn in her honour, "draws her golden bow, rejoicing in the chase, and sends out grievous shafts."

When embarking on important ventures in peace or war, leaders in the Greek world often consulted oracles and always sacrificed animals at temples or sacred altars. Every city adopted a patron god to whom its people dedicated their principal temple. In their civic centres they created ceremonial spaces and sacred ways for religious processions. The primary purpose of performing plays in their theatres and athletic contests in their stadiums was to honour the gods. The Romans worshipped their own version of the Olympian gods, but renamed them, and created their own mythology. For example, Zeus changed to Jupiter, Athena to Minerva, Aphrodite to Venus and Poseidon to Neptune. However, Apollo remained the same. Some emperors considered themselves to be divine and expected the people to worship them too, but, having fulfilled their obligations, the populace could worship in any other ways that they desired. The Romans believed in ritual and decorum; religion played an important part in civic life.

In addition to the Olympian gods and their Roman counterparts, the Egyptian God Serapis was worshipped in several cities of western Anatolia. Brought into being on the order of Ptolemy I of Egypt to unify the Greeks and Egyptians of Alexandria, he combined the attributes of Osiris and Apis, and was represented in human form like Greek gods. The substantial trade between Alexandria and the Greek and Roman cities led to substantial Egyptian communities in Ephesus, Miletus and Pergamon where Temples of Serapis existed beside those of the classical gods.

ARCHITECTURAL PRINCIPLES AND STYLES

The Greeks based their architecture on a post and lintel system in which vertical columns support horizontal beams. They discovered that columns standing in front of walls, shining in sunlight and casting shadows on the surfaces behind them brought the architecture to life. It seems natural, therefore, that their architects should devote care and artistry to the refinement of the columns and the entablature that they carry. Vertical grooves, known as flutes, accentuate the height of columns and disguise the joints between the separate 'drums' of stone; the columns taper with a slight curve (entasis) which gives them an organic appearance that straight lines could not convey; capitals celebrate the transition from the

Orders of architecture

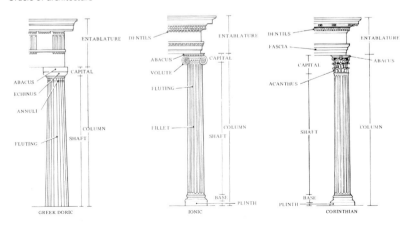

column to the architrave. The architects took great care with the proportions of the columns and the spaces between them.

The Greeks developed three styles of columns, known as orders. On the Greek mainland and in Italy and Sicily the Doric order was the earliest to appear. It was rather plain with a rounded capital supporting a square block (the abacus) on which the architrave, a horizontal beam rests. In Ionia an alternative style appeared whose capital, with spiraling volutes, based perhaps on rams' horns or seashells, is more decorative. While Doric columns rest on the platform of a temple without a transitional element, Ionic columns stand on molded bases. Since Doric columns appear sturdier than the slender Ionic ones, it has been suggested that the two orders represent masculine and feminine qualities. Since the first Doric temples were built of wood, various elements reflect details of traditional carpentry perpetuated in stone. This is evident in the frieze, a horizontal band above the architrave where triglyphs, three vertical strips of wood separated by grooves, simulate the ends of beams resting on them. The triglyphs alternate with metopes, square panels often containing sculpture. The Ionic frieze is often ornamented with a band of sculpture. Above the frieze, on all three orders, the projecting cornice is designed to throw off rainwater. The triangular gable end of a temple or portico, known as the pediment was a place for the display of sculpture.

The Corinthian order first appeared in the late fifth century BCE and became popular in the Hellenistic era. Like much of the ornament in Greek architecture, it was inspired by a plant form, the acanthus leaf. Corinthian shafts and bases are the same as those of the Ionic order, but the capital, with leaves carved around it, possesses an exuberant quality that appealed to the Romans. Large-scale civic and religious buildings in the Corinthian order appear triumphal and convey imperial power.

Roman post and lintel architecture

The Romans, who admired Greek architecture, continued to use the post and lintel system for temples and many important buildings. They articulated facades by grouping columns in various combinations with entablatures and pediments. Since stone lintels could only span short distances they exploited the arch, the vault and the dome to cover larger spaces and carry heavy walls above.

The Library of Celsus, Ephesus. Columns and their entablatures articulate the façade. The pairs of columns standing forward to support an entablature form aedicules

(L) Barrel vaults on massive walls flanking the central space in the Baths of Faustina at Miletus. These supported the groin vault over the calidarium (hot room) which has collapsed. (R) Barrel vaulted passage giving access to the seating of the theatre at Miletus demonstrates Roman efficiency.

Arches, vaults and domes in Roman architecture

The barrel vault, the simplest type, is like a very thick arch. When built on massive walls or piers it could support a heavy structure. To cover larger spaces, like the caldarium of the Baths of Faustina in Miletus, two barrel vaults intersected to make a groin vault, the groin being the line of intersection. A dome is like an arch rotated through 360 degrees. It required thick supporting walls to withstand the outward thrust of the heavy masonry. The Romans built domes of concrete, brick or stone. In important vaulted or domed buildings they applied columns and entablatures to the interior and exterior walls to ornament them in a symbolic manner. In such cases the arches and vaults provided the structure while the columns and entablatures endowed them with architectural quality.

CITY PLANNING

Hippodamus of Miletus has been credited with the invention of the grid plan that gave order to his own city and to Priene, but actually this type of street layout with rectangular blocks of consistent size appeared much earlier in Greek colonies in Anatolia and elsewhere. Hippodamus, by writing about it theoretically, has been awarded the credit. A significant characteristic of Greek cities is the placing of important architectural elements such as temples, agoras, bouleuteria organically in the landscape. In contrast the Romans developed powerful axes and placed their temples symmetrically in forums. However, since the Romans inherited Greek cities that had already established their plans according to Hellenic principles, Roman organization is rare in the western Anatolian cities discussed here. Certain, virtually standard architectural forms appear in every city; they are the standard elements in the townscape.

The Stoa

The stoa is a portico fronted with a colonnade (a row of columns) offering shelter from the sun or rain. It is a place to meet, conduct business or simply promenade. It may have openings in the back wall leading to shops. If war trophies or religious objects were displayed on its wall, it possessed ceremonial significance. Stoas surrounded agoras, (the central squares or market places of cities) and palaestras (the courtyards of gymnasiums). On archaeological sites a long, straight row of small column bases generally indicates where a stoa once stood.

The Agora

The agora was the heart of a city, serving many important purposes. It was the political meeting place, where citizens listened to proclamations from rulers and officials, attended ceremonies and conducted political activities. It was the principal business centre, but was also used for strolling and gathering. The agora was surrounded by stoas. In some cities temples were placed in the agora, but more usually they stood in their own sacred precinct. The most important civic buildings, such as the prytaneum (town hall), the bouleuterion or ecclesiasterion (assembly buildings), were placed by the agora, as well as fountains, altars and statues. In larger cities a purely commercial agora, was built separately. Shops lined the stoas and market stalls filled the central spaces. In smaller cities, civic and commercial agoras were combined. Unlike Roman forums, which were symmetrically planned with the temple on a central axis, Greek agoras were generally less formal.

The Temple

The Greeks were a deeply religious people; they sacrificed to the gods on all important occasions. So the design and erection of temples was an essential part of building cities. The earliest temples probably followed the form of megarons, the palaces of Mycenean kings. They were rectangular rooms with mud brick walls, pitched roofs and a front porch with two columns between sidewalls. These sidewalls were called antae and a temple

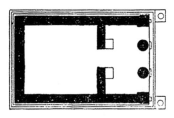 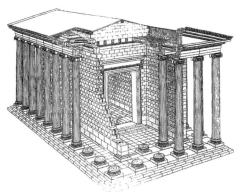

(L) A temple in antis with two columns between the antae.
(R) A peripteral temple with with two columns in antis in the pronaos. The Temple Athena Polias at Priene (H. Schleif)

with columns between projecting walls is described as in antis. Early in the archaic era the roofs spread wider, with their eaves supported on a peristyle of columns. Once the cella, the enclosed cult chamber, was surrounded by these freestanding vertical elements, the temple came alive with the effects of light and shade. At first temples were of wood, but in the early sixth century stone, with its greater durability, became the favoured material.

A temple with a single row of columns around it is described as peripteral; one with a double of columns is dipteral. When the roof spreads as wide as on a dipteral temple, but there is no inner row of columns, it is described as pseudo-dipteral. The pteron, the covered walk around the cella wall, in this type appears unusually spacious. I will explain these types as I discuss specific temples. The three orders, Doric, Ionic and Corinthian, offered different character, and architects altered proportions to suit the site and even the identity of the god to whom the temple was dedicated. Consequently no two temples in Aegean Turkey are identical.

The temple was not built to hold a congregation of worshippers; sacrifices took place at an open-air altar close by. Its purpose was to shelter the image of a god, which stood in the cella, only visible to the public through a doorway. Thus, it was conceived as an earthly residence for the deity, entered only by the priests. Since religious processions were of great importance, architects carefully designed the approaches to temples. They avoided axial symmetry and preferred to lead people along turning paths from which the architecture would gradually be revealed. The first view of a temple was often an oblique one, so that it would be seen three dimensionally. Here the Greeks differ greatly from the Romans, who preferred to approach temples on a central axis from which only a frontal façade could be seen.

The Bouleuterion and Prytaneum

The Greeks developed the first urban democracies. As long as their city-states were independent, and not ruled by tyrants or oligarchies, the citizens governed themselves. The ekklesia, the assembly of all adult male citizens, who made major political decisions, usually met in the theatre if the bouleuterion was not large enough. The boule, a deliberative and advisory council considered in advance the issues that were brought before the ekklesia. Its members were chosen by lot or in a few cases elected. The boule met in the bouleuterion, a covered space with tiers of seats on a rectangular or semicircular plan. The day-to-day administration of a polis was conducted by the prytaneis, an executive committee of the boule, whose members were chosen by lot and met daily for a period of one tenth of a year. During their tenure they lived and ate together in the prytaneum. This was usually built like a large peristyle house. It contained the sacred hearth with the sacred flame that had been brought by the first settlers from their mother city, and constantly tended. The best examples in the Greek world of the bouleuterion are found in Priene, Ephesus and Miletus.

The Gymnasium

Physical fitness was important to the Greeks. Strength and endurance were vital for warriors and success in athletic contests signified manhood. Athletes obviously cared personally about winning and cities were proud of teams that triumphed in panhellenic games such as those at Olympia. But the real purpose of athletic contests was to honour the gods to whom the games were dedicated. The main space of the gymnasium was the palaestra, an open, rectangular court with stoas on all four sides of it. Every major city possessed at least one gymnasium and there are excellent examples in Ionia. The boys exercised and competed in the nude, a tradition possibly based on the Greek appreciation of the male body. The gymnasium also served as a school where young boys engaged in intellectual pursuits, studying philosophy, mathematics and rhetoric.

The Stadium

Most cities possessed stadiums, which were always long with either U-shaped or elliptic tiers of seats around them. Although the Olympic games were founded in the eighth century BCE, the formal stadium was not built at Olympia until the fifth century. It never possessed stone seats; races were run on open ground between natural slopes. The finest classical stadium in the whole Mediterranean region is at Aphrodisias.

The Theatre

Like athletic contests, theatrical performances were given in honour of the gods. It is believed that Greek theatre began with choric dances honouring Dionysus. They took place where spectators could sit on a hillside curving around a flat area, known as the orchestra, where the chorus performed. A platform was raised behind it for the dancers. Dating to about 500, the theatre of Dionysus, below the Athens Acropolis, may have been the first such place. It provided the natural bowl for the audience that was gradually covered with stone seating. This form, which evolved slowly, represents the standard from which hundreds of others are derived. The many theatres in Aegean Greece attest to the importance of the festivals in which plays were performed.

The Greek theatre consists of standard elements composed in a traditional way. The orchestra occupies a little more than a semicircle contained by the lowest tier of seating. Here the chorus, wearing masks, spoke and moved in unison. Behind them on the raised stage, the actors played the principal roles. The cavea consisted of tiers of seats. The audience reached them by steps placed radially at intervals. The priests and most important people sat on throne-like marble seats in the front row. The Romans enlarged many Greek theatres in Aegean Turkey to hold vast audiences. In some cases they provided access to the upper tiers through vaulted passages. While Greek theatres opened to the landscape, Roman theatres were more enclosed, with a scenae frons, a high stage, building shutting off the view. Elaborately designed stage buildings generally included copious sculpture.

Libraries

Educated Greeks and Romans valued literacy and regarded books as precious possessions. Until the development of parchment in Pergamon in the second century BCE, most books were written on papyrus imported from Egypt and rolled up in scrolls. Scholarly individuals collected them in their houses, but by the Late Classical era the first public libraries were built. Ptolemy II, Alexander's successor in Egypt, founded the largest and most famous in Alexandria in 290 BCE, which, before its destruction by fire in 48 BCE, amassed a collection of 750,000 scrolls. The Hellenistic library in Pergamon rivaled it with 200,000 scrolls and the Roman Library of Celsus in Ephesus possessed 12,000. Since books needed to be copied by scribes, these huge numbers of scrolls required untold hours of work by a multitude of scribes, mostly slaves. Callimachus in Alexandria developed the first system for organizing the books by subject and alphabetically by author. It is likely that most of the Greco-Roman cities described in this guide built libraries, but few have been identified. The Library of Celsus, the best-preserved example, clearly expresses the architectural ambitions of its patron.

New Roman building types

The civic and social life of the Romans demanded new types of building never conceived by the Greeks. These included basilicas, baths and nymphaia. Apart from temples, which the people did not enter, and bouleuteria, which were rather small, the Greeks did not create interior spaces for public assembly. The Romans, on the other hand, built spacious basilicas serving as halls of justice, places for public gatherings and proclamations by officials. Such spaces usually contained a tall central nave with its roof supported on columns, flanked by aisles on both sides. Splendid examples of basilicas existed in most cities of Roman Asia; one of the finest, adorned with copious sculpture, stood in Aphrodisias. None of them has survived because their post and lintel structure succumbed so easily to earthquakes; only their column bases and fallen fragments have survived.

In contrast to the fragile construction of basilicas, the massive masonry walls and vaults of many Roman thermae (public baths) still bear witness to the Roman passion for bathing. Emperors and prominent citizens endowed ambitious thermae as a means of gaining popularity and embellishing their cities. These grand establishments not only served functional needs with their prolific water supply, advanced heating systems, and rooms for different purposes; they also delighted the eye and edified the mind. Marble revetments faced the walls and sculpture honoured the gods or evoked beauty and virtue. For example, the nine muses, offering inspiration in the arts and science, graced several thermae. Every Roman bath included an apodyterium, (changing room) a tepidarium (offering tepid water), a caldarium (with hot water) and a frigidarium (with cold water).

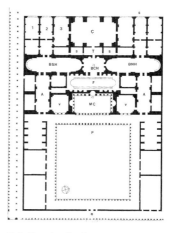

Bath Complex, Sardis

Larger baths included a natatio (a swimming pool) and sometimes a sudatorium (steam room). In addition, smaller rooms served for massage. Under the floors, hot gases from a subterranean furnace circulated between the brick columns of hypocaust systems to provide radiant heat in the floors. Most thermae included a palaestra for exercise and athletic contests. All these elements can be seen in the Baths of Faustina at Miletus (See p. 313). Roman architects clearly enjoyed the challenge of designing baths. Rather than conforming to a standard plan, they organized the spaces in a variety of ways, thus creating unique architectural conceptions.

Nymphaea, which appeared in many Roman cities, notably in Miletus and Ephesus, also celebrated the Roman love-affair with water. They were often built where water flowed into a city from an aqueduct, thus transforming a practical urban function into a playful work of art. To the delight of citizens, water splashed over surfaces alive with marble goddesses, water nymphs and fishes onto rocks below. The nymphaeum shows that the Romans, for all their imperial pomp, possessed a sense of fun.

Houses

Very little remains of the houses in the rich cities on the Aegean coast of Anatolia. Unlike the Roman houses in Pompeii and Herculaneum, which were preserved with astonishing detail under volcanic ash, the residences of this region were long ago stripped of furnishings, artifacts and decorations. Archaeologists have been able to find the foundations of Greek houses in several cities and this has helped us to understand how their inhabitants lived. Greek men were more engaged in civic activities than in domestic life; they preferred to spend their time in the elegant public spaces than in their houses. However, the larger houses included rooms in which men entertained their friends at symposia. The best examples, discovered in Priene, enabled Theodor Wiegand and his colleagues to identify a pattern, which appears to be widespread in the region (See p. 285). It is a typical Mediterranean type arranged around a small courtyard, entirely inwards-looking for security and privacy. Wiegand's drawing has been reproduced in countless books on passive solar energy to show how the Aegean Greeks understood principles that we should observe today for both comfort and energy saving. A portico, fronting the principal room, shaded the interior in summer when the sun is high, while admitting the low winter sun. Many houses were smaller with narrower courtyards, and others were two stories high.

The houses of Priene were divided into separate quarters for men and women. Since women played no part in public life they must have spent a lot of time in their homes, usually in rather cramped rooms. Principal rooms in which men entertained their friends at symposia generally opened onto the court. Roman houses were also built around courtyards; the larger ones were lavish, with more rooms, mosaic floors, frescoes on the walls and the dynamic forms of arches to enliven the spaces. The best examples to be seen are a series of houses in Ephesus which step up a hillside. Like the houses of Pompeii in Italy they look entirely inwards, with very little presence on the street. Their exteriors were lined with small shops so that only the entrances were visible (See p. 286).

VISITING THE SITES

Practical details

Brown road signs show the way to the archaeological sites. Most of them offer parking places, the larger ones charging a fee. Some sites, such as Troy and Ephesus are highly organized and you will be required to keep to paths. On many sites, certain areas that you might want to penetrate are closed off and can only be seen over a fence or from a high place like the upper tier of a theatre. On others, for example Priene and Miletus, you will find more scope for exploration. The archaeologists working at a few cities have provided direction signs and boards with up-to date information and reconstruction drawings; at others you will find little guidance.

Some of the buildings shown on plans are difficult to find. I point out several unmarked paths to places of great interest where you will probably be quite alone, because few people know of them; but they may be difficult to find. Be prepared for long grass full of thistles, thorny shrubs and marshy ground.

Troy VI: Reconstruction (© Christopher Haußner)

TROY

Archaeologists have discovered at least nine distinct layers of habitation at Troy, going back five thousand years. Following cycles of repeated destruction and rebuilding from the Bronze Age to the Roman era, each new city rose over the debris of an earlier settlement. Yet, because of the power of a single literary work, we are mesmerized by the drama that unfolded in the ten-year span of the Trojan War. Homer, in the *Iliad* actually concentrates on a much shorter time, the last months of the war: He tells us of the actions and emotions of a few characters; he exposes their flaws as well as their nobility; he also gives vivid descriptions of the place. The names of the Achaean Greek warriors, Agamemnon, Achilles, Odysseus, Patroclus, as well as the Trojan king Priam, his wife, Hecuba and son Hector, resonate with us, but the millennia before and after the legendary war tend to remain as historical voids.

A visit to Troy leaves many questions unanswered but gives us a richer perspective; it fills in gaps with intriguing revelations. Historians today no longer doubt that the Trojan War took place; however, they believe that its cause was economic. We will never know whether Paris, son of King Priam of Troy, stole away Helen, wife of the Spartan king Menelaus, inciting a war of revenge, but increasing evidence has narrowed the gap between myth and history. It is possible that the Achaean Greeks used the abduction of the beautiful queen as an excuse to attack a rich and powerful kingdom on the other side of the Aegean.

The intersection of myth and history is tenuous, but always fascinating. The bards, telling stories around the fires in palaces and villages, certainly embellished facts, but potent oral traditions kept the legends alive; kernels of truth prevailed. In the case of Troy the debate about fiction and truth will never end. For those who are prepared to devote time and imagination to deciphering the ruins, Troy can powerfully evoke the Trojan War. But, obscured by new layers of building and disrupted by early archaeological efforts, the site is bewildering.

The Trojan War of the *Iliad*

The Greeks, a people with a passion for art and literature, kept their obsession with the Trojan War alive through poetry, drama, sculpture and painting; they also passed their fascination on to the Romans. Artists depicted episodes from the war on ceramic vessels, bringing the stories into everyday life in palaces and houses. Heroic scenes, carved in marble, adorned temples, altars and civic monuments throughout the Greek world. Their deep connection with the heroes of the war is a panhellenic phenomenon; it represents a common heritage shared by Greeks in faraway places, almost as strong as their reverence for the same gods.

Western culture has also embraced the Trojan War. Of all the conflicts in history and mythology it remains, perhaps, the most enduring in our collective memory. The reason lies in Homer's poetry. But what do we know of Homer? Was he a single individual or only one of many poetic voices, gradually combined in the astonishing work of literature, the *Iliad*? Either way, Homer stands out from all the bards who created historical epics for his ability to convey not only dramatic events, but also vivid characterization and psychological depth. Although he lived about four hundred years after the siege of Troy, his descriptions suggest first-hand knowledge of Bronze Age life; he knew the landscape of the Scamander valley, the line of the shore and the presence of Mount Ida in the distance. He also penetrated the human mind as he wove together the elements of the story: prophesy, sexual passion, jealousy, vengeance, brutal conflict, cruelty, deep bonds between friends, compassion, fate. The *Iliad* speaks to us because it deals with timeless emotions and universal issues.

The *Iliad* is also important as an historical document because it sheds vivid light on the relationship between the Greeks and their gods. The seemingly almost human deities of Mount Olympus become deeply involved in the lives of men and women. They observe the unfolding drama, take sides, exert influence, and behave capriciously.

Homer's narrative does not cover the entire war but focuses on events near the end. The larger story begins with a terrifying nightmare. Hecuba, the queen of Troy, dreams that her belly is on fire; a soothsayer tells her that the son she is about to bear will bring destruction to her city. When the baby is born, a servant, ordered by King Priam to kill him, abandons him in a forest on Mount Ida. Miraculously, he is suckled by a she-bear and taken home by a sheepherder. He grows up as a handsome shepherd named Paris. All is well until Eris, the goddess of discord, intervenes. Angry that she is not invited to a wedding feast, she throws a golden apple into the banqueting hall, announcing that it is "for the fairest." A dispute follows between the goddesses present as to which of them is the fairest. Zeus refuses to decide who deserves to win and urges the three who remain in the contest to bring Paris from Mount Ida as judge. Naturally the three goddesses bribe him with extravagant promises: Hera offers power and Athena promises wisdom. It is not surprising that the young man chooses Aphrodite, the goddess of love, who promises to reward him with the most beautiful woman in the world, a more appealing prize to a virile young man.

Paris hands the golden apple to Aphrodite who soon takes him to the court of Menelaus, King of Sparta, and his wife Helen, a daughter of Zeus, renowned for her beauty. Menelaus, a gracious host, trusts his guest and leaves on a journey to Sicily. When he returns, he finds that Helen has sailed away to Troy with Paris taking treasure with her. Menelaus calls on all the chiefs and kings of Greece to invade Troy and bring Helen back to Sparta. Under the command of Agamemnon, King of Mycenae and brother of Menelaus, the Achaeans assemble a fleet of a thousand ships and a potent force of warriors. Among them, Odysseus and Achilles resist the call to war, but are eventually persuaded to go. Artemis, angered when one of her favourite deer is killed by an Achaean soldier, sends a persistent north wind, to prevent their departure. They cannot sail until Agamemnon, in a desperate act of appeasement, has sacrificed his daughter Iphigenia.

When they reach Troy, the Achaean warriors draw up their ships on the shore, set up a fortified camp and launch their first assault on the city. The strong walls and well-armed defenders keep them at bay. Since King Priam has allies among his Anatolian neighbors, this is not just a war between the besiegers and the occupants of the city, but a more complex struggle. The war is said to have continued for ten years, with the advantage going back and forth between the Trojans and their attackers. All of the fighting described by Homer takes place outside the walls; he tells, in vivid detail of the combat between the heroes, but says little about the common soldiers. The Achaeans defend their camp near their boats on the shore, but often command territory near the walls. He does not mention the fate of the lower city, outside the walls.

The Achaeans maraud for food and anything valuable in the surrounding towns; soldiers take it for granted that they can seize women as booty and claim them as honourable prizes. A central subplot in the *Iliad* is the episode in which Agamemnon abducts Chryseis, the daughter of the priest of Apollo at Chryse, a town at the southern end of the Troad. Agamemnon is outraged when her father demands her return, even though he offers a ransom. The victim's father prays to Apollo, asking him to inflict a plague on the invading army. So, once again, a god intervenes, causing Greek soldiers to fall sick and die. Achilles, having heard the opinion of a soothsayer, demands that Chryseis be sent back to her father, but Agamemnon insists on taking Achilles's concubine Bryseis, in return. It is now the turn of Achilles to be angry. His mother, Thetis, a sea-nymph supports his position and looks for help from the gods on Mount Olympus. Achilles sulks in his tent and refuses to fight while a new battle raged.

Without Achilles, the Achaeans lose their advantage. The Trojan prince Hector, known as the "horse trainer," and his brothers are powerful and skilled warriors. At times the invaders are driven back towards their ships. One of the most dramatic episodes in the *Iliad* occurs when the opposing armies are fighting close to the walls; a truce is called and Menelaus challenges Paris to single combat that could have resolved the whole issue. If Paris wins, the Greeks will sail home, leaving Helen in Troy. If he loses, they will take her with them. Menelaus is gaining the upper hand when Aphrodite, who from the beginning has championed Paris, suddenly spirits him away. Agamemnon declares Menelaus the winner and demands the return of Helen. At this point Hera, who also takes the Achaean side, intervenes, urging a Trojan soldier to break the truce by shooting an arrow at Menelaus. It does not injure him severely, but impels the resumption of the war; the tide now turns against the Greeks.

Odysseus tries to persuade Achilles to return to the fray; instead, Achilles allows his friend Patroclus, to fight in his armor. The appearance of a Greek warrior they believe to be Achilles terrifies the Trojans, but Hector mortally wounds Patroclus and takes the armor. The death of his dearest friend arouses Achilles from his torpor. Wearing new armor, made for him by Hephaistos, the blacksmith of the gods, he forces the Trojans back into their city, leaving only Hector outside. Achilles pursues him three times around the city wall, but Athena forces Hector to stand his ground and fight. In a powerful interchange, Homer relates Hector's desperate attempts to make a pact with Achilles that neither will defile the other's body, but Achilles's only thought is to avenge the death of Patroclus. Homer conveys the scorn and hatred as Achilles rejects him with Athena at his side; he drives his spear into Hector's throat, strips the armor from his bloody corpse and drags it around the walls behind his chariot. Only with the intervention of Zeus can grief stricken Priam, laden with valuable treasure, intercede with Achilles for the return of Hector's body.

After a nine-day truce for Hector's burial rites the war resumes again. The tide could turn when a large army of Ethiopians arrives to support the Trojans, but Achilles kills their leader Memnon. Finally, Paris shoots a poisoned arrow that strikes Achilles in the foot, the only part of his body that is vulnerable. Odysseus and Ajax vie for his armor and, when Odysseus is voted the most worthy, Ajax kills himself. Achilles's son avenges his father's death by killing Paris.

Homer's *Iliad* concludes before the final sack of Troy; he only mentions the Trojan Horse in the *Odyssey*, the story of the long drawn out journey of Odysseus home to Ithaca. The Roman author Virgil (70-19 BCE), writing the Aeneid, about eight hundred years after the time of Homer, gives his account of the Achaeans' entry to the walled city in the belly of a wooden horse dissembled as a gift, and then continues to the fiery end of Troy, in other chronicles also tell the story. Archaeology confirms that invaders attacked Troy and that fire destroyed it. While no firm evidence proves that the invaders were Achaean Greeks, these warlike, seagoing people with a reputation as raiders seem to be the obvious suspects.

Barry Stauss, author of *The Trojan War: A New History* (2006), argues that although no contemporary records of the war exist, we know a lot about warfare in the Middle East from literate societies of the same time. He points out, for example, that the description of "champions on both sides, carving paths of blood through the enemy as if they were supermen," echoes accounts from the Hittites and the Assyrians. In the Bronze Age people believed that the gods played powerful roles in human wars.

Rediscovery and Archaeology

Troy did not disappear when the Trojan War was over. After a hiatus, it was colonized by Greeks and remained predominantly Greek in the classical era. Alexander the Great with a copy of the *Iliad* in hand, sacrificed there and paid homage at the tomb of Achilles, before engaging the Persians in the Battle of Granicus. The Romans, believing the Trojan prince Aeneas to be their ancestor and founder, felt a special bond with Troy. They named it Novum Ilium and made major additions to the city, including a forum, temple and theatre. The Emperor Constantine even considered making Troy the capital of his eastern empire. But Byzantium, which possessed many advantages, was his final choice. The fortunes of Troy declined when, in the Hellenistic Age, the harbour silted up.

By the time that European antiquarians were seeking the ruins of the fabled city in the nineteenth century, it lay far from the sea, uninhabited, concealed by a deep layer of silt and a few Roman ruins. Other mounds contended with it as the place where evidence of ancient Troy might be found.

Frank Calvert, a British diplomat in Istanbul with a passion for ancient history, and a love of Homer, became convinced that a mound named Hisarlık was the site of Troy. In 1847, his brother Frederick bought a farm that covered part of the mound and the two of them began excavations on a small scale. They were correct but Heinrich Schliemann, a ruthless German businessman and adventurer, with far more resources at his disposal overshadowed Calvert as the discoverer of Troy. The story of Schliemann's life reads like an improbable novel.

When Schliemann was seven, a book of world history for children captured his imagination. He was particularly fascinated when he read about the Trojan War, and became obsessed by a picture of Aeneas carrying his father Anchises from burning Troy. When his father told him that nothing remained of the city, he became determined to prove him wrong. But first he needed to be rich. Although forced by poverty to leave school at fourteen, and suffering ill health, he possessed a prodigious aptitude for business as well as a phenomenal memory. In only a few years he worked his way from a grocer's assistant to wealthy merchant. Meanwhile he taught himself fifteen languages and travelled the world. His fortune, based on trading indigo in Russia, banking in California during the Gold Rush, and war profiteering in Crimea, finally allowed him to employ hundreds of workers to dig for the city of King Priam.

By 1871, when he began work at Hisarlık at the age of forty-nine, he had married Sophia, a young and beautiful Greek woman willing to share his goals and work with him on the site. At that time, the field of archaeology remained undeveloped. In any case, the meticulous recording of the data practiced by later professionals, would not have appealed to Schliemann. His goal, to find Priam's treasure, blinded him to the greater cause of revealing history accurately. In the autumn of that year, with eighty laborers, he cut a deep trench into the hill starting on the north side. The following spring he continued with almost twice the workforce. He knew what he was looking for and when buildings that appeared to date from later eras stood in his way, he simply demolished them without even making records.

Sophia sorted pottery that he found in a little house that they built above the trench, but at that time no scientific method had been developed for dating the findings in each stratum. He dug too deep, going far below the city of King Priam, and demolishing valuable evidence as he went. But Schliemann's instincts were often rewarded with luck. In the summer of 1873, he noticed a copper object and something glistening behind it. He sent the workers away, and with the help of Sophia, dug out an astonishing collection of gold jewelry, vessels of precious metals and bronze. The objects that excited Schliemann the most were two gold diadems, intricately fashioned out of thousands of minute pieces. Calling them "Priam's Treasure," and convinced that they had been worn by Helen, he put one of them on Sophia's head so that the gold framed her whole face. In his mind, she was the new Helen. As he admitted later, the treasure he had found belonged to a society that lived in Troy 1250 years before the Trojan War.

The "Great Treasure"

Schliemann's permit to excavate required him to give half of his findings to the Turkish government, but he concealed the jewelry and smuggled it to Athens. It was later placed in the Pergamon Museum in Berlin, but at the end of World War II it was taken by the Russians to Moscow. The Turkish government was upset with him for absconding with his "treasure"; so he shifted his attention to Agamemnon's citadel at Mycenae in Greece. He left the mound at Hisarlık in a dreadful state having worked in such a destructive manner. Surprisingly he was able to return there in 1878 and excavated under the watchful eye of Turkish officials for several more seasons.

Wilhelm Dörpfeld, an architect with archaeological experience at Olympia in Greece, joined him in 1882 and began to impose professional methods on the process of excavation. He pioneered the system of stratigraphy that allowed archaeologists to date the layers of a site by comparing the pottery found in them with known examples from other places. This method would have been extremely valuable during Schliemann's early years. Schliemann died in 1890, but Dörpfeld returned in 1893-4. During his last campaign he determined that the superimposed settlements at Troy could be divided into nine distinct layers, as opposed to Schliemann's seven. He numbered the layers with Roman numerals. Troy I to Troy IX

Carl Blegen from the University of Cincinnati conducted excavations at Troy from 1932 to 1938. As he deepened his analysis, he identified two separate phases of history in the layer that Dörpfeld had designated as Troy VII. So he distinguished VIIa from VIIb. Most significantly, he found evidence that the city in VIIa had been brought to an end with violent warfare, followed by fire, establishing a credible link between the ruins he was investigating and the Trojan War.

After Blegen's productive years at Troy, work stopped until 1988 when Dr. Manfred Korfman of Tübingen University began a new archaeological campaign. He identified the position of the Trojan harbour and proved that the lower city of Troy, outside the walls had been much larger than previously believed. He worked with the Turkish authorities to establish a National Park around Troy and UNESCO accepted Troy as a World Heritage Site. With support from the Çanakkale-Tübingen Troia Foundation, he wrote an excellent guidebook entitled Troia / Wilusa.

William Aylward, Classics Professor of the University of Madison-Wisconsin, began a new campaign of excavation in 2013.

History

The original inhabitants of the city we call Troy were native Anatolians not Greeks; they spoke Luvian, an Indo-European language common to various parts of Anatolia. Their kingdom, named Wilusa, was known to the Hittites with whom they developed relations and who sometimes oppressed them. They traded with the Achaean Greeks, who called the city Wilios, and later Ilios. It appears that many Trojans spoke Greek and absorbed Greek culture.

Benefiting from their fertile territory in the Scamander Valley, they grew plentiful crops, raised animals and bred horses, but one significant advantage helped Troy to become the richest Bronze Age city in the whole Aegean. Her strategic position at the mouth of the Hellespont gave her the ability to exert a measure of control over Black Sea trade. She profited from the ships forced to wait for favourable winds in her harbour, causing envy and enmity among her rivals. The phases of Troy's history correspond with the different layers that have been identified by the archaeologists. Please note that some of the numbers and dates have been revised recently and may differ from those published earlier.

Troy I (2920-2550 BCE) The first inhabitants of Wilusa lived simply, relying on fishing and animal husbandry. They protected themselves with walls of roughly coursed stones forming an irregular oval about ninety metres long. The only dwellings that survive are a row of long houses, of mud brick on stone foundations built adjacent to each other, with no

A wall of Troy I with a tower in the distance

A row of houses from Troy I in Schliemann's trench

space between. A fire of unknown cause destroyed this city, leaving a layer of ash and decayed mud brick, which marks the top of the first of the nine layers of Troy.

Troy II (2550-2250 BCE) The same people, whose city had been leveled by fire, rebuilt it on a larger scale in the form of a citadel. It appears that a ruling class had gained power and sought to express an exalted status. They expanded the walled area to enclose a larger oval of irregular shape about 30 m/100 ft. wider. The walls of stone blocks, reinforced by towers, reached a height of 6 m/20 ft. Two monumental gates approached by wide stone-paved ramps led into the citadel through covered passages. Within an inner set of walls, they erected a palatial structure similar to a Mycenean megaron and beside it some smaller megarons. Whether these were palaces or shrines, is unclear. Unlike the long houses of Troy I that shared common walls, these were free standing structures with porches on the south ends. By this time other houses clustered outside the walls.

The lower city, covering an area of 90,000 square metres and surrounded by a wooden palisade, accommodated a greatly increased population.

We know from a rich hoard of bronze weapons, jewelry, and vessels of precious metals, that the people of Wilusa enjoyed prodigious

Reconstruction of Troy II showing ramps leading to the two gates and the Megaron behind an inner line of walls (© Christopher Haußner)

The paved ramp leading to the southwest gate of Troy II

wealth about 1250 years before the Trojan War. Schliemann recognized his discovery as "King Priam's treasure." These artifacts, supplemented by many others unearthed by later archaeologists, bear witness to the widespread trade links forged by the Trojans. Tin, essential for making bronze may have come from as far away as Central Asia? Items of exquisite craftsmanship available only in Egypt and Mesopotamia, and ceramic vessels from various Mediterranean sources, tell us about the extravagant tastes of the Trojan elite.

In the three-hundred-year span of Troy II, three great fires burned there; the final one, probably caused by an unknown enemy, destroyed it completely. This must have been one of the most spectacular cities of the Mediterranean world at that time, but we know too little about it. Lacking inscriptions or records from trading partners with a written language, we do not even know the names of the kings who reigned there or the nature of their religious practices.

Troy III, IV & V (2250-1740/30 BCE) After the fiery end of Troy II, the surviving inhabitants set to work to reconstruct their city, but they did so in a less ambitious manner, with smaller buildings placed closer together in the citadel. Houses were often built side-by-side with common roofs. During the next six hundred years little expansion took place, but seven more conflagrations occurred. Each time, the level of the floors rose a little, as decaying mud bricks and ashes from wooden roof beams added a new stratum.

Troy VI (1740/30-1300 BCE) In about 1740 BCE in the Middle to Late Bronze Age an ambitious new spirit arose in Troy. After the previous rather dormant phase, new leaders more than doubled the space enclosed by walls. Fortifications of dressed stone, with strong towers, encircled a citadel, 180 metres long and 125 wide. The height of the walls was increased two more metres of mud bricks surmounting the six-metre-high stonework. As a precaution against earthquakes, the walls leaned slightly inwards. Slight offsets, visible in vertical lines at intervals along them, may have been purely aesthetic, with the aim of articulating the stone surfaces. An ingeniously curved entrance passage, leading to the east gate, made any attack with a battering ram impossible. In contrast, the south gate, guarded by a large, square tower, opened straight into a street.

On the south side of the citadel, a series of large houses built on the new ground added just inside the walls, suggest a much higher standard of living than the wealthier Trojans had enjoyed earlier; some of them rose to two stories. But all evidence of the palace of the king, at the

The walls of Troy VI. The east entry. The passage curves to the left before it reaches the gate. The remains of a square tower stands in the lower left corner. The walls of a large house can be seen above it

The entrance passage curved before reaching the east gate. The steps inside the east gate

highest point of the hill, vanished when the Romans built their Forum and Temple of Athena on the highest point of the citadel. During this period, trade expanded and the population continued to grow. The lower city, which expanded to 300,000 square metres, absorbed most of the increase. Fatefully, at the height of Troy's success an earthquake struck. It seems that the walls largely survived, but most of the mud brick houses must have collapsed with severe loss of life.

Late Troy VI i (formerly VII a) (1300-1180 BCE) Amazingly, the population recovered and rebuilt the city. Trade continued actively, but there appeared to have been anxiety about defense. Storerooms put up in the citadel look like preparations for a siege. The tall square tower by the east gate was erected and some minor entrances were blocked with stone. This appears to be the city of the legendary King Priam, the setting for the Trojan War. Many archaeological discoveries point to destruction caused by foreign invaders. Why should they not have been the Achaean Greeks led by the kings of Mycenae and Sparta?

Reconstruction of the city described in the *Iliad*   A length of wall added to the walls from Troy VII

Troy VI j (1180-1130 BCE) After the fall of Troy a simpler people, with cultural links to those of the previous period, lived in smaller buildings inside the walls. They do not appear to have imported valuable ceramics, but made what they needed themselves.

Troy VII b (1150- 950 BCE) During this period ceramics similar to wares made in the northeastern Balkans appeared in Troy, suggesting occupation by a different cultural group. This population diminished and for a while the citadel was virtually uninhabited.

Troy VIII (700 -85 BCE) At the beginning of this period Aeolian Greeks, whose forebears had migrated across the Aegean from mainland Greece, occupied the citadel. Aware that this was the historic Troy, they named it Ilion and built a temple to Athena. They cleared away the remnants of Bronze Age buildings from the highest point of the hill to create a large temenos with stoas on three sides. They also erected other temples. The Greek city lasted through many centuries from the Dark Age to the Hellenistic era; so it clearly went through many changes. Alexander came to make sacrifices at the tomb of Achilles, which the inhabitants appear to have identified.

Troy IX (85 BCE – 400 or 600 CE) The Greek city, though not particularly important in the Hellenistic era, must have contained fine

A sanctuary from Troy VIII Part of the wall of Troy II stands behind it

The Odeon

architecture, but we know little of it. In 86 BCE the Roman general
Gaius Fimbria led a violent campaign in Asia and, using a dishonest
ruse to enter Troy, massacred the people and destroyed the city. While
most Romans, proud of the Trojan heritage they claimed through
Aeneas, respected Troy, this evil man dealt a cruel blow to the innocent
inhabitants.

The Emperor Augustus, the founder of the Roman Empire, who ruled
from 27 BCE to 14 CE rebuilt the Temple of Athena. Other emperors
including Hadrian and Caracalla restored the Greek odeon and gradually
transformed it into a Roman metropolis. Predictably, they brought fresh
water from springs on Mount Ida to elevate Troy up to Roman standards
of hygiene. Meanwhile the lower city, now entirely planned on a grid,
increased in size.

Visiting Troy

The first sight of the walls of Troy comes as a shock; they seem so
small. But, rising originally to ten metres, they were much higher than
they are today and were finished with a uniform crenellated top. They
were wide enough to hold many defending soldiers, and tall towers protected the gates. These fortifications stood here for more than a millennium and, as far as we know, excluded all adversaries until the city was
finally sacked. The curved passage that leads to the gate demonstrates a
brilliantly simple means of foiling attacks.

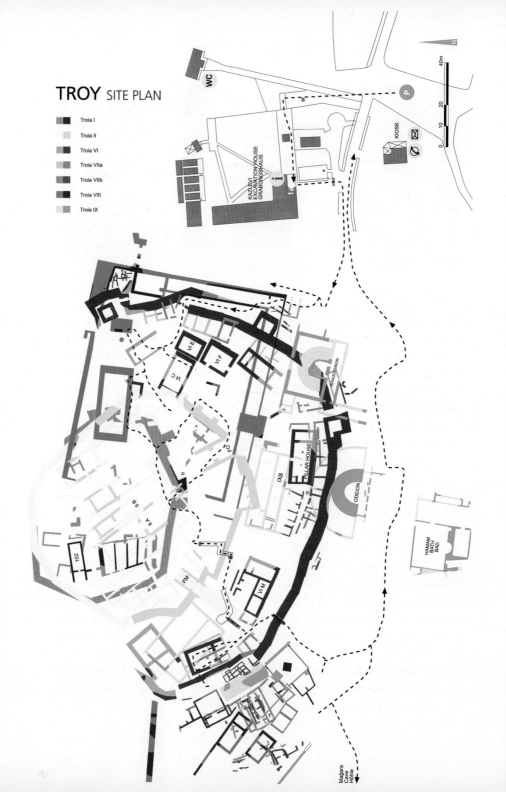

TROY SITE PLAN

- ■ Troia I
- ■ Troia II
- ■ Troia VI
- ■ Troia VIIa
- ■ Troia VIIb
- ■ Troia VIII
- ■ Troia IX

N

40m

20

10

0

P

KIOSK

WC

KAZI EVI
EXCAVATION HOUSE
GRABUNGSHAUS

i

BOULEUTERION

VI E

VI F

VI C

FÖ

Ir

II B

II A

102

FM

IX B

PILLAR HOUSE

ODEON

VI M

HAMAM
BATH
BAD

Mağara
Cave
Höhle

(L) Schliemann's trench with strata marked to show historic periods. (R) The remains of a wall from Troy II and the remains of a Megaron from Troy II/III protected by a canvas roof. A powerful contrast between archaeological methods

These walls are the most coherent part of Troy. After you pass through the opening where the gate once stood, and climb the steps to the upper level, the site becomes confusing. You will go almost straight from the walls of Troy II and the remains of houses from Troy VI, just inside them, to some fragments of the Roman temple from the first century CE. Not only do you see elements from different periods out of sequence, you encounter the trench cut by Schliemann, through the many strata. In one part of the trench, small plaques, marked with Roman numerals, show how the strata correspond with the historic periods.

To protect the fragile remains, a one-way path leads visitors around the site and barriers prevent you from straying. But the archaeologists and the Çanakkale-Tübingen Troia Foundation have made the exploration of Troy as rewarding as possible by placing a series of well-designed information boards in key positions around the site. Each one explains the sights nearby and provides an historical context. They have also executed exemplary restorations. Two of the most intriguing structures to see are now sheltered by a sail-like canopy created in 2003. One of them is a section of the brick wall from Troy II, baked by the fire that destroyed the city. The archaeologists have protected it by adding a few courses of brick that they made by an ancient method. Next to this wall are the remains of a Megaron from Troy II or III. When I look at this abode of about 2200 BCE, I cannot help wondering what stories were told around its central fire. I do not doubt that forerunners of Homer, who passed an oral tradition to him, drew from the events of earlier days to conceive their own epics.

The Baths of Herodes Atticus. Three of the arches still stand.

ALEXANDRIA TROAS

Alexandria Troas, originally a small Aeolian settlement, possessed the advantage of a fine harbour not far from the opening to the Hellespont. In 310 BCE Antigonus I, one of the successors to Alexander the Great, founded a new city there and named it Antigonia in his own honour. Lysimachus, who defeated Antigonus at the battle of Ipsus eight years later, changed the name to Alexandria. Soon, to distinguish it from many other cities of the same name, it became Alexandria Troas. To help realize its economic potential, Lysimachus forced the populations of seven nearby cities to move to the site. Since the sea had receded from Troy, leaving the fabled city landlocked, the port of Alexandria Troas became the busiest in the region. It thrived as a transfer point between Aegean shipping and overland trade with central Anatolia, and attracted wealthy traders; it soon rivaled nearby Assos. Among the goods exported from there to Rome were granite columns of stone quarried near Neandria eight kilometres to the east.

The Emperor Augustus, who founded a Roman colony there considered making it the capital of his empire, renamed it Augusta Troadensis. During the reign of Hadrian the city functioned as the administrative centre of the Province of Asia under the leadership of Herodes Atticus whom he appointed as prefect in 125 CE. This scholarly Greek, a philosopher who became a Roman senator, and a great philanthropist, is best known for building the Theatre of Herodes Atticus in Athens in 161 CE. In Alexandria Troas, he commissioned the longest surviving monument, the Baths that bear his own name as well as an aqueduct supplying it with water and a large theatre. The city remained prosperous into the fourth century CE, when the emperor Constantine considered making it his eastern capital. But the final selection of Byzantium as the capital, and its dazzling transformation into Constantinople signaled the decline of Alexandria Troas. Earthquakes also took their toll. Ironically, the excellence of the harbour sealed the city's fate. The ease of loading stone quarried from the buildings onto ships, made it a good source of materials for Ottoman mosques and palaces. For example, in the seventeenth century, Sultan Mehmet IV's architect, building the Yeni Valide Mosque on the Golden Horn in Istanbul, took limestone for walls, domes, and columns as well as marble revetments to embellish surfaces.

Alexandria Troas played a role in the history of Christianity in the region. St. Paul sailed from there on his first journey to Europe and returned there later. He preached there again in 59 CE and caught the attention of the populace by reviving a man named Eutychus who fell out of a high window and was believed to be dead. After a few days, St. Paul left to walk over the mountains to Assos. The city was the seat of a series of bishops during the Byzantine era.

Visiting Alexandria Troas

The narrow, winding coastal road, leading north from Assos and Chryse towards Troy, passes close to Alexandria Troas. A brown sign will show you where to turn off onto a small loop road, and another sign announces your arrival. But there is no parking place or ticket office to indicate that this is an archaeological site. If you look up, on the east side of the road you will see a tall stack of masonry rising above the trees. A path to the left of it takes you to the muscular remains of the Baths of Herodes Atticus. A second path, to the right of the first one, leads to a place where it is easy to climb up onto the high structure. From this position you can look out over the whole site. In the foreground, three arches span between massive abutments, but the walls and vaults they carried have collapsed. The voussoirs (wedge-shaped stones) of the nearest arch demonstrate the brilliant structural logic of this device. Almost two thousand years after they were built the voussoirs stand alone: twenty-two small stones defying gravity, as they soar over a wide opening.

In April 2013, I scrambled up to this aerie and sat comfortably while surveying the site, with the Aegean beyond it, I found it hard to believe that a hundred thousand people once lived here. Looking inland I could see the nearby ridge occupied by Neandria, a city whose population was forced by Lysimachus to move to Alexandria Troas. I remembered exploring Alexandria Troas twenty-two years earlier and identifying the outline of the theatre and the foundations of a temple. Now the vallonea

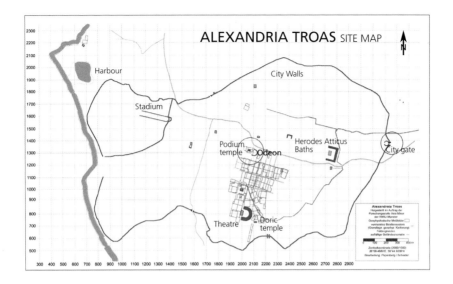

ALEXANDRIA TROAS SITE MAP

Harbour

City Walls

Stadium

Podium temple Odeon Herodes Atticus Baths City gate

Theatre Doric temple

oak trees covering the ground have grown taller and thicker, making it almost impossible to walk in any direction. Only the most tenacious travelers will be inclined to trace the substantial remains of ten kilometers of walls or search for vestiges of architecture within them.

A team of German archaeologists from the University of Münster in association with the universities of Ankara and Çanakkale has been excavating there since 1993 and have recently discovered a stadium, but this is not a site that demands a visit unless you are passing nearby. The picturesque village of Dalyanköy, which offers simple waterside restaurants, occupies the ancient harbour, which is now separated from the sea by a sandbar.

Statue base with sacred symbols of Apollo uncovered at the Baths

CHRYSE (Smintheion, Gülpınar)

While Alexandria Troas was not founded until the Hellenistic era, Chryse goes back to the Bronze Age. According to the geographer Strabo, writing at the end of the first century BCE, a group of Cretans emigrating to the Aegean coast of Anatolia and seeking a good site, received advice from an oracle that they should settle in the place where they were attacked by the 'earth-born.' While they were sleeping near the shore where they landed, mice came out of the ground and not only ate their provisions, but gnawed at the leather straps of their armor. Understanding that they had arrived at the favoured place, they founded their city and honoured Apollo as their patron god. They dedicated their first temple to Apollo Smintheus, the mouse god. Strabo claims that they were ancestors of the Trojans.

In the *Iliad*, Homer names Chryse as the city of the priest named Chryses, whose daughter Chryseis was seized by Agememnon as a concubine. Her abduction, as a prize of war, and her joyful return in Odysseus's ship were pivotal episodes in the quarrel between Achilles and Agamemnon. The story also sheds light on religious rituals of the Homeric era. Homer describes the beaching of the ship with Chryseis in the prow, and loaded with bulls and goats for sacrifice to Apollo in expiation for the insult to Apollo. According to tradition the most prized portions of meat would have been reserved for Apollo, the rest consumed by the Greek oarsmen and the people of Chryse. As we stand on the site we can imagine the roasting of meat over many fires, as well as the scene of feasting and singing before the drunken companions of Odysseus fell asleep on the shore.

The Smintheum (or Smintheion) we see today was built a millennium later than the event described by Homer. This temple, in the Ionic style, is an early example of a type described as pseudo-dipteral, which means that the roof projected far beyond the walls of the cella, without the

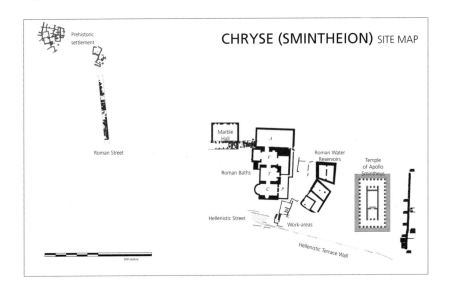

Prehistoric settlement

Roman Street

Marble Hall

Roman Baths

Roman Water Reservoirs

Temple of Apollo Smintheus

Hellenistic Street

Work-areas

Hellenistic Terrace Wall

100 metre

support of an inner row of columns. It may have influenced the great architect Hermogenes of Priene, who designed two beautiful temples of this type a generation later at Teos and Magnesia. Another significant feature of the design is the frieze showing scenes from the Trojan War, the

Reconstruction proposal for Apollo Smintheus temple

earliest known example of this subject in Anatolia. Some panels from this frieze can be seen in the small museum on the site which is open during the excavation season (usually June to September). Strabo mentions a fine wooden statue of Apollo by the famous Greek sculptor Skopas, who at one time worked with Praxiteles. The ruin of the temple was hastened in Byzantine times when marble blocks from it were taken to build a Christian church, and then used again for a mosque.

The Hellenistic Smintheion with restored steps c.200 BCE

A scene from the Trojan War in the frieze of the Smintheion

Temple of Athena, Assos c.530
A unique Doric temple built in the archaic period.

ASSOS

Homer described the population of Assos as pirates and seamen. The city became the capital of an indigenous Lelegian population. In the tenth century Greeks of Thracian origin migrated across the narrow gulf of Edremit from Methymna on the island of Lesbos to colonize the site. Assos emerged from the Dark Age as one of the principal Aeolian cities. Little is known of the early development of the city, but by the mid-sixth century BCE it was prosperous enough for its people to build an impressive temple to Athena, overlooking the water towards Lesbos. This sacred site, an acropolis on an extinct volcanic peak, dramatically celebrates the bond between architecture and landscape that was so dear to the Greeks. Below it, on a series of terraces stepping down towards the harbour, stood the principal buildings of the polis, the Agora with its stoas and Bouleuterion and a theatre set naturally into the hillside. The remains of the civic architecture mostly date from the Hellenistic era, but, in the previous centuries, civic activities took place in the same areas.

Athena's helmeted head appears on one side of a coin minted there in the sixth century BCE, with a griffin on the reverse. Later coins, celebrate the agricultural riches of the city with the heads of cows, wheat and grapes. Like its neighbors, Assos was conquered by King Croesos of Lydia in 560 BCE and in 546, after his ignominious rout by the Persian king, became subject to the Persian Empire. After the Athenians defeated the Persians, Assos gained independence; it joined the Delian League as a founding member in 478. At this time the population was probably about 4,500.

In the mid-fourth century while Hermeias was king, the cultural life of Assos thrived. In a fascinating course of events, Hermeias, a slave and eunuch belonging to Eubolos the ruler of the nearby city of Artaneus, was sent to study in Plato's academy in Athens, where he became a friend of Aristotle. On his return to Aeolis, he became king of Assos jointly with

Eubolos whom, by some accounts, he murdered. Hermeias maintained close relations with Athens and his city competed in the Olympic games. Wanting to preside over a state where intellect could rule, he invited Aristotle and other philosophers to join him there. Aristotle enjoyed a privileged position in the city; he married Hermias's niece Pythia, who bore him a daughter. He led the discourse of a lively school of philosophers, including Callisthenes, Theophrastus and Xenocrates. It is believed that he started to write his Politics there as well as a work that has been lost: *On Kingship*.

But this golden age of civic pride and philosophical inquiry was brought to a tragic end in 341 when the Persians invaded. The scholarly and liberal-minded king Hermeias was tortured to death and the philosophers fled with Aristotle to Mytilene on the island of Lesbos. Seven years later, in 334, Alexander the Great, who had been tutored by Aristotle in the Macedonian palace at Pella, defeated the Persians and Assos was freed from Persian rule.

When Alexander's successors, the Diadochi, fought over the empire after his death the region became less stable. For sixty years, the Galatians, a Celtic people with large territories to the north, ruled Assos, but in 241 King Attalos I of Pergamon succeeded in defeating these invaders and annexed the city. Both Pergamon, the richest polis in the region, and Assos benefited from the patronage of the wise and benevolent Attalos. This political change launched a period of outstanding civic architecture. It was during this time that the Agora was enlarged and a second stoa built, probably by Pergamene architects. Attalos III, the grandson of Attalos I willed his kingdom, on his death, to the Roman republic. So, in 133 BCE Assos passed peacefully into the orbit of Rome.

Under the republic and later the Empire, Assos continued to prosper; Roman traders settled there; new architecture was built and additions were made to the theatre. In 17 CE the eastern provinces were given to the popular general Germanicus as a reward for his victories over the Germanic tribes. The next year, when he visited Assos with his wife Agrippina, the Assians erected a statue of him in the Bouleuterion and flattered the couple with an inscription to Gaius Caesar Germanicus and the goddess Agrippina. When their youngest son Caligula became emperor, Assos sent five delegates to Rome to celebrate his accession and to make sacrifices to

Jupiter at the Capitol. During this period the city of Alexandria Troas, a few kilometers to the north, began to eclipse Assos in importance.

The coming of Christianity to Roman Asia made a big impact on Assos. In c. 59 CE, Saint Paul, on his long journey from Corinth to Jerusalem, met Saint Luke and preached there. Although he usually traveled by ship, he had walked from Alexandria Troas. In the Byzantine era Assos was the seat of a bishop, and in 325 participated in the Council of Nicea, a gathering of all Christian bishops called by the Emperor Constantine. Evidence of five churches remains. The lower walls of all these structures can still be seen. In the fifth century CE Christians, desiring to obliterate pagan symbols, destroyed several Roman buildings, and burned marble sculpture in limekilns.

Assos was captured by the Seljuks in 1080 and by the Ottomans in 1330. During the next few hundred years the city was kept alive by trade. The most prominent Ottoman monument, the Hüdavendigar Mosque built by the Sultan Murad I in the late fourteenth century, still stands near the upper entrance to the site. It was a fine mosque in its time, but has been somewhat altered. More noteworthy, but easily missed is the Ottoman bridge with four arches over the Tuzla River to the east of the road from Ayvacık. Built of cut stone, with excellent workmanship it is one of the best examples of its type.

Damage from earthquakes and frequent attacks by pirates decimated the population. Gradually the residential areas moved to the site of the present village of Behramkale, on the north side of the Acropolis, to avoid pirate raids.

Rediscovery and Archaeology

As early as the seventeenth century, Assos captivated western travelers with a classical education and romantic dispositions. They perceived in the architectural remains the embodiment of the Greek polis as described by Aristotle. John Covel, chaplain to the ambassador of Charles II of England to the Ottoman court, discovered Assos in 1677 and described the ruins in his journal. A French ambassador in Constantinople the Comte de Choiseul Gouffier wrote a vivid account of Assos in his *Voyage pittoresque dans l'Empire Ottomane*. In 1800, William Martin Leake, an English military man and diplomat with antiquarian interests, visited Assos and wrote:

The Agora today with much of the architecture described by Clarke missing

"The whole gives perhaps, the most perfect idea of a Greek city that anywhere exists." The first excavation was by a French team in 1835, under the direction of an architect, Charles Texier. Three years later, with the help of the French navy and permission from the Ottoman Sultan Mahmud II, they removed some sculpture to the Louvre in Paris. A description written in 1839 by the English traveler and artist, Sir Charles Fellows, shows how much more was visible on the site than we can see today:

"Immediately around me were the ruins, extending for miles, undisturbed by any living creature except the goats and kids. On every side lay columns, triglyphs, and friezes, of beautiful sculpture, every object speaking of the grandeur of this ancient city. In one place I saw thirty Doric capitals placed up in a line for a fence. I descended towards the sea, and found the whole front of the hill a wilderness of ruined temples, baths, and theatres, all of the best workmanship, but all of the same grey stone as the neighboring rock."

Much of the masonry seen by Fellows was systematically carted away in the years that followed when the site was used a source of stone for new construction in Istanbul.

Fortunately, serious and expert archaeological work soon began. In 1879 two adventurous young American architects, Joseph Thatcher Clarke and Francis Bacon arrived in a 20-foot sloop to investigate the site. They

The village of Behramkale, the mosque and a bastion of the ancient walls.

were so convinced that the site should be excavated that they were able to persuade Charles Eliot Norton, the professor of classics at Harvard as well as leaders of the recently founded Archaeological Institute of America, to raise funds for a proper archaeological survey. Under the leadership of Clarke, and with Bacon as draftsman, the site was excavated for three seasons in 1881-3. The German architect Robert Koldeway joined them in the second season and cut his teeth in archaeology. His experience at Assos launched a career culminating in the discovery of the Ishtar Gate and the Hanging Gardens at Babylon. The Institute published the impressive findings of the team in 1882 and 1898 in two well-illustrated volumes.

Clarke's journal shows the excitement he experienced as he tried to visualize the city in its heyday:

The past week we have been busy surveying and planning future work. The place grows on us daily. It is something enormous! The south slope of the Acropolis must have been a wonderfully picturesque place! A large terrace just above the theatre, with a portico at the back 300 feet long, flanked at each end by temples or other secular buildings. What a place it must have been for youth and beauty to promenade in the cool stone porch before the performance in the theatre below! The portico and terrace lined with sculpture and works of art! 'Tis high up over the sea, the blue mountains of Mytilene opposite! Then there are the hundreds of sarcophagi and monuments at the Street of Tombs, and the imposing fortification walls around, crowned on top by the old temple, and when one thinks of the fertile valley and the cool river flowing through it right down from Mt. Ida, everything goes together! The clean cut Greeks and their surroundings of Temples, Tombs and Porticos! Long live the memory of the bright and merry Greeks!

A postscript to the late nineteenth century excavations at Assos is that Francis Bacon's younger brother Henry, who joined the team of archaeologists there, went on to become a successful architect in the United States and gained acclaim for his design of the Lincoln Memorial in Washington DC. Dr. Bonna Westcoat suggests that the architect absorbed principles at Assos that allowed him to create a symbol of American reunification and emancipation that was "purely Greek" and "centred on freedom." Thus she evokes a connection between the architecture of this Aegean city and the place where Marianne Anderson sang and Martin Luther King made his "I have a dream" speech.

After decades of neglect, archaeological excavations began again in 1979 under the direction of Dr. Ümit Serdaroğlu with support from the Turkish Ministry of Culture and Tourism. Dr. Bonna Westcoat of Emory University joined the excavations for several seasons and, after years of measurement and analysis, has developed a comprehensive theory on both the original design of the temple's entablature and the meaning of its sculptural ornamentation. The latest phase of the work is receiving support from the Archaeological Institute of America.

Visiting the site at Assos

I recommend beginning at the temple so that you can get an overall sense of the site and enjoy the panorama. It is a short walk from the parking area and bus stop through the attractive village of Behramkale, where you will pass small hotels and restaurants. After visiting the Acropolis, you can follow the road down and enter the lower levels of the city through gates that are not locked. The first leads through the necropolis to the Agora; the second to the theatre. The road continues down to the picturesque little harbour, which is worth seeing. When you reach the water you will be able to imagine the hard climb to the Agora and the temple that faced travelers arriving in the city in ancient times. I do not recommend trying to go on foot from the Agora to the temple.

Health Centre

to Ayvacık

to Kadırga Cove

to Gülpınar

ASSOS SITE MAP

Ayazma Church

City Walls

Necropolis

to harbour

Ahır Church

Mosque

Entrance

Acropolis

Cistern

Temple of Athena

Eastern
Gate

Western
Gate

Gymnasium

Agora

Houses

Bouleuterion

Western
Church

Theatre Church

Theatre

Long walking route ·····
Short walking route ·····

Hotels and Restaurants

Gendarmerie

Parking Area

Ancient Harbour

Harbour

Coastal Church

AEGEAN SEA

The Temple of Athena

Standing 236 m/ 775 ft. above sea level, the Temple of Athena, built
in about 530 BCE, is the only Doric temple in the eastern Aegean. With
its columns tapering to a narrow neck and the widely flaring capitals, it is
typical of the archaic era, somewhat reminiscent of columns of sixth century temples in Corinth and Paestum. But the columns are more widely
spaced than was usual. The choice of the Doric style suggests the influence of Athens, although scholars have regarded this example as distinctly provincial. The most unusual feature is the presence of sculpture on the
architrave, whose surface remains unornamented in all other Doric architecture. In the Ionic order, the commonest order on the Anatolian coast,
the architrave was traditionally adorned with sculpture, so it appears

The frieze of triglyphs and metopes and the carved architrave (Istanbul Archaeological Museums)

that the architect created an unusual hybrid under the influence of local practice. Bonna Westcoat, author of *The Temple of Athena, Assos*, has argued that although academics tend to look for conformity with architectural rules, the architects at Assos should receive credit for "placing visual communication at the forefront of their enterprise." She points out that the frieze on the architrave is in the most visible place possible for a continuous narrative in low relief.

Only ten of the original sixty-eight metopes survive. The subjects they represent include the abduction of Europa by Zeus, King Priam pleading for the return of Hector's body during the Trojan War, two sphinxes facing each other and fights between animals. Part of the entablature can be seen in the Istanbul Archaeological Museums.

As on the metopes of the Parthenon in Athens, centaurs appear on several sections of the architrave. But these creatures, half man and half horse, are not illustrating the same story, the battle of the Lapiths and the centaurs, that is enacted on the Parthenon in Athens. The sculpture at Assos represents the Labors of Heracles. The scene illustrated shows Heracles in an incident on his way to capture the Erymanthian boar, when he chases away drunken centaurs that have attacked him. It is interesting to note that while the front legs of most centaurs in Greek art are like those of horses with hoofs, some of those at Assos have human front legs and feet.

Part of a mosaic of black and white marble placed in the cella in the Hellenistic period was found by Clarke and Bacon but none of it remains today. The temple was damaged by an earthquake before Assos joined the Roman Empire; it appears not to have been used during the Roman era.

In 2010, under the direction of the archaeologist Nurettin Arslan, the stylobate of the temple and six standing columns were restored using the local stone of which they were originally built. The lower shafts of other columns align with the complete ones, helping us to envisage the whole peristyle. Rising from an orderly base, the columns of this unique archaic temple proclaim the sacred nature of the place.

When you stand beside the ruins of Athena's temple and gaze over Lesbos and the Aegean, as Aristotle did twenty-three centuries ago, you can picture the role of Assos as a shining light in the Hellenic world.

The Fortifications

The andesite walls surrounding Assos, originally three kilometers long, are the most complete in the Hellenic world. They include two impressive gateways, the largest of which, the West Gate, rises almost fifteen meters high. It remains sufficiently intact to give an idea of the city's defensive power. This gate is approached by an ancient paved road that passes through the necropolis. The oldest sections of the walls, built in the sixth century BCE, can be identified by their polygonal blocks of masonry, differing from the early fourth century fortifications, which

The fourth century walls near the West Gate

The West Gate of Assos seen from the Necropolis with an open sarcophagus in the foreground.

were built with fine cut stone. These walls offer an excellent example of military engineering in the late classical era.

The Necropolis

Below the southwest side of the Acropolis lies the fascinating necropolis of Assos with impressive tombs of the Hellenistic and Roman eras. The sarcophagi possess an intriguing attribute, inherent in the type of stone used: the ability to decompose bodies quickly. The Greek word sarcophagus literally means, "flesh eating." It is not surprising that Assos exported sarcophagi.

In addition to the smaller tombs, foundations of larger ones survive, most notably that of the wealthy Roman, Publius Varius. This tomb with

(L) A typical sarcophagus (R) Tomb of Publius Varius

its barrel-vaulted interior provided the archaeologist Francis Bacon with a cool place to enjoy his lunch each day while excavating the site. He surmised the unusual form of the superstructure.

The city plan

Responding to the terrain, the city was laid out on a series of bow shaped terraces on the contours, which began to curve at the two ends of the Agora. The civic buildings stood in the centre, while residential quarters were mostly built to the east.

The Agora, the centre of activity in Assos, was entered through a formal gate beside a temple from the second century BCE that was built, in the Roman manner, on the axis of the civic space. Consistent use of the Doric order unified the architecture of the Agora, which was all carved from the hard, grey andesite quarried nearby. Only the capitals were of white marble. On the north side stood a stoa two stories high, not unlike the Stoa of Attalos in Athens. Since both were designed by Pergamene architects, the similarity is not surprising. It was not built directly against the steep slope above, but set slightly forward to avoid dampness and to let the cool air from behind it to circulate.

This Stoa would have been an elegant, covered market, capturing the winter sun, but comfortable in the hot summer. The slightly earlier stoa on the other side presented only one story to the Agora but, profiting from the change in level, it was four stories high on the other side. At the east end of the Agora stood a large Bouleuterion built in the early second century. This was the council house of Assos, with an interior space about 20 meters square sheltered by a wooden roof. It was built as a gift to the city by a private citizen. Since there is no sign of stone tiers of seats, we can assume that the seats for members of the boule were built up of wood. At the other end of the

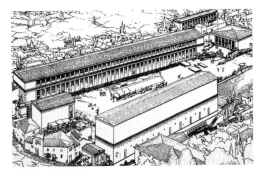

Reconstruction of the Agora

(L) The Bouleuterion at the eastern end of the Agora (R) The Roman bath below the South Stoa. The back wall of the North Stoa and the cliffs of the Acropolis are visible in the background .

Agora, a raised platform is all that remains from the Doric temple from the Hellenistic era.

The Roman Bath below the South Stoa, according to an inscription found by the American archaeologists, was dedicated to Julia, Aphrodite and to the people the city by Lollia Antiochis, She was a member of the imperial family and a prominent citizen of Assos in the first century CE. Only the back wall stands; the area in front of it is covered by debris from excavations.

The Gymnasium, built in the second century BCE, stood to the northwest of the Agora. It was a replacement for the gymnasium where Aristotle may have taught the young men of Assos. It was severely damaged while the site was used as a stone quarry, but the bases of walls and columns give an idea of its layout. Typical of Greek gymnasia it was essentially a palaestra, a spacious courtyard, with rooms opening off one side. While the shafts of the surrounding Doric columns were of grey andesite, the capitals were of marble. A barrel-vaulted cistern from the Roman period can still be seen under the gymnasium. A small church built in the Byzantine era filled the northeast corner of the court, encroaching on its original space. The foundations of the apse of the church are visible. The **Western Church,** on the left, a little further down the road can be seen over a fence with an information board beside it. The lower walls reveal the typical Byzantine, apsidal plan with a nave almost twenty meters long. Thatcher and Clark found mosaics in good condition on the floor. One could probably walk to it from the theatre, but there is no path through the dense growth. The **Theatre Church,** a little beyond the theatre has not been excavated and is virtually inaccessible.

The Theatre of Assos built in the third century BCE and enlarged by the Romans

The Theatre

The Theatre at Assos, built in the third century BCE, offered its 5000 spectators one of the most beautiful settings in the Hellenic world with the Aegean as a backdrop. We do not know about the performances that took place there but some details have emerged. For example, inscriptions show that leather workers and ironsmiths had seats reserved for them. The theatre was enlarged by the Romans, and restored with carefully matched andesite blocks in the twentieth century. Further restoration was begun in 2011. I suggest that you sit on one of the upper tiers while a traveling companion declaims a lively passage from a classical drama. You will experience the acoustic quality of the theatre with the speaker's voice bouncing off the orchestra floor, but creating no echoes.

The Harbour

While many town sites were chosen for their natural harbour, the Greeks who colonized Assos gave priority to defensible terrain and an ideal site for a temple. To compensate for the lack of protection from high seas, they built two stone breakwaters. These have been reinforced over the years and still enclose two small harbours. The picturesque, stone built village, with hotels and restaurants attracts many summer visitors. To reach it, follow the sign to Antik Liman.

Temple of Trajan

PERGAMON

Pergamon, rising dramatically on a hilltop four hundred metres high above the valley of the River Kaikos, is among the most exciting places in Aegean Turkey to visit. Since it lies inland from the sea it did not attract Greek colonists during the Dark Age; a small indigenous population occupied the site. The legend of the mythical founder Telephos, the son of Heracles, that is depicted in sculpture on the Altar of Zeus, probably arose from a desire to enhance the city's stature in the Hellenic mind. During the archaic period it remained a small hilltop city with a commanding and easily fortified position. In about 470 BCE King Gongylos of Eritrea, who supported the Persians, ruled there. In 399 BCE the Spartans, attempting to gain territory in Anatolia after the Peloponnesian War, seized it for a short while with the help of the historian and mercenary Xenophon; but they failed to hold it.

After his victory at the Battle of Granicus in 334 BCE, Alexander the Great bypassed Pergamon on his march south to Sardis and Ephesus. But his successors, the Diadochi who fought each other for the control of his empire impacted the city's future: Lysimachus held Pergamon, but after his rival Antigonus died at the battle of Ipsus (301 BCE), he gave the command of the city to Philetairos, a Greek from the Black Sea region, who had earlier supported Antigonus, but changed sides in the conflict. Lysimachus also entrusted him with the safekeeping of his war booty worth 9,000 silver talents that he had deposited in the citadel there. Philetairos served Lysimachus until 282 BCE, when he betrayed him by suddenly turning over both the citadel and the treasury to his enemy Seleucus. But within a few months Lysimachus and Seleucus had both been slain, opening the way for Philetairos to rule Pergamon. Despite his repeated treacheries, Philetairos governed wisely until his death in 263. Making use of the rich treasury, he initiated a major campaign of building on the Acropolis, strengthening its walls and raising temples to Demeter and to Athena, the patron goddess of the city. He gave generous support to art and culture, for which Pergamon was celebrated for centuries. Thus, his city rivaling Alexandria and Athens, was revered for architecture, sculpture, philosophy and, above all, its library. It also led the Greek world in the field of medicine.

Pergamon remained, nominally, under Seleucid control but Philetairos enjoyed autonomy. Although impotent and unmarried, he founded the Attalid dynasty of kings that ruled until 133 BCE. He adopted his nephew Eumenes and passed the reins of power to him after his death. The generations of Attalids that followed cultivated friendship and military solidarity with the Athenians and the Romans, but remained steadfast against the ambitious Macedonians and Seleucids. By limiting warfare mainly to fighting those who directly threatened them, they gained wealth and territory. Eumenes I (r. 263-241 BCE) strengthened the Attalid hold on Pergamon when he joined with Ptolemy II to defeat the Seleucid king Antiochus I in 261. After this victory, he presided over a period of peace, disturbed only by attacks from marauding Galatians, a Celtic people from Central Anatolia known to the Romans as Gauls. Eumenes probably kept them at bay by paying the tribute they demanded. He was succeeded by his cousin Attalos whom he had adopted.

Attalos I (r. 241- 197 BCE) defeated the Galatians decisively and was acclaimed with the name of "Soter" (saviour) He sided with the Romans

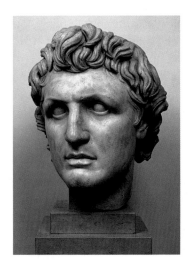

Attalos I

against Philip V of Macedon. While warding off invaders and gaining favour with the Romans, Attalos I established a long period of stability. His admiration for Athenian culture led him to send his son Eumenes to be educated in Athens. Attalos I acted as a benefactor to other cities, including nearby Assos, by sending skilled craftsmen to assist them with their architectural ventures. He also dedicated a stoa at Delphi. The reign of his son Eumenes II (r. 197-159 BCE) was a golden age for Pergamon. As a student in Athens he fell under the spell of the Acropolis

The Stoa of Attalos, built by Eumenes II, as a gift to the Athenians in their Agora was rebuilt in replica by the American School of Classical Studies in Athens in 1952. It conveys an idea of the of the Stoas he built in Pergamon.

and felt inspired by it to add to the architectural glory of his own city. Near the foot of the hill he erected a propylon, a formal gateway to the Acropolis, the beginning of a unique urban promenade from which the architecture of the city would gradually be revealed. His greatest achievements included the enlargement of the theatre, the steepest in the Greek world, which seated 10,000 spectators; building the library which was second only to the library at Alexandria, and constructing the Altar of Zeus, one of the greatest monuments of the Hellenistic world. He also levelled terraces on the lower slopes to allow for new buildings and urban spaces. He added a Lower Agora and a vast gymnasium. The local andesite stone gave most of the architecture a grey colour that fused it to the hill, but white marble allowed Pergamene sculptors to create some of the finest sculpture of the Hellenistic era. In appreciation of his education in Athens, he gave support to the city's philosophical schools and built the impressive Stoa of Attalos in the Athenian Agora. During his reign, agriculture and manufacturing thrived, most significantly the making of '*charta pergamena*,' parchment prepared as an alternative to papyrus for the production of books. He also founded the sacred city of Hierapolis in Caria and, in order to expand trading opportunities, he established Attaleia, now known as Antalya, on the Mediterranean coast.

Eumenes followed his father as a military leader, resisting attacks by the Galatians and the kings of Pontus, holding back Macedonian expansion, and opposing the Seleucids. He allied himself with the Romans against the Seleucid king Antiochus III, who, as a champion of Greek freedom tried to drive the Romans from mainland Greece. The Romans defeated him at Thermopylae in 192 BCE and followed him to western Anatolia, where Eumenes joined them with his own army. In 190 BCE, Eumenes helped the Roman commanders Cornelius Scipio Asiaticus and his brother Scipio Africanus to defeat Antiochus in the fateful Battle of Magnesia.

At this time, the Romans had no ambition to administer new provinces in Anatolia; they believed that the strong Pergamene Kingdom could provide a bulwark against the Seleucid threat. Therefore, after the treaty of Apamea in 188 BCE which mandated harsh terms against the Seleucids, the Romans gave Eumenes control of all the Seleucid territories in Western Anatolia. Thus, the Attalid kings of Pergamon, after little more than a century of rule, became the masters of the independent Greek cities on the Aegean coast without attacking any of them. Pergamon, now the capital of an empire, which had never been invaded, represented Hellenistic architecture and sculpture at its peak.

After the death of Eumenes, whose son Attalos had not reached his majority, the throne passed to his brother Attalos II "Philadelphus" (r. 160-138 BCE) who ruled jointly with Eumenes at the end of his reign and distinguished himself as a military commander. He made several diplomatic missions to Rome and supported the arts and sciences. His nephew Attalos III (138-133 BCE) who succeeded him, was less popular with his subjects, but ruled during a period of peace. He devoted time to studying medicine, botany and horticulture, gaining respect from Galen, the most celebrated doctor of his era. With disregard for other human beings, he used prisoners as subjects in his experiment on poisonous plants. Having no male heirs and, perhaps seeing the inevitability of Roman rule in Anatolia, he bequeathed Pergamon and all her possessions to the Roman republic. The transition, which might have ensured peace and continued prosperity, turned out to be painful. A force of peasants, mercenaries, slaves and other opponents, assembled by an illegitimate son of Eumenes II, prevented the Romans from grasping their prize; three years passed before they controlled the city. Fifty years later the citizens of Pergamon showed their aversion for Roman rule again when they joined with Mithridates VI of Pontus who occupied the city and attempted to eject the Romans. A brutal massacre of Romans ensued. Soon after the quelling of this revolt, the cities of the Pergamene Empire became the Roman province of Asia. Pergamon was chosen as the capital of the province until that role was transferred to Ephesus.

During the Roman period Hellenistic buildings dominated the city, but the emperor Augustus restored and embellished several of them and Caracalla rebuilt the Temple of Dionysus in marble. Hadrian, who inherited the imperial throne as Trajan's adopted son, made the most substantial addition to the Acropolis with the monumental Temple of Trajan. Both Trajan and Hadrian were worshipped there. The Corinthian columns of this temple, the tallest elements on the citadel today, give an idea of the grandeur of Roman Pergamon.

In the Christian era Pergamon became the seat of a bishop and, around 90 CE was named by John the Divine in the *Book of Revelation* as one of the 'seven churches of the Apocalypse.' The words in John's letter to the Church of Pergamon 'I know where thou dwellest, where the throne of Satan is' have been associated with the Altar of Zeus, but more likely referred to the Temple of Trajan, where the emperor demanded to be venerated as a god. A Christian named Antipas was burnt at the stake for refusing to worship at the imperial temple. After Constantine had given legitimacy to their faith in 313 CE, the Christians of Pergamon built a church inside the roofless Roman temple to the Egyptian gods. Under Byzantine rule, Pergamon which had suffered earthquake damage began to decline; as Muslim raids became a threat new defensive walls were built, using spolia from collapsed buildings including carved panels from the Altar of Zeus.

Rediscovery and archaeology

The German passion for Greek architecture reached a peak in the mid-nineteenth century when many civic buildings, particularly in Munich, were built in the Greek revival style. No doubt the spirit of Hellenism gripped Carl Humann when, in 1864, he discovered panels of sculpture from the Altar of Zeus built into Byzantine fortifications at Pergamon. At the time, he was overseeing the construction of roads in the region, but he felt compelled to change from engineer to archaeologist and devote the rest of his life to Pergamon. It took until 1878 for him to obtain the support of the Berlin Sculpture Museum and permits from the Ottoman authorities to begin excavation on the site and take possession of the items he found. In the first campaign (1878-86), with Alexander Conze and Richard Bohn, he unearthed the upper city and moved the sculpture from the Altar of

(L) Carl Humann and Richard Bohn in the Sanctuary of Athena (DAI) (R) The Altar of Zeus reconstructed in the Pergamon Museum, Berlin. This recreated version of the altar in the Berlin Museum runs the full width of the original, but is reduced in depth, and eliminated the elevated courtyard

Zeus to German warships for transport to Berlin. Between 1901 and 1909 the Pergamon Museum was built there with great fanfare, to display the archaeological discoveries. Later campaigns of excavation (1900-13) revealed the middle city and, under Theodor Wiegand, the Heroon, the Asklepion and the Red Courtyard were brought to light (1927-1936). The German Archaeological Institute, collaborating with Turkish colleagues continues the work today. I would recommend anyone who visits Pergamon to make a stop in Berlin on the way to see the missing elements.

VISITING PERGAMON

The Acropolis of Pergamon towers over the northern end of Bergama. It is divided, into the upper and the middle cities with residential areas between them on slopes too steep for civic buildings. On more level ground below, the sanctuary of the Egyptian gods, known as the "Red Basilica" stands within the modern town while the Asklepion lies on its south-western edge. The Bergama Archaeological Museum, containing significant archaeological finds is nearby on the main street of the town. Until 2010 it was possible to drive to a car park near the top of the hill. Now, a cable car carries visitors to an arrival point on the east side of the Acropolis, from which the walk to the summit is fairly easy. If you intend to see the impressive gymnasium and sanctuary of Demeter in the middle city, you should only buy a one way ticket and make your way down on foot. The well-preserved and protected mosaics and of a structure known as Building Z make the walk specially worthwhile. As you look at the plan and explore the site you will see that the upper city, built on a series of terraces, fans out to the south-west, while the more rectilinear middle city orients to the south-east. The desire of the Attalid kings to create inspiring architecture on such precipitous terrain led to spectacular townscape.

After you leave the cable car, (1) turn left at the top of the ramp and walk slightly downhill towards the trees standing on the base of the Altar of Zeus. Immediately to the left you will see the **Heroon** (2) where Attalos I and Eumenes II were worshipped as god-like heroes after their deaths. Arranged around a peristyle court, this building was like a large house; it did not contain a tomb. A spacious banquet room opened off the court for ceremonial meals; beyond it was a cult room. You will immediately come to the rectangular, level terrace created by Eumenes II for the **Altar of Zeus** (3). Although nothing remains but the steps of its base, the commanding position and the sense of order proclaim its significance. The Altar of Zeus shows both the ambition and the versatility of Pergamene architecture. Ionic colonnades, raised up on plinths, define an elevated courtyard which contained the offering table, approached by a broad flight of steps. The sculptural friezes that adorn the plinths represent a high point in Hellenistic art and proclaim the virtuosity of the Pergamene

The stepped base on which the Altar of Zeus stood

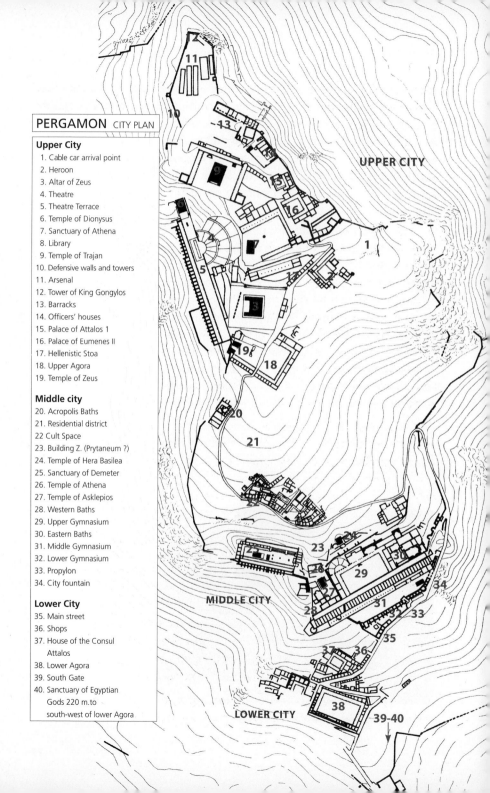

PERGAMON CITY PLAN

Upper City
1. Cable car arrival point
2. Heroon
3. Altar of Zeus
4. Theatre
5. Theatre Terrace
6. Temple of Dionysus
7. Sanctuary of Athena
8. Library
9. Temple of Trajan
10. Defensive walls and towers
11. Arsenal
12. Tower of King Gongylos
13. Barracks
14. Officers' houses
15. Palace of Attalos 1
16. Palace of Eumenes II
17. Hellenistic Stoa
18. Upper Agora
19. Temple of Zeus

Middle city
20. Acropolis Baths
21. Residential district
22. Cult Space
23. Building Z. (Prytaneum ?)
24. Temple of Hera Basilea
25. Sanctuary of Demeter
26. Temple of Athena
27. Temple of Asklepios
28. Western Baths
29. Upper Gymnasium
30. Eastern Baths
31. Middle Gymnasium
32. Lower Gymnasium
33. Propylon
34. City fountain

Lower City
35. Main street
36. Shops
37. House of the Consul Attalos
38. Lower Agora
39. South Gate
40. Sanctuary of Egyptian Gods 220 m.to south-west of lower Agora

UPPER CITY

MIDDLE CITY

LOWER CITY

sculptors. The wings that thrust forward on either side of the staircase help to emphasise the dynamic integration of architecture and sculpture in an almost Baroque manner. Eumenes II built the altar to commemorate his father's victories against the Galatians, and his own military triumphs. The friezes, 113 m. long, containing a hundred over-life-size figures do not refer to the specific battles in which the Pergamenes triumphed; rather, they represent the gigantomachy, the conflict between the Olympian Gods, led by Zeus, and the underworld forces of Chaos. The choice of this mythological drama links Pergamon to the Parthenon of Athens on which some of the metopes told the same story. The writhing bodies of gods and monstrous giants symbolize the idea of Greek ascendancy over barbarians, or good over evil. The sense of violent movement and emotion, captured in a series of dramatic moments, exemplifies Hellenistic sculpture. A separate set of friezes in the upper court concerns the origins of Pergamon and the role of the mythical founder Telephos, the son of Heracles, who as a baby, abandoned on a hillside, had been suckled by a lioness. Experts on Hellenistic art believe that one sculptor conceived and directed the entire narrative program, assisted by about forty stone carvers from many parts of the Greek world.

The Altar of Zeus initiated a new architectural type; it provided a model for altars built later at Magnesia and Priene. In the sixth century the altar was completely demolished at the behest of the Christian zealot John, the Bishop of Ephesus, who was charged by the Byzantine emperor Justinian with the task of rooting out idolatry. The spolia, including the low relief panels of the frieze were built into defensive walls, shortly afterwards, to protect against the Persians.

From the northwest corner of this sacred precinct, you can access the upper tiers of the **Theatre (4)**. Make the transition from the horizontal plane surrounding the altar to dramatic curves of this auditorium and enjoy the view up to the Temple of Trajan. It is well worth descending to the **Theatre Terrace (5)** below to experience the full height of the cavea. The long terrace leads to the Temple of Dionysus; above it the tiers of seating rise sixty-five metres. These two elements belonged together as a sanctuary of Dionysus, here honoured, whose image stood in the temple.

The Theatre, perhaps the most amazing feature of Pergamon, is the steepest in the Hellenic world; since there was no room for it to expand

The theatre at Pergamon, the steepest in the Hellenic world

sideways into the usual semicircle, it is narrow. The eighty tiers of seats, divided into three sections by horizontal aisles, rise dramatically up the slope to accommodate 10,000 spectators. They were built of local andesite, except for a marble royal box in the centre of the lowest section. Begun in the early days of the Attalid Kingdom, it was greatly enlarged by Eumenes II. During the Hellenistic period a temporary wooden stage was put up at the time of each Festival of Dionysus. In the Roman era, walls bolstered the sides of the theatre and a stage building was constructed behind the orchestra. Nothing remains of these additions. The tower above the top right hand side of the cavea dates from the Byzantine era when new fortifications were built.

The Theatre Terrace (5) almost 250 m. long made a magnificent promenade, lined on the west side with elegant Doric stoas that opened to the valley. At the northern end of the axis the exquisite prostyle Ionic **Temple of Dionysus** (6) stood at the top of a flight of steps. It was originally built of the same stone as the theatre, but it was refaced in marble by the emperor Caracalla (211-17) who wished to be worshipped as the New Dionysus. Enough of the temple remains to give an idea of the refinement of the design. The lower shaft of one column still stands and another lies close by.

In the base of the Byzantine tower at the top of the theatre, you will find an opening into a vaulted passage that emerges via a flight of steps

(L)The remains of the Temple of Dionysus and the long theatre terrace that also served as a promenade
(R) Reconstruction of the Ionic Temple of Dionysus (DAI)

beside the stylobate of the **Temple of Athena** (7). As the reconstruction shows, the temple is skewed from the geometry of the surrounding stoas and oriented to the south. This Doric temple, built by Philetairos in the third century BCE is one of very few in Anatolia. It reveals the association with Athens fostered by the Attalids. Other cities in the region revered Athena as their patron goddess, but this temple shows a direct influence from the Parthenon and the temple of Hephaistos in the Athenian Agora. With six columns across the front and two columns in antis in the south

(L) The sanctuary of Athena, with the library behind the stoa on the left. The buildings with peristyle courts at the top are palaces of the Attalid kings (from a model at Pergamon Museum, Berlin).
(R) Columns of the North Stoa of the Sanctuary of Athena. The back wall of the Library can be seen directly behind them.

The restored propylon of the sanctuary of Athena. Pergamon Museum, Berlin

and north porches it is closer to the latter. However, with only ten columns on the sides, it was shorter. In the Hellenistic manner the columns were more widely spaced, with three triglyphs to each column, as opposed to two on the fifth century Athenian temples.

Philetairos built stoas on three sides of the sanctuary leaving the west side open to the view over the theatre and the landscape beyond. Eumenes II added a beautiful propylon as a formal entry to the sacred precinct. His architect combined the sturdy Doric order on the lower story with the lighter Ionic above, thus giving the façade a human scale. The symbols of an owl for Athena and an eagle for Zeus appeared in the frieze below the pediment. An inscription declares that this building was dedicated by King Eumenes to the victory-bringing Athena.

Images of weapons captured from the defeated enemy emblazoned the panels between the second story columns of the propylon; the same motif may also have ornamented the upper stories of the stoas. Eumenes also celebrated his military triumph in a group of bronze sculptures on a long pedestal on the open side of the sanctuary of Athena. Unlike most depictions of vanquished enemies, *the dying Gaul* and the *Galatian Chieftain killing his wife and himself*, attributed by the Roman author Pliny to the Pergamene sculptor Epigonos, known to us through Roman copies, show their subjects as heroes. Celebrated as quintessential examples of Hellenistic art, each of these sculptures, expresses pathos as it captures a tragic end to a valiant human life. The Galatian neck rings, moustaches and their dishevelled hair identify them as barbarians, but rather than cowering under the feet of their conquerors they possess dignity. Ironically, this treatment of the victims ennobles Eumenes the conqueror, implying his overthrow of a worthy enemy. A bronze statue of Augustus was placed in the first century CE.

The Great Library (8)

The Attalid kings all exhibited a passion for literature, but Eumenes II, a dedicated collector, whose agents scoured the Greek world for books, founded a library surpassed only by the one built by the Ptolemies in Alexandria. Since Athena was associated with learning, the siting of the library in the sanctuary of Athena seems appropriate. Eumenes placed it above the north stoa of the temenos, and probably remodelled the stoa at the same time so that the library could be entered from its upper story. The lower part of the rear walls still stand, and archaeologists have assembled enough data to understand its form. A statue of Athena Parthenos, a small copy of the great statue by Phidias in the cella of the Parthenon presided over the reading room. A stone bench ran round three sides of the room to separate patrons from the bookshelves along the walls. It appears that attendants working behind the bench brought books to them. At its peak the library held 200,000 scrolls and codices. Tall windows in the east wall illuminated the room, but before the use of glass windows in the first century CE, they needed to be protected against rain with shutters. The upper stoa served as a reading room; curtains between the columns offered protection from the weather. Scribes probably worked in the other rooms and a residence stood behind the library.

The Pergamenes contributed significantly to the development of parchment as a writing material. Although the practice of writing on specially prepared animal skins goes back centuries in the Middle East, the word parchment is derived from charta pergamena (paper of Pergamon.) When King Ptolemy V, infuriated by the rapid growth of the Pergamene Library and determined to stem its rivalry with Alexandria, forbade the export of papyrus, it appears that the Pergamene librarians turned to parchment as a substitute and made improvements in its manufacture. It seems likely that they also aided in the crucial development of the codex which substituted folded paper or parchment for scrolls. Books made by this method were more convenient to read than long paper scrolls. In later years Christians produced most of their books as codices. After Julius Caesar inadvertently set fire to the library at Alexandria, by burning ships in the harbour, Mark Antony, in an arrogant act of cultural imperialism is said to have given all the books in the Pergamene collection to Cleopatra.

To create a level terrace on which to build the Temple of Trajan, Hadrian's engineers constructed massive stone barrel vaults beneath it. The open ends of these vaults can be seen above the highest seats of the Theatre (see p. 8)

The Temple of Trajan (9)

The Emperor Hadrian (117-138) was a prodigious builder, responsible for the Pantheon in Rome, his own villa at Tivoli, Hadrian's Wall across the north of England and countless other monuments. The temple he built for Trajan (98-117), in gratitude for making him heir to the empire, is still the dominant architectural feature of the Acropolis. The triumphal character of its Corinthian order perfectly expressed the imperial glory to which Hadrian aspired. A capital with exuberant acanthus leaves, standing at eye level, conveys an idea of its vast scale. Despite the dedication to Trajan, the discovery of colossal heads of the two emperors suggests that they were both worshipped there. The heads are now exhibited in Berlin. Like most Roman temples its precinct was defined by stoas, but, with one side open to the glorious view, it differed from the enclosed forums of imperial temples in Rome. The North and South Stoas opened at the level of the paving, while those on the east side, adapted to the steep rocky slope by stepping up onto higher ground.

After visiting the Trajaneum, continue up the hill to a stretch of **walls with towers** (10) which give a good idea of Pergamene fortifications. Beyond these walls the **Arsenal** (11), consisting of five wooden buildings

The Temple of Trajan, or Trajaneum built by Hadrian. A Corinthian capital of the Trajaneum

on stone foundations lying north of these walls, was built in the reigns of Attalos I and Eumenes II to store weapons, grain and other essential food. Large numbers of andesite balls found in their ruins, were made to be hurled at invading enemies by a palintonon, a siege engine like a giant catapult. Weighing up to 75 kilos, they are now arranged in piles in the Lower Agora. At the highest point, King Gongylos built a fortified **square tower** (12) in the late fifth century BCE as his residence. It was probably here that Philetairos stored the treasure that enabled him to execute his ambitious plans for Pergamon. The lower part of two of its walls still stand. Turning south-east you will reach the **Barracks** (13). They clearly chose this high position, near the palaces, with a commanding prospect over the surrounding territory, for strategic advantage.

One of the most complete sections of the defensive walls stands above a precipitous slope on the east side of the barracks. From this area you can enjoy the splendid view over the valley of the river Ketios, a tributary of the Kaikos, which has recently been dammed to form a large lake. The Romans, skilled hydraulic engineers, also achieved great feats of water supply. Using the principle of syphonage, they brought water under pressure in ceramic and lead pipes from Madra Dağ, a mountain 45 km. away,

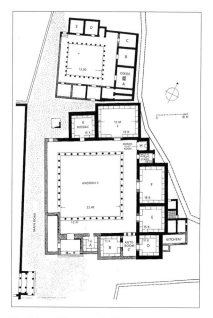

The Palace of Eumenes II, Plan

to the heights of Pergamon, to serve the royal palaces and fountains in the upper city. One of the aqueducts that carried it is visible in the valley to the north near cultivated ground. The many cisterns built throughout the Acropolis to collect rainwater, were controlled by strict laws. Washing laundry in the public fountains incurred severe penalties.

Continuing down the northwest side of the Acropolis you will pass the scanty remains of houses (14) where officers probably lived, and reach the **Palaces of the Attalid Kings**. It is hard to visualize the splendor of these royal residences. Archaeologists have been able to reconstruct their plans and have found superb mosaics, but today only the lower walls remain; we have to imagine the opulent details. The first palace (15) with a small peristyle court has been identified with Attalos I, while the second (16) with a court 25 m. square appears to have been built by Eumenes II. It included a small cult room in the northwest corner and five spacious rooms. The largest, used for banquets, had sufficient space for 22 dining couches along the walls. It was lavishly decorated with floor mosaics and decorative stucco on the walls. After visiting the palaces, turn west on the path to the Altar of Zeus. You will pass the site of a **Hellenistic Stoa** (17), of which virtually nothing remains, and take the path leading downhill leaving the Altar of Zeus on your right.

The Middle City

Go south and cross the **Upper Agora** (18) on a paved path that divides it. To the right you will see the foundations of a small **Temple of Zeus** (19) which was once the focus of the Agora. Continuing downhill you will pass the site of the **Acropolis Baths** (20) of which a few walls remain. A major residential district once covered the barren hillside to the left (21). Experts at the German Archaeological Institute, after analyzing the evidence of the few walls that still exist, have reconstructed the pattern of houses on curving streets that follow the contours, intersecting with stepped alleys climbing up the slopes. Following the traditions of Hellenistic design, all but the smallest houses were built around peristyle courts. Continue to the first of two new structures. The first one protects the interior of a complex containing a **cult room** (22), a small bath house and a narrow Odeon. The wall decorations displayed here are copies of the originals in the Bergama Museum.

From here you will get a good view of the sanctuary of Demeter far below. Straight ahead down the path you will see the new shelter that protects the well-preserved mosaics and wall coverings of a building identified by the DAI as **Building Z** (23). Erected in the time of Eumenes II, "Building Z" probably served as the **Prytaneum**, a place for entertaining guests of the city. Later additions adapted to the steep slope by stepping down onto a lower terrace. It was enlarged and remodeled again in Roman times, when elaborate mosaics were installed. But, in 178 CE, an earthquake destroyed it, burying the mosaics. The German Archaeological Institute excavated it in 1990-93 under the direction of Wolfgang Radt, who devised the means of keeping them in place. The elegant shelter, which remains architecturally distinct from the ancient city, opened in 2004, allowing visitors to view the mosaics from catwalks.

The largest mosaic with a geometric border embodies sixteen octagonal panels, each one with a theatrical mask, except for the four in the centre which depict birds and animals. In a square recess off the room, a mosaic shows Silenus, the companion and tutor of Dionysus, wearing a festive wreath and carrying the child Dionysus in his arms. This mosaic suggests use of the recess for a religious ritual.

Immediately east of Building Z, the **Sanctuary of Hera Basileia** (24) stood on a narrow terrace above the Upper Gymnasium. It consisted of a small Doric prostyle temple, a stoa and an exedra erected by Attalos II.

The Sanctuary of Demeter (25) is the oldest religious site at Pergamon. Recent research reveals that devotees of Demeter worshipped here as early as the fourth century BCE, before the Attalid dynasty held power. They continued to do so for at least five hundred years. In the third century Philetairos rebuilt the sanctuary and, a generation later, Apollonis, the

Demeter Sanctuary

wife of Attalos I, enlarged it in honour of her mother Boa. She built new stoas and added a fountain and a propylon. At an annual festival during the Hellenistic era, women, with no men present, thronged the space that seems so empty today; they performed *Thesmophoria*, ceremonies to intercede with Demeter for bountiful harvests and fertility. The rituals related to the myth of Demeter, the rape of her daughter Persephone by Hades, and Persephone's abduction to become queen of the underworld. The release of Persephone, after Demeter's agonizing search for her, represents the emergence of new life in the spring, leading to the fecundity of summer. Her descent into underworld for part of each year foreshadows the coming of winter and the burial of seeds in the ground. The rituals also strove to mitigate fear of the afterlife in the gloom of Hades. On the first day, the women sacrificed piglets, interring them in a pit; the next day they fasted and purified themselves; on the third day they raised up the decomposing animals to symbolize the fertility imparted to the earth by the rotting flesh. Feasting and festivity followed. When the Romans ruled Pergamon the rituals continued, but became closer to those of the mystery religion performed at Eleusis in Attica. At this time men also participated.

While most Greek temple sites remained open to the surrounding landscape, walls enclosed this one to allow secrecy. The only entrance, a propylon built by Apollonis and remodelled in the Roman era, stood in the southwest corner. Today, two columns with palm leaf capitals flank its entrance. At the west end of the temenos, the foundation of the small Ionic temple remains, and in front of it the presumed position of the sacrificial pit. When archaeologists excavated the site, they found unusually rich soil in the pit. A flight of ten steps forty metres long in front of the eastern end of the North Stoa provided tiered seating for spectators.

Just south of Building Z outside the propylon of the sanctuary of Demeter lie the remains of a **Temple of Athena** (26) and, directly below that, the foundations of another small **Temple of Asklepios** (27) rebuilt in the Ionic Style in the second century BCE on the site of a Doric temple of the third century. The large and important sanctuary of Asklepios 1.5 km. to the southwest had existed since the fourth century BCE. This one gave the god of healing a presence in the city. Its proximity to the gymnasium reminds us of the connection in the Greek mind between health, education and athletics. From these sites you can get an excellent view of the gymnasium far below them.

The **Upper Gymnasium** (29) was a magnificent work of architecture occupying a broad terrace bolstered on the south side by a tall retaining wall. It dates to the Hellenistic era but was extensively rebuilt by the Romans. While the two gymnasia on narrower terraces below it served the needs of adolescent boys and, at the lowest level, children, the upper one for young men was known as the 'Ceremonial Gymnasium.' The palaestra 74 m. long was surrounded, as was usual, by stoas. The one on the south side, extending beyond the palaestra along the edge of the terrace to a length of 210 m, provided a covered stadium for running; in the basement below it a similar space served the same purpose in winter and high summer. The stoas on the other sides rose to two stories; they gave access to rooms for education and for civic events. Important ceremonies took place in the Ephebium, the largest room in the centre of the north side which focused on an apse with a half dome on a wall lined with columns opposite the entrance. The space to its east, with apses covered with half-domes at both ends, was reserved for the worship of the emperor. In the Hellenistic era it had been two rooms, but the Romans removed the wall between them and lined the walls with marble of various colours, perhaps at the time of an imperial visit.

An unusual addition to a gymnasium, a theatre, opening off the west end of the North Stoa, seated a thousand spectators. Since it did not include an orchestra it was not intended for dramatic or musical performances, but for lectures and orations. A fountain in the northeast corner of the palaestra surrounded by stone paving allowed sweating athletes to splash water over themselves; a room behind the West Stoa provided stone basins, which can be seen today, for more serious washing. These facilities may have sufficed in Hellenistic times but did not meet Roman standards of luxury. The **Western Baths** (28) as well as the **Eastern Baths** (30), offered the usual marble lined rooms with water at different temperatures and floors warmed by hypocausts. The small piers supporting

The Upper Gymnasium from the northwest. The North and East Stoas are relatively well preserved, but the South Stoa has entirely collapsed. While it remained standing, the palaestra was an enclosed environment without the current view. The Eastern Baths are visible top left

the raised floor can be seen in one of the spaces. These baths served the residential district immediately to the north as well as patrons of the gymnasium. The water reached them, under pressure, through pipes installed in the time of Eumenes II.

From the southern edge of the Upper Gymnasium, you can look down into the covered running track that was under the Southern Stoa. It is believed to have been vaulted. Passing its eastern end you can reach the **Middle Gymnasium** (31) on the level below; it was a much simpler facility but a long stoa ran along its north side. Symbols of power and nobility confronted the boys of Pergamon at an early age. Their gymnasium included statues of heroes as well as a small prostyle temple dedicated to Hermes and Heracles, the gods of physical exercise. The Romans rededicated the temple to include homage to the emperor. A staircase, built in the nearest of three towers in the Byzantine walls leads to a fascinating vaulted and stepped passage built during the reign of Eumenes II. This reaches the **Lower Gymnasium** (32) for pre-adolescent boys which contained no buildings. It was an irregularly shaped space, now modified by Byzantine walls and towers that rose above it. Between the western end of the Lower Gymnasium and the city fountain is the **Propylon** (33) that opens to the way up to the gymnasia. **The City Fountain** (34) was a long pool from which residents could fill their water jars. A row of twelve columns supporting its roof stood in the water.

Below the propylon, the **Main Street** (35) built of huge stone blocks, with ruts made by chariot and cart wheels, leads down to the Lower Agora. First constructed in the Hellenistic era, it received repairs and improvements to the drainage under the Romans. Twenty-one small shops (36), on the right as you descend, stood between the road and a large residence, identified as the **House of the Consul Attalos** (37). It was designed in a formal manner for a lavish life-style and planned for shade in the summer and warmth from the sun in winter. The oikos, the principal reception room of the house, faced south onto the large court, with its walls exactly aligned with the colonnades of the peristyle. The columns were Doric on the lower floor and Ionic above. Four other large rooms opened off the court; mosaics and frescos, protected by a roof, have survived in the room in the middle of the north side. A staircase in the north-west corner gave access to an upper story. Since the main floor was built of precisely cut blocks of andesite laid dry and the upper floor was of irregular stones set in mortar, we can assume that the upper floor was a Roman addition. A bathroom and a pool in the basement were also Roman.

The Agora on the Acropolis of Pergamon, complete with a Temple of Zeus, was reserved for religious and civic ceremonies; in contrast the **Lower Agora** (38) at the foot of the main street opposite the shops, was a bustling market place. Eumenes II built it in the early years of his reign as he enlarged the city. Surrounded by two-story, double-aisled stoas in the Doric order, it provided space for many shops opening off its back wall. The size of these shops may seem minimal to modern travelers; however, they are no smaller than those in the Grand Bazaar in Istanbul, where a vast quantity of merchandise changes hands. The second story of the North Stoa connected with the street above. Inscriptions on stone tablets in the Agora proclaimed laws about building houses and roads, as well as the maintenance of water systems. A fine head of Alexander the Great, found in the Agora during excavations can be seen in the Istanbul Archaeological Museums. The German archaeologists built their residence within the court of a large peristyle house discovered to the west of the Lower Agora. To the south, the city spread onto the relatively flat ground, covering up almost all the remains of the ancient buildings.

When Eumenes II built the outer walls round the foot of the Acropolis, his architect devised the **South Gate** (39) in an ingenious manner requiring those entering to make a turn inside a square tower. Its foundations survive among houses.

The Sanctuary of the Egyptian Gods, (40) erected in the second century CE, during the reign of Hadrian, expressed the popularity of the Egyptian religions in the Roman Empire. This vast red brick building complex, that greets travelers before they ascend to the Acropolis of Pergamon, looked entirely different in classical times. Multi-coloured marble covered the towering masonry, and a courtyard two hundred metres long, now half covered with houses, created a high walled temenos where huge crowds of devotees could gather. Undeterred by the River Selinus flowing diagonally across the site, the builders channeled its torrent from the Kozak mountain range through two vaulted conduits under the courtyard. A colonnade running across the east end of the court and supporting a roof, acted as a monumental gateway to the most sacred area which contained three temples. Its four central columns stepped forward for emphasis. Beyond them, a huge hall stood symmetrically between two courtyards, both dominated by round towers in the centre of their east sides. Stoas running around three sides of these smaller courts created shade and a pleasant character. An arched door 14 m. high, approached

(L) The Red Hall, standing roofless and without its east wall
(R) The northern round tower

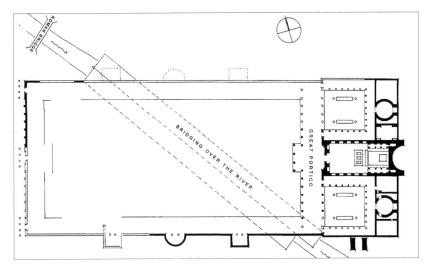

Plan of the sanctuary of the Egyptian gods, showing the course of the River Selinus in a culvert under the court. The temples stand at the west end of the court. The main hall in the centre is flanked by courts, each dominated by a round tower

by a flight of marble steps, opened into the lofty hall, spanned by a wooden roof 26 m. wide. The threshold of the door, a monolithic block of marble weighing at least sixty tons, clearly possessed symbolic properties. Twelve tall niches recessed into the walls, five on each side and two flanking the entrance, probably displayed statues of deities; above them high windows illuminated the space. The windowless eastern end, only accessible to priests, and separated from the rest by a wide water channel, remained dim and no niches penetrated the walls. In this inner sanctum stood the colossal statue of a god that astounded the faithful by uttering god-like pronouncements. The large pedestal that supported it survives, revealing a passage way through which a priest climbed into the hollow interior to give voice to the deity. A complex arrangement of underground tunnels connected with staircases linked all the buildings and rose to the roof, allowing for mysterious visions and sounds to amaze the worshippers. The back wall was flat, but a large niche made a recess in its exterior, probably for a tall statue. The wall was demolished in the Byzantine era. The columns of the stoas in front of the round towers in the small courts, took the form of atlantes, male figures representing Atlas,

A fragment of one of the atlantes dressed in an Egyptian manner

back-to-back with female caryatids. These figures displayed a distinctly Egyptian character. It is unlikely that all the columns of the courts shared the same form. The round towers were illuminated through oculi, circular openings, in the crowns of their domes. We do not know how the towers were used.

Scholars have not conclusively proved that this temple was dedicated to the Egyptian gods Serapis, Isis and Harpocrates. Osiris, Apis and Helios are also mentioned on an inscription. Nor is it known what kind of rituals took place in the courtyards and round towers. However, inscriptions and other types of evidence confirm that this functioned as a thriving sanctuary of Egyptian cults. Several water basins and the channel lined with alabaster, dividing the public and sacred ends of the hall, suggest the ritual washing required in Egyptian religions. The unidentified patron of this vast complex, possibly the emperor Hadrian himself, must have lavished a vast sum on it. Since building in brick was uncommon in western Anatolia, it has been suggested that skilled brick layers were sent from Rome. In the Byzantine era, after the roof had collapsed Christians removed the pagan images and built a church dedicated to St. John with a nave and aisles within the hall; they took down the east wall to construct an apse. The Ottomans demolished the church and converted the north tower into a mosque which is still in use today. At one time the south tower held an olive press; today it serves as an exhibition area. The German Archaeological Institute is continuing to study this unique building complex and is carrying out stabilization and restoration work.

THE ASKLEPION

According to legend, Asklepios, the son of Apollo and a mortal woman named Koronis learned the art of medicine from the centaur Chiron. By the classical era he was uncontested as the god of healing. His reputed birthplace at Epidaurus in Greece became the principal sanctuary for the practice of his healing arts. As early as the sixth century BCE it attracted sick people from all over the Greek world; by the Hellenistic era, it was a rich city with a flourishing centre for the treatment of disease with one of the largest theatres in the Hellenic world. In a process described as incubation, the people who went there seeking a cure spent a night in a large hall where, they believed, Asklepios himself came to them in their dreams to tell them what they needed to do to become healthy. The cult of Asklepios spread to at least 200 other places, including Athens and the island of Kos where the ruins of a splendid sanctuary survive today. The Asklepion at Pergamon became the most important in Anatolia.

Although founded in the Hellenistic era, little remains from that time except the sacred spring and a fountain. Most of the architecture we see today dates from the second century CE when it was extensively remodeled to compete with the Asklepion of Kos. The emperor Hadrian, who possessed a passion for building, visited Pergamon in 123 CE; he built the stoas that define the large courtyard and the circular treatment centre. These and other improvements were completed before the great physician **Galen** (129-161 CE) practiced there. Galenos, as he was named in Greek, was the son of a successful architect with broad, scholarly interests. When he was about sixteen, Asklepios appeared to his father in a dream and ordered him to send him to study medicine. Galenos had already been exposed to philosophers and scientists, but he then spent four years in the Asklepion. After his father died, leaving him with ample funds, he travelled widely, visiting the important medical school at Alexandria while preparing for a career based on scientific observation as well as tradition.

On his return to Pergamon, he was appointed by the High Priest of Asia as the physician of the gladiators. Previously, most severely injured gladiators died, but as a result of his care, the majority survived their wounds to fight again. While treating them with such success, and carrying out dissections of monkeys and pigs, Galenos discovered critical principles and wrote treatises that formed the basis of medical science for the next fifteen

The Sacred Way leading from the city to the Asklepion   The main court

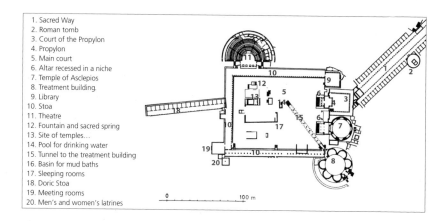

1. Sacred Way
2. Roman tomb
3. Court of the Propylon
4. Propylon
5. Main court
6. Altar recessed in a niche
7. Temple of Asclepios
8. Treatment building.
9. Library
10. Stoa
11. Theatre
12. Fountain and sacred spring
13. Site of temples…
14. Pool for drinking water
15. Tunnel to the treatment building
16. Basin for mud baths
17. Sleeping rooms
18. Doric Stoa
19. Meeting rooms
20. Men's and women's latrines

hundred years. His understanding of the circulation of the blood was only surpassed in 1626 when William Harvey proved that the heart acted as a pump. While in his early thirties, he left Pergamon for Rome, where he served as personal physician to several emperors. Before leaving Pergamon, Galenos contributed significantly to the reputation of the Asklepion, attracting many Romans as well as Greeks from far-away places. Three Roman emperors, Hadrian, Marcus Aurelius and Caracalla, received medical services there. The remedies that Galenos advocated included diet, exercise, herbs, water, mud packs, massage, music and other common-sense treatments as well as supernatural means such as incubation.

The architecture of the Asklepion has survived well enough to convey an idea of its former magnificence: the Sacred Way (1) with many of its columns still standing, led from the edge of the city a kilometer away, past the Roman theatre, to the sanctuary. Stoas lined the section nearest

(L) The tunnel leading to the treatment centre
(R) The corridor of the treatment centre

the Asklepion. Comparable to the stately Arcadian Way at Ephesus, it remains one of the best preserved Roman colonnaded streets in Anatolia. To its south a well-built tomb from the Augustan era can be seen (2). The public entered the sanctuary through a colonnaded court (3) and a grand propylon in the Corinthian order. This gateway, with a portico like a temple front on the inside, led into the large court where many Ionic columns of the surrounding stoas remain (5). Two altars (6), flanking the propylon, were recessed into niches. To the south, stood the temple of Asklepios-Zeus, a miniature version of the Pantheon, the original domed temple built by Hadrian in Rome only a few years earlier. It was commissioned in 142 CE by a consul, who clearly wanted to bring state-of-the-art architecture to Pergamon. As in Rome, a tall Corinthian portico and a vestibule preceded the domed rotunda; an oculus, a circular opening in the crown of the dome, illuminated the interior; rectangular and rounded niches alternated in the walls. A statue of Asklepios stood in a niche opposite the entrance, while the others contained statues of lesser gods associated with healing. Unfortunately only the lower walls of this remarkable building remain. In contrast much of the massive masonry of the treatment building (8), immediately to the south of the temple, still survives. This enigmatic building, connected to the court through a tunnel, was planned on two levels around a circular central space with six vaulted lobes radiating around it and a wooden roof covering the central part.

The **Library** (9) in the corner of the court to the north of the propylon, contained not only medical books, but also literature, to entertain

(L) Nude statue of Hadrian from the Library (Bergama Museum) (R) The Asklepion Theatre, seating 3000 spectators

and engage the minds of patrons. A statue of Hadrian in a wall niche dominated the space; his pose as an idealized nude gave him god-like attributes. It can be seen in the Bergama Museum today. The theatre (11), dedicated to Asklepios and Athena Hygeia at the western end of the North Stoa seated 3000 spectators. The dramas, performed there in honour of the gods, contributed to the alleviation of disease; the pleasure of witnessing them also encouraged people to extend their stay at the Asklepion. Today, we can look from the theatre seats into the North Stoa, but, like other Roman theatres in the region, a stage building articulated with columns enclosed the theatrical space. Although quite small in scale, it was the first *frons scenae* in Anatolia to be built three stories high.

Just south of the theatre, the **sacred spring** (12) and a pool beside it provided water for patients to bathe in and to drink; a nearby receptacle covered with a roof (14) stored more drinking water. Recent tests have shown that the water is slightly radioactive. In the west side of the courtyard patients could take mud baths or smear their bodies with mud. The foundations of three small temples, south of the sacred spring, show the integration of religious practice and health care. They were dedicated to Apollo, Asklepios, and his daughter Hygeia who devoted herself to the prevention of disease. Another shrine celebrated Telesphorus, a boy-deity associated with healing. Nearby rooms were provided for sleeping; their exact position remains uncertain. Beneath the South Stoa and accessible by staircases, lay a long basement roofed with groin vaults supported on cylindrical columns. Its purpose is not known, but it may have been one of the places used for incubation.

Sceptics can be reassured by reading the inscriptions left by satisfied patients to show their gratitude for cures. The extant writings of the famous Greek orator Aelius Aristides (117–181 CE), who spent thirteen years at the Asklepion, shed light on the treatments he received. Although clearly a hypochondriac, he willingly submitted to indignities prescribed for him. For example, under a doctor's instructions, one bitterly cold winter's night, he smeared himself with mud, ran three times around the fountain and washed it off with freezing, sacred water. While at the Asklepion, he made speeches in the theatre and arranged choirs of boys and men to sing hymns of praise to Asklepios. At the end of his life, after winning accolades as an orator, he became a priest of Asklepios in his native Smyrna. Researchers today continue to analyze both the archaeological discoveries and the documentary evidence. It is hoped that we will gain further understanding of medical practices in the Asklepion.

The Roman Theatre, Amphitheatre and Stadium

Eight-hundred metres to the northeast of the Asklepion, along the sacred way, stand the ruins of the **Roman Theatre**, and beyond it the **Stadium** to the east and the **Amphitheatre** to the west. These buildings are still unexcavated, but give evidence of the Roman expansion of the lower town. The Roman theatre, seating thirty thousand, superseded the Greek theatre on the Acropolis for theatrical performances, and gladiatorial games took place in the amphitheatre, before audiences as large as fifty thousand. When naval battles were enacted, the waters of a stream, channelled beneath a vault, could be diverted into the arena.

The Bergama Museum, 10 Cumhuriyet Cad. Bergama

The archaeological museum on the main street of Bergama was the first museum in Turkey related to a specific ancient site. It exhibits significant sculpture, mosaics and artifacts as well as a model of the Altar of Zeus.

Cybele, the patron goddess of Smyrna,
Roman (Izmir Museum)

SMYRNA (IZMIR)

Smyrna occupied a beautiful position below Mount Pagos at the head of a deep gulf. Although it was a significant example of an early *polis* in the archaic era, and a fine city in the Hellenistic period, virtually nothing survives from either phase of Smyrna's history. The evidence has disappeared under the modern urban development of Izmir, the third largest city in Turkey. The only archaeological remains that can be seen are a few fragments of the archaic city and the well-preserved Roman Agora. However, the museum exhibits important sculpture and artifacts from the region that go back to the Bronze Age.

Greek colonists settled at Old Smyrna before the end of the second millennium BCE. They selected an easily defended site on a small peninsula connected to the mainland by a narrow isthmus between two good harbours. Fertile agricultural land nearby could support a growing population, and the Hermos River, connecting it to the interior of Anatolia, ensured trade.

Six streams flowed from Mount Pagos and other nearby hills into the Gulf of Smyrna. One of them was the Meles, which several ancient writers associate with Homer. Scholars have reached no consensus in identifying the Meles or the nearby cave frequented by the poet. However, George Bean argues convincingly that the springs that fed it are the same ones that flow, at a constant rate year round, to provide drinking water to Izmir today. They are now inaccessible behind walls. The assertion that Homer was born in Smyrna is challenged by the island of Chios, another reputed birthplace of Homer, but there is plenty of evidence that he knew the terrain of Smyrna well. Strabo mentions the Homerion, a heroon in the form of a peristyle house with a shrine and a statue of him.

Smyrna was one of the earliest Greek cities of Aeolis and a founding member of the Aeolian League. However, in about 800 BCE it was captured by Ionians from Colophon while the inhabitants were at a festival of Dionysus. The Smyrnaeans, cast out of their own polis, dispersed to other Aeolian cities but the Panionic League denied Smyrna's new citizens the right to join them.

By the seventh century the small peninsula was tightly packed with houses. A Temple of Athena stood at the highest point; a girdle of walls surrounded it. The inhabitants were able to repulse an attack by King Gyges of Lydia, and they subsequently strengthened the defensive walls but these precautions proved insufficient in the long run. Gyges's grandson Alyattes II conquered and destroyed the city in about 600 BCE. He achieved that goal before the day of sophisticated siege engines by piling up earth, so high that some of it still remains on the site. Smyrna then broke up into a cluster of villages and did not recover before the Hellenistic era. Possessing little wealth and few ships, it never joined the Delian League.

When Alexander the Great came from Sardis to Smyrna, he rested after hunting by the temple of the two Nemeses on the slope of Mount Pagos (Kadifekale). He dreamed that the goddesses came to him, and told him to move the city to Mount Pagos. The oracle at Klaros, consulted by a Smyrnaean delegation, declared: "Thrice and four times happy will those men be who are going to inhabit Pagos, beyond the sacred Meles." After the plan was executed in the early fourth century BCE under Alexander's successors, Antigonus and Lysimachus, the new city prospered. Hellenistic Smyrna, a place of great architectural and scenic beauty, stretched from the shore of the bay and around the slopes of Pagos. It included a Temple of Zeus Akraios on its western slope and a theatre on the northern slope. A stadium occupied a ledge below the Acropolis and a temple of Cybele, the patron goddess of Smyrna, stood outside the city to the east.

During the era when the Attalids of Pergamon ruled most of the Aegean coast, the Smyrnaeans resisted their hegemony, instead forging a bond with Rome. As a means of appealing to the Romans for support, by combining diplomacy with religion, they initiated a new cult of the previously unknown goddess Roma and built a temple to her. The plan succeeded but after 133 BCE the Pergamene and Roman empires became one. Subsequently the cult of Roma, invented in Smyrna, flourished both in Rome and the provinces. During the Roman era, as the harbours of the two great trading cities, Miletus and Ephesus, silted up, Smyrna became the more powerful trading city but Ephesus was chosen as the capital of the Roman Province of Asia.

With a growing Christian community in the first century, Smyrna was named by St. John in the *Book of Revelations* as one of the seven churches of Asia. An early bishop Polycarp, ordained and installed by St. John, became a martyr in about 155 CE when he was burnt at the stake in the Stadium at the age of 86. A century later, under the emperor Decius, St. Pionius was burned as a martyr in the same place.

Rediscovery and archaeology

The distinguished Turkish archaeologist Ekrem Akurgal of Ankara University and John Cook, the head of the British School of Archaeology in Athens, began excavating the site of Old Smyrna in 1948. They made discoveries dating back to 3,000 BCE and were able to learn about many aspects of the first Hellenic settlement that dated from about 1,100 BCE. Work has continued there and is currently directed by Meral Akurgal.

Rudolf Naumann and Salahattin Kantar excavated the State Agora between 1932 and 1941 for the Turkish Historical Society and the General Directorate of Museums. Since 1997 the Metropolitan Municipality of Izmir has carried out a program with the aim of enlarging the site. It has acquired property, demolished old buildings and handed their sites over to the archaeologists. They also provide support for those working on the project. Among new discoveries are a short section of the road that led from the harbour and the Faustina Gate of the Agora.

Visiting Izmir/Smyrna

For those exploring the central part of the coast, Izmir, is easily reached by bus and plane, and makes a practical starting point. Cars can be rented there. Buses from the airport and the Otogar (bus station) run to the central bus station on the waterfront near Konak Square, which is not very far from the Izmir Archaeological Museum or the Agora. The traffic and parking in Izmir are so challenging that motorists with time limitations may choose to bypass it on the motorway and spend more time on the other sites. If you decide to stop there, make sure that you have a good map of the city before you arrive.

Old Smyrna

The site of old Smyrna in the district of Bayraklı, lies about 8.5 km. north of both Konak Pier and the Roman Agora, and about 600 m. inland from the waterfront, a few blocks behind the Central Hospital. Archaeological work is in progress there, but the site may not always be accessible to visitors.

Akurgal and Cook found evidence establishing occupation of the site contemporary with Troy I and II in the third millennium BCE. The arrival of Greeks in the tenth century BCE is proved by plentiful pottery of the proto-geometric style. The lower stone courses of the walls survived in places but the upper parts of mud brick, probably reinforced with wood, decayed long ago. The reconstruction is conjectural. The most imposing remains are the temenos walls and the platform of the Temple of Athena from the seventh century. Akurgal described the capitals and column bases that he unearthed in broken fragments, as the oldest and most beautiful in the Hellenic world.

The emperor Marcus Aurelius and his wife Faustina rebuilt the **Agora** after 178 CE, when much of the city was destroyed by an earthquake. Two stoas on the east and west sides enclosed a space 120 x 80 m. while a large basilica defined the north side. Many tall columns of the west stoa, complete with capitals, convey the grand scale of the Roman architecture. The undercroft beneath it, which functioned as a bazaar, shows the Roman use of vaults to level sites for important buildings and use urban land efficiently. The Basilica, currently undergoing restoration was also raised above a vaulted basement, which served as a granary. An altar of Zeus in the centre of the Agora was ornamented by marble figures of Greek gods. Akurgal suggests that those of Demeter, goddess of the harvest, and the sea god Poseidon, standing in a prominent position, symbolized Smyrna's domination of both land and sea. This sculpture can be seen in the Izmir Museum.

During the Ottoman period, the Agora served as a cemetery. The many tombstones piled up in the southeast corner bear witness to that use. A number of large illustrated boards with text in Turkish and English provide historical information.

A visit to the Izmir **Archaeological Museum** will reveal much about the Greek and Roman cities of Aegean Turkey, including rarely visited

The Roman Agora, the west colonnade of the West Stoa. The vaults of a basement beneath the floor are visible in the foreground

places with sparse remains. It exhibits pottery from Miletus going back to Mycenean times, fine examples of ceramics from the sixth and seventh centuries BCE, displays on the archaeology of such sites as Clazomenae, Teos, Pitane, and Metropolis. The sixth century painted terracotta sarcophagi from Clazomenae are particularly fine. Visitors will also find Hellenistic and Roman sculpture from various sites. One of the rarest pieces is a late Hellenistic bronze athlete found in nearby Cyme harbour. As the Izmir Archaeological Museum is overflowing with artifacts, some buildings in the International Fair ground of Izmir have been converted recently to the Izmir Museum of History and Art displaying items of terra cotta, stone and precious metals from the Archaeological Museum.

Temple of Dionysus, designed in 220-205 BCE by the architect Hermogenes of Priene

THE ÇEŞME PENINSULA

The Çeşme peninsula projects westward into the Aegean between the Bay of Izmir and the Bay of Kuşadası. Today, with its sandy beaches, spas hotels, private villas and restaurants, it is the summer playground for Izmir. A highway carries visitors quickly to the busy resort of **Çeşme**, which lies at the western end, only a dozen kilometers from the Greek island of Chios. In contrast, the ancient ruins at **Clazomenae** and **Teos** belong to another world. They occupy peaceful sites that provide a link to the days of the Ionian League.

TEOS

Teos was first settled during the tenth century BCE, in the Dark Age, by Greeks from Orchomenos, an important Bronze Age city in Boetia, to the north of Thebes. The excellent town site between two harbours also attracted migrants from Athens and other parts of Ionia. Spurred by the large capacity of its harbours, Teos developed important trade routes to many Mediterranean and Black Sea cities. By the seventh century, Teos became famous for its wool. In the sixth century BCE, it joined with other Hellenic cities in building a temple at Naukratis in Egypt, an indication of its strong commercial interests there.

Thales of Miletus, the father of Greek philosophy and a wise statesman suggested in the early sixth century BCE that Teos should be the political centre of the Panionion, the league of Ionian cities, but this advice was not taken. When the Persians invaded in 546 BCE, rather than defend their city, the Teians sailed to form a colony at Abdera in Thrace. This migration may have been partly motivated by the precious metals mined near there. However, before long, many of them returned and reoccupied Teos. The two cities maintained close political, religious and commercial relations and, in the sixth century, minted similar coins representing a griffin, the mythical creature associated with Dionysus.

By the time of the Ionian Revolt against Persia (499-493 BCE) the city had grown wealthy enough to provide seventeen ships for the Ionian fleet, which they lost in the fateful battle of Lade in 494. After Alexander the Great's liberation of the Greek cities, and its acquisition by the Attalids of Pergamon, Teos thrived; its prosperity continued into the Roman era. African grey marble with spots of white and red quarried 3 km. northeast was exported to Rome. Emperor Hadrian visited the city and ordered the rebuilding of the Temple of Dionysus in marble.

In addition to success in trade and renown for its festival of Dionysus, Teos gained a reputation as a place of intellectual and literary pursuits. The epic poet, Antimachos, a contemporary of Homer and Hesiod, lived there in the eighth century. Although his work was known in classical times, little has survived. The most famous Teian poet Anacreon (582-485) wrote lyrical poetry well suited to this city of Dionysus. The themes of love, wine and the pleasures of life made his poetry popular. He went to Abdera with his compatriots but returned to Teos and was lured by Polycrates, the tyrant of Samos to provide entertainment at his court. He received the ultimate reward for his wit in 522 BCE when Hipparchos of Athens sent a fifty-oared galley to bear him gloriously to Athens where he remained for several years, before returning to spend his last years in Teos. A statue of him stood on the Acropolis in Athens, and several coins minted in Teos depicted him with his lyre.

The philosopher Protagoras (490–420 BCE) was born in Abdera but appears to have lived in Teos. Plato named him as the original sophist. He is best known for making the revolutionary statements: "Man is the measure of all things", and: "Concerning the gods, I am not able to know to a certainty whether they exist or whether they do not." A century later, Nausiphanes a follower of the naturalistic system of Demokrates taught a number of pupils in Teos. The famous philosopher Epicurus (or Epikouros) traveled from Samos to study with him. Apparently Epicurus fell out with Nausiphanes, but nevertheless based his atomistic principles on his teaching. He rose to fame in Athens and generated a following throughout the classical world.

Teos was also the home base in the early second century BCE of an association of Dionysian actors, poets, singers and musicians, who performed all over the region, until they quarreled with the city authorities and moved to Ephesus. They probably returned to Teos for the two principal festivals of Dionysus – the Dionysia and the Anthesteria – as well as the Heracleia in honour of Heracles and the Dia, dedicated to Zeus.

Rediscovery and archaeology

In 1763, the Society of Dilettanti, intending to produce a new volume of *Antiquities of Ionia* sent the architect R. P. Pullan to Teos to make drawings of the temple. A French team worked there from 1824 to 1825, followed by a series of Turkish archaeologists from Ankara. Since 2010 Musa Kadıoğlu from the Classical Archaeology Department at the University of Ankara has been directing excavations and restoration on the site and has published a short guide to the site.

Visiting Teos

Signposts from the small town of Seferihisar point the way to Sığacık and from there, through an intimate landscape of valonia oaks and small fields to Teos. Low hills slope down to the romantic ruins of the Temple of Dionysus, which lies in open space among ancient olive trees. The bases and lower shafts of several columns and a few fallen Ionic capitals convey its former beauty but few vestiges of this important city remain. The theatre and several other elements shown on the plan posted on the site are barely visible but the large Bouleuterion was unearthed in 2011.

The Temple of Dionysus, the largest in Anatolia dedicated to the god, was designed in the late third century BCE by Hermogenes of Priene (ca. 220-190 BCE). He based his conception on the Temple of Athena Polias (ca. 350 BCE) in Priene, designed by the famous architect Pytheos, but he applied his own system of proportion to it. The Roman architect Vitruvius, who admired Hermogenes, described his aesthetic system as eustyle.

Ionic capital from Temple of Dionysus

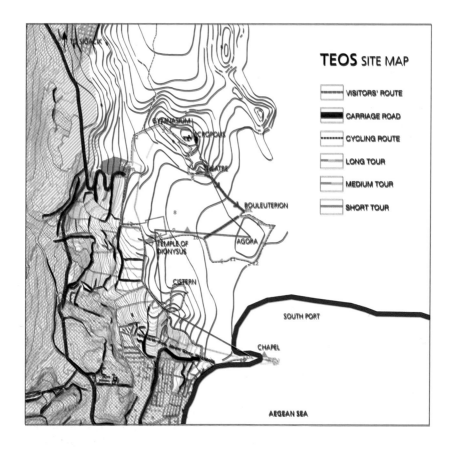

TEOS SITE MAP

VISITORS' ROUTE

CARRIAGE ROAD

CYCLING ROUTE

LONG TOUR

MEDIUM TOUR

SHORT TOUR

According to Hermogenes, the space between the columns should ideally be two-and-a-quarter times the lower diameters, while the column should be nine-and-a-half times its diameter. The architect created a spacious and elegant temple, by placing the six columns on the ends and the eleven on the sides far from the cella wall. This is an early work of Hermogenes, who went on to design the Temple of Artemis at Magnesia, to which Vitruvius and Strabo gave the highest accolades.

Roman Emperor Hadrian commanded a radical restoration of the temple, replacing the original limestone with marble exactly to the design of Hermogenes. The capitals we see today, though faithful copies, are actually Roman. Archaeologists have found none of the original blocks of the frieze, so they do not know whether the Romans made exact copies of them or

A Section of the frieze showing the Roman copies of a Dionysiac Thiasos (the ecstatic retinue of the god) Izmir Archaeological Museum.

made significant changes. Since Romans constantly made copies of Greek sculpture for their own use, the former alternative seems likely. Panels from the frieze on the entablature showing the *thiasos* can be seen in the Izmir Archaeological Museum. The temple was enclosed in a temenos with Doric stoas on the north and south sides and Ionic stoas to the east and west.

To the east of the temple, you will come to the site of the **Agora** and a temple of unknown dedication, where nothing but foundations stand above ground. Northwest of there, is the recently excavated and well-preserved **Bouleuterion** arranged with sixteen rows of seats divided by stairways into four sections. An inscription dated to 200 BCE shows that musical and rhetorical performances took place there as well as political meetings. Continuing northwest, you will reach the sparse remains of the **Theatre**. The foundations of the stage building are visible, but almost all of the stones of the seats have been removed for construction elsewhere.

Above the theatre, continuing in the same direction, you can climb up to the **Acropolis** where a level stone platform has been exposed. A temple on an east-west axis, probably dedicated to Zeus Kapitolios, dominated the city from here.

The **Gymnasium**, a short distance to the northeast of the Acropolis, has not been excavated, but an inscription carved

The Bouleuterion

The Theatre

in the second century BCE refers to the philanthropy of a citizen named Polythros, who contributed to the salaries of teachers. It states that: "Girls and boys attending the Teos Gymnasium were taught reading, writing and literature by three different teachers, who were paid an annual salary of 500-600 drachms. The music teacher was paid 700 drachms annually and two sports teachers were paid 500 drachms each."

South of the Temple of Dionysus is a large **Roman Cistern** built with stone arches and vaults, and lined with stucco. Continuing southeast of the cistern, you will come to the **Southern Port**. Most of the huge blocks of stone that reinforced it have been covered in sand, but some are visible in the water. At the southern end are the lower walls of a small chapel with double naves and apses. Its history is unknown.

CLAZOMENAE

Clazomenae (or Klazomenai) was settled after the Dorian invasion, probably by Greeks from the Peloponnese. It was an early member of the Ionian League. This polis was at first founded on the mainland but for

Painted terracotta sarcophagi, sixth century BCE (Izmir Archaeological Museum)

fear of the Persians, its inhabitants moved to an offshore island from which they later returned. For a while Clazomenae was split between the two locations. At the order of Alexander the Great, the island was connected by a causeway that still exists.

This city was the birthplace of the pre-Socratic philosopher

(L) Reconstruction of an olive press and a well (R) An olive press recreated on the basis of archaeological evidence.

Anaxagoras, the first to take Ionian philosophy to Athens where Socrates was his pupil. He postulated a more complex order in the universe than his Milesian forerunners Thales and Anaximenes, and made significant scientific discoveries.

Almost nothing remains of the architecture at Clazomenae, beyond some foundations and a single Corinthian capital but a large number of painted sarcophagi were produced here. Some striking examples from the sixth century BCE are on view in the Izmir Archaeological Museum. A connection has been made between these lively artifacts and Greek black figure vase painting of the same era.

For those interested in the production of olive oil, a commodity of immense importance in the region since the Bronze Age, Clazomenae has something unique to offer. Elements from an olive press dating from the sixth century have been unearthed here that allowed archaeologists from Ege University to understand the process and to reconstruct a press of the same type. It involves both vertical grinding wheels and horizontal presses. This is the only surviving example of an olive press of this type; it is two centuries older than any other olive press in the Greek world.

With support from a Turkish producer of olive oil and a German company producing natural building materials, the team has also recreated buildings based on evidence of local vernacular structures. The traditional method of extracting and purifying the oil is explained in clear diagrams. Rows of newly made amphorae of the type used to store oil are on show.

The Marble Court seen from the Palaestra

SARDIS

Sardis lies about 90 km. inland from the Aegean, in the upper Hermos valley. Its early history is hard to establish. Homer mentions the site in the *Iliad* as the territory of Maeonians. Herodotus states that Greek warriors, "sons of Heracles" established a kingdom there. As the Hittite Empire declined, Lydians, a people of obscure origin, speaking an Indo-European language, migrated into the region and established their rule over the indigenous people. Herodotus described Lydia as "a fertile country rich in gold." Indeed, Sardis, drawing plentiful gold from the river Paktolos (Sart Çayı), a tributary of the Hermos (Gediz), was renowned for its wealth. The site possessed several links with Greek mythology. Euripides, in his play the Bacchae, identified snow-capped mount Tmolos that overlooks Sardis as the birthplace of Dionysus and it was connected with the mythical ruler Tantalos, whose son Pelops founded the Peloponnese and the royal dynasty of Mycenae. The region was also associated with the Anatolian earth mother goddess Cybele, whom the Greeks transformed into their goddess Artemis. While the sources of Homer and Herodotus in ancient myths were often contradictory, discoveries of Mycenean and Greek Proto-geometric pottery confirm a Hellenic presence in Lydia from about 1200- 900 BCE.

In the Archaic era the Lydians gradually absorbed Greek culture and wrote in the Greek alphabet. By the sixth century BCE Sardis was economically powerful, minting the world's first coins, manufacturing valuable goods and trading widely. The earliest coins were made of electrum, a naturally occurring alloy of gold and silver; later they issued them

Lydian electrum
trite c.600 BCE

Tumuli of Gyges and Alyattes north of Sardis, from the north, with Sardis and the Tmolos range in the background

in both pure gold and silver. Archaeological evidence of gold-working industries near the Paktolos supports the belief that the river was a major source of the precious metal.

A series of strong kings fought to protect and expand their territory. King Gyges (680-652) resisted the Cimmerians, a barbarian tribe who had overrun Phrygia and sacked Sardis. His son Ardys (651-625) defeated them decisively and also occupied the Ionian Greek city of Priene.

Under the ambitious King Alyattes II (609-650) the Lydians captured Smyrna in the west and the Phrygian capital Gordion in the east. They also made peace with the Medes, former adversaries further to the east. These kings were buried under vast tumuli that can be seen to the north of the site. Herodotus described the largest one as equal to the pyramids of Egypt.

King Croesus (595-547? BCE), whose wealth gave rise to the expression "rich as Croesus," overpowered the remaining Greek cities on the Aegean coast and ruled them from Sardis. He was a relatively benign ruler, who admired the Greeks, and did not harshly oppress his subjects. Indeed, he became their benefactor when he sponsored the reconstruction of the great Temple of Artemis at Ephesus, which had been ruined by a flood. Little writing by Lydians survives to shed light on their culture but Greek writers left records. Several Greek poets, philosophers, scientists, and musicians travelled to Sardis. Even the Athenian statesman Solon visited and the great philosopher Thales of Miletus may have served as an advisor to Croesus. In addition Greek artisans and scholars flocked there to work for the wealthy ruler. The Lydians developed a reputation for music but perhaps their most enduring inventions were the games of knucklebones and dice.

Croesus could have created a brilliant empire if success had not gone to his head. He felt threatened by the expansion of the Persian Empire under Cyrus the Great and, not content with merely defending his borders, he set his sights on conquest. He consulted the oracle of Apollo at nearby Didyma, to which he had already made valuable donations, but received no clear reply. The Delphic oracle, also receiving his ostentatious gifts, pronounced that if he waged war on the Persians a great empire would fall. Convinced that the oracle referred to the Persian Empire, he crossed the river Halys (Kızılırmak) and attacked the forces of Cyrus the Great. After several skirmishes without victory on either side, Croesus returned to Sardis for the winter, but Cyrus followed him and defeated his army on the plain of Thymbra. It is said that baggage camels, ridden by the Persian cavalry in a sudden charge, so terrified the Lydian horses that they bolted.

Contrary to the hopes of Croesus, it was his own empire that was doomed. Sardis fell to the Persians after a short siege and, according to legend, Croesus was burnt on a flaming pyre. In some versions of the story Croesus was saved at the last minute by Apollo, who sent a violent rainstorm to extinguish the fire.

The Persians virtually destroyed the city and pulled down the massive defensive walls that surrounded it. Cyrus then conquered all of the Greek cities on the Aegean coast, reducing some of them to ruins. Sardis became the Persian administration centre in Anatolia governing all the satrapies in Ionia. It was linked by the Royal Road through central Anatolia and Mesopotamia to the Persian capital of Susa far away near the Persian Gulf. In 499, when the Ionians, led by Miletus, revolted against their Persian overlords, they sacked and burned Sardis. The loosely allied Greek cities were no match for the vast army of Cyrus's successor Darius who retaliated by razing Miletus completely. The Greek cities under Persian satraps continued to be ruled from Sardis, but they were allowed religious freedom.

In 334 BCE the city surrendered without a fight to Alexander the Great, but in the unstable period of his warring successors it suffered conflict. Sardis was captured in 282 BCE by Seleucus I and in 213 BCE Antiochos

III destroyed the city. The few remains of Hellenistic architecture date from rebuilding after this invasion. In about 180 BCE Eumenes II of Pergamon conquered Sardis and other Greek cities; less than half a century later, Attalos III, the last Pergamene king, donated it with his entire empire to the Romans, who made it their administrative centre for the region. The city thrived during the Roman era and several emperors paid ceremonial visits.

Sardis was severely damaged by an earthquake in 17 CE, but the emperors Tiberius and Claudius both contributed money for rebuilding it. At this point a grand colonnaded street was built, paved with large marble slabs. Unfortunately much of this is lost under the modern highway that runs from Izmir to Ankara. The principal architectural monument of this era is the Bath-Gymnasium Complex, whose splendor shows the wealth and ambition of the city under Roman rule. In the third century, part of the bath complex was converted into a synagogue.

Christian Sardis

Sardis was the seat of a bishop in the late first century CE and was one of the Seven Churches of Asia addressed by St. John in the *Book of Revelation*. John rebuked the Sardians, writing: "I have not found thy works perfect before God." In the second century the bishop Melito (d. ca. 180) was an influential Christian scholar, revered as a prophet; he was also known as a millennialist, believing that Christ would reign for a thousand years. He travelled to Palestine and studied writings in the library at Caesarea. In ca. 161 he wrote an apology for Christianity, which he sent to the emperor Marcus Aurelius. His most lasting legacy was coining the term "The New Testament." Several churches were built between the third century CE and the Byzantine era.

Jewish Sardis

There is some evidence that a Jewish population existed in Sardis as early as the sixth century BCE. During the Hellenistic era Antiochos made a significant contribution to the demography of the region, when he resettled two thousand Jewish families from Mesopotamia in Lydia and Phrygia, including many in Sardis. It appears that their descendants continued to prosper there under Roman rule: the Emperor Augustus mandated special rights for them including the practice of their own religion. Inscriptions and other archaeological finds in the shops suggest that Christians and Jews as well as the general Greco-Roman population coexisted as they plied their trades and carried out commercial activities. They also prove that Jews were among the prominent citizens of Sardis and members of the city council or *boule*.

Rediscovery and excavation

Between 1910 and 1914, archaeologists from Princeton University excavated the Temple of Artemis and also unearthed over a thousand Lydian tombs. Since 1958 Harvard and Cornell Universities have sponsored excavations, led by George Hanfmann, whose main achievement has been the discovery and partial restoration of the Roman gymnasium bath complex and synagogue, where he found many inscriptions and mosaics. Today the American teams continue their work and Turkish archaeologists are taking leading roles.

Visiting Sardis

Easily reached by the modern highway from Izmir, Sardis with its significant history, the Temple of Artemis as well as the splendid bath-gymnasium complex with the unique synagogue, it is worth the journey. The highway bisects by the site, leaving the bath-gymnasium complex and synagogue to the north and the Temple of Artemis to the south. A local road leading south, close to the Paktolos river gives access to the temple. You can see the other places in the southern area before crossing the highway to explore the bath-gymnasium complex. The tumuli of Gyges and Alyattes lie about 8 km. across the Hermos river to the north.

The Temple of Artemis

There was a large enough Greek population in Sardis during the archaic era to build a temple to their patron goddess Artemis. Ironically, this was destroyed when the Greeks burnt the city during the Ionian revolt and only rebuilt after the city was taken by Alexander the Great. Built in the Ionic style over a long period from ca. 300 BCE to 150 CE, the new temple was the fourth largest in the classical world. With eight columns along the front and twenty on the sides it was designed in the pseudo-dipteral manner. Although only two complete columns and a few lower shafts survive, its magnificent siting, and orientation to Mount Tmolos makes it an inspiring site. The well-preserved Ionic capitals with some floral decoration show the willingness of the architects to experiment with details. An altar to Artemis next to the west end of the temple may have served for the worship of the goddess for at least two hundred years before the temple was first built. It was stepped in the manner of the altar of Zeus at Pergamon, but on a much smaller scale. We can only speculate on its original form.

In the first few centuries CE the Temple of Artemis went through significant changes. 17 CE, an earthquake caused severe damage, but it was repaired; most of the surviving columns are Roman. During the second century the imperial cult gained strength. In ca. 140 CE the Emperor Antoninus insisted that the temple should be divided into two chambers so that the citizens could worship him at the east end and his wife Faustina at the west end. In the fourth century CE, as Christianity superseded the pagan religions and the temple fell onto disuse, stone was removed for use in new buildings. A small church built in the fourth century, right against the northeast corner of the temple, shows that Christianity gained ground in Sardis during the reign of Constantine. It is one of the oldest surviving churches in Anatolia. Hardly large enough for a congregation, its purpose may have been to sanctify the place of pagan worship; it also served as a chapel for a nearby cemetery. A second apse with three arched windows was added in the sixth century.

(L) Temple of Artemis, Sardis c.300 BCE – 150 CE. The Acropolis rises dramatically in the background
(R) Ionic capital detail

A fourth century Christian church.

Returning northwards alongside the local road, you will pass a fenced area described as Paktolos North, where excavation revealed complex layers of foundations and lower walls of buildings. They range from Lydian houses, an altar of Cybele and gold workshops of the sixth century BCE to a late Roman bath and two Christian churches. The difficulty of digging among walls of different periods at various levels and protecting the findings, made it hard for the archaeologists to offer access to visitors and to expose the remains to view. In some areas they have taken the step of reburying what they found, in order to protect it. However, the discoveries in this area yielded valuable information about life in Sardis over more than a millennium. The gold processing workshops, which include water channels, furnaces and areas for cupellation (a process of separating gold from ores and other metals), show that the Lydians practiced advanced techniques in metallurgy. The Lydian houses revealed copious pottery but most furnishings and ornament had vanished. Excavation of the Early Christian church of the fourth century revealed beautiful mosaics.

Further to the east the remains of the only significant Persian architecture can be seen, a few steps of a pyramid tomb from the time of Cyrus the Great. This seems to be similar in design to some tombs in the capital of Cyrus I at Passargadae. Northeast of the tomb the collapsing seats of the Roman theatre are visible on the unstable slope of the Acropolis. Below it, almost completely covered by soil, lies the unexcavated Roman stadium.

On the south side of the highway, near a space identified as a small chapel, archaeologists discovered the remains of a building known as the **House of the Bronzes**. They found several bronze vases and items associated with Christian worship. This elegant house with Christian symbols incised in the marble floors may have been the residence of the bishop of Sardis. Among the discoveries was a small shovel for embers intricately designed with a Greek cross within a circle supported by two dolphins. Scholars are still puzzling over the presence of a statue of Bacchus, the pagan god of wine, in the corner of one room. The house appears to have been destroyed by fire, possibly in anti-Christian riots that occurred in the fifth century CE. Another room, dating from centuries earlier, appears to have been a pottery workshop. Vases and shards from the early Iron Age up to the time of Croesus suggest that it served that purpose for centuries. Unfortunately none of these buildings can be seen today.

The Bath-Gymnasium complex

The restoration of the gymnasium complex by archaeologists from Harvard and Cornell allows us to see the grand and opulent facilities that the imperial administration created for citizens. Now that the façade rises again to its original height with wings on both sides to enclose the Marble Court, we can appreciate the grandeur of the whole concept. This building stands at the west side of the vast palaestra; the synagogue is on its south side and column bases define its other borders. It is now possible to imagine large-scale athletic events taking place here. It has been suggested that the Marble Court was associated both with the imperial cult and Dionysian rituals. The façade, with a distinctly Baroque character, is architecturally similar to the stage building of a Roman theatre: its columns stand forward in front of walls to create strong contrast of light and shade. Central columns with spiral fluting add to the drama. Originally, statues standing between the columns would have enlivened it in a traditionally Roman manner; the details of the Corinthian capitals are crisp and exuberant. An inscription proclaims that this complex was dedicated by the citizens of Sardis to Caracalla and Geta, sons of the emperor Septimus Severus and his wife Julia Domna.

In contrast to the lively and graceful post and lintel architecture of the facade, the halls of the thermae, enclosed in massive masonry, express a static character, but the architects brought the solid walls to

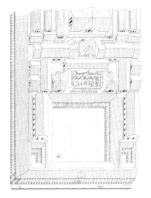

(L) Sardis Bath-Gymnasium complex and Synagogue reconstruction
(R) The almost Baroque architecture of the Bath-Gymnasium complex in the Corinthian order

life with many niches carved into them and broad curves in the apsidal ends of two long halls. Like most Roman baths the whole facility was symmetrically planned. A powerful central axis, beginning at the eastern entrance, traversed the palaestra, continued through the marble court to the frigidarium, across a hall with a long swimming pool and on to the central hall with niches for statuary. This imposing space was flanked by identical apsidal tepidaria. The axis terminated in the large, vaulted caldarium. To maintain the symmetry, the changing rooms through which the public entered, and the rooms for massage were exactly the same on the two sides. All the interiors were originally lined with polychrome marble, but today only the unadorned lower walls survive. The western part has not yet been excavated.

The Synagogue

By the early third century CE the Jewish community possessed sufficient status and numbers to be awarded the privilege by the Emperor Lucius Verus to convert the spacious south hall of the Baths into a synagogue. This impressive building 20 m. wide and 80 m. long was large enough to provide for a congregation of one thousand worshippers.

The synagogue was entered through an atrium with a central marble pool rather like the peristyle court of a Roman house. From there, three doors gave access to the long main hall, which terminates at the

(L)The atrium of the synagogue, *ca.* 450 CE
(R) Restored wall decoration in the synagogue

west end in an apse. In most apsidal synagogues the apse was on the side towards Jerusalem and contained the Torah, but since the building already existed with the opposite orientation, two pedimented aedicules, one of them for the Torah, stood on the east wall between the entrance doors. The southern aedicule is identified by a Hebrew inscription as the place for the Torah. Six large piers about 9 m. tall on each of the side-walls supported a wooden roof. Clerestory windows beneath the ceiling illuminated the space. The lower walls were lined with marble and the upper surfaces were adorned with mosaics and paintings. Surviving fragments of these decorations show birds, fish, vines and pomegranates. One section of the wall has been recreated to suggest the decorative

The prayer hall of the synagogue looking eastwards

(L) A detail of the floor mosaic
(R) The table at the west end of the nave
with two lions flanking it on each side

scheme. Fortunately, the floor of the colourful, mostly geometric mosaic that covered it is intact. This has been expertly reset on a fresh base so that it can be enjoyed by visitors. The only seats formed a semicircle in the apse. A nearby table probably served as a lectern, standing before the apse, with eagles carved on its supports. Two lions, possibly created much earlier for rituals in honour of Cybele, appear to act as guards on either side of it.

Small shops behind stoas lined the south side of the complex, facing the principal street of the city. The shops at the western end date from the Byzantine era.

The Museum at Manisa

Many of the finds at Sardis are displayed in the museum in Manisa, which lies about 60 km. northeast of Sardis. The museum is also worth visiting because it is in the külliye (complex) of the beautiful Ottoman Muradiye Mosque (1583-86) designed by the renowned Ottoman architect Sinan. The busy commercial town also contains other significant Ottoman architecture.

Manisa Museum, Lion from the synagogue at Sardis

A view southwards through Frontinus Gate
towards the Byzantine Gate

HIERAPOLIS

This Phrygian city lies on a high plateau above the valley of the river Lykos, a tributary of the upper Maeander. The name Hierapolis, means "sacred city." Hot springs and strange vapors rising from a cave explain the belief, in prehistoric times, that this was the entrance to the underworld kingdom of Hades. Creating a powerful duality, the ground beside this symbol of darkness, became a sanctuary of Apollo, the god of wisdom and music, associated with light. The city's position at the junction of trade routes from the Aegean Sea to eastern Anatolia, and the Royal Road from Susa in Persia to Sardis and the coast, brought wealth from trade. The rich agricultural land of the Lykos valley was able to support a large population; flocks of sheep that thrived there, and the lucrative wool trade also ensured prosperity.

The water that gushed from springs at a temperature of 35° C (95° F), laden with calcium bicarbonate, cascaded over the edge of cliffs below the classical city. In the course of countless millennia it laid down beds of travertine creating a fantastic landscape of terraced pools with stalactites at their edges. This process provided vast quantities of stone for the architecture of Hierapolis. The curative powers of the water, derived from the valuable minerals induced many wealthy Romans suffering from illnesses to come here for treatment. Drinking it was considered particularly beneficial to the heart and kidneys, while bathing in it alleviated the pains of arthritis and cured skin diseases. Spas still attract invalids for the same reasons today, but the majority of tourists come to Pamukkale today to see the spectacular travertine terraces. Because of its amazing whiteness the Turks name the place Pamukkale, meaning "Cotton Castle."

History

Little is known about the history of Hierapolis before 188 BCE when it was passed from the Seleucid Kingdom to Eumenes II of Pergamon after the Peace of Apameia. The Seleucid king Antiochos III may have founded it a few decades earlier, but we can credit the passionate builder Eumenes with initiating the architectural program that launched it as a great city. Since a series of earthquakes over several centuries destroyed the early buildings, little remains from his time, but the Hippodamian grid plan, laid out in the Hellenistic era set the pattern for the city's development. Today we see the architecture erected under a series of Roman emperors, who took an interest in this Asian metropolis. In the reign of Nero (54-68 CE) an earthquake caused serious damage. Hadrian (117-138 CE) may have visited the city; during his time the vast civic Agora was built. One of the greatest periods of growth and new building came in the time of Septimius Severus and continued through the Severan dynasty (193-235 CE). In the fourth century, as Phrygia became less secure, Emperor Theodosius (379-395 CE) ordered the construction of walls around the city.

A large population of Jews, descended from some of those resettled in Lydia and Phrygia by Antiochos III in the fourth century CE, lived in Hierapolis. Their presence probably aided in the growth of Christianity there, as early as the first century. St. Paul probably did not visit Hierapolis, but the Apostle Philip is believed to have preached in the city and met his death there as a martyr. A bishopric was established there by the second century CE and in the sixth century CE the city became the Metropolis of Phrygia. The new cathedral was built at that time.

Early in the seventh century Persian invasions threatened Phrygia and further earthquakes struck Hierapolis, from that time decline set in. Makeshift buildings were put up over the ruins of fallen structures.

Rediscovery and excavation

In 1740 an ardent English traveler named Richard Pococke, passing through the Middle East on his way from Egypt to Greece, stopped at Hierapolis where he marveled at the travertine terraces and the necropolis. He published an influential book on his travels, which included descriptions of the Temple of Apollo, the nymphaeum and the theatre. His work probably encouraged other Englishmen such as Robert Chandler to go there. The ubiquitous Frenchman Charles Texier, who visited in the mid-nineteenth century, produced some picturesque engravings; other antiquarians and architects followed. The first serious archaeological study was conducted in 1898 by Carl Humann working with German colleagues, but the site lay dormant until the Italian archaeologist Paolo Verzone, in partnership with the leading Turkish archaeologist Arif Müfid Mansel, began work in 1957. Since then, the Italian Archaeological Mission, with Turkish collaboration has continued the excavation, re-erected columns and turned unruly piles of rubble into coherent, if only partial skeletons of buildings. Thanks to their dedication, it is now possible for the public to visualize the architecture and townscape of Hierapolis.

In 1980 the Roman Baths, with a magnificent barrel vaulted space still intact, were converted into a museum, and in 1988 Hierapolis-Pamukkale became a World Heritage site. Soon after that, hotels on the archaeological site were demolished. One exceptional project has been the rebuilding, using original elements, of the *scenae frons* (stage building) of the theatre under the direction of Daria de Bernardi Ferrero. This process is called anastylosis. When completed it will be the only theatre in Aegean Turkey with an entire story standing behind the stage. Support for this venture has been provided by Fiat of Istanbul and the Koç Foundation. The current director of the Italian Mission, Francesco D'Andria, has published a book on the city that includes many photographs of site before and during restoration projects.

Visiting Hierapolis

Visitors enter at both ends of the classical city. The southern gate can be approached on foot or by car at the top of the travertine terraces; the northern one is reached from the town of Pamukkale by a winding road that climbs steeply to the level plateau where the city was built. I will describe the itinerary starting at the north end. From the car park and ticket office you will walk through the north necropolis, which lies outside the city walls and does not conform to the grid. After passing the massive Bath Basilica and going through Frontinus Gate, you reach the absolutely straight main thoroughfare, Frontinus Street, which stretches ahead for over a kilometer. To the west (on the right) there is only space for short streets that end at the edge of the white cliffs, but the urban fabric stretches up the lower slopes of hills on the east side. As in Priene, the grid accommodates to irregular ground, but here the linear quality dominates. On one side of the splendid city the irregular wooded hills

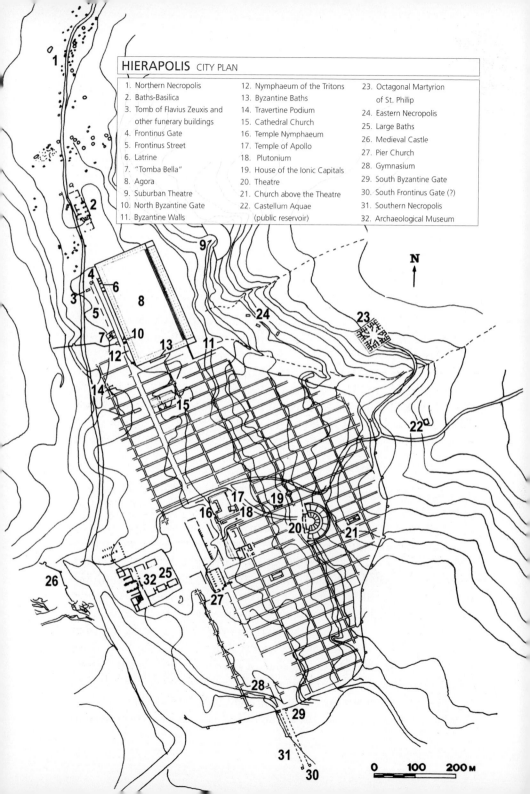

HIERAPOLIS CITY PLAN

1. Northern Necropolis
2. Baths-Basilica
3. Tomb of Flavius Zeuxis and other funerary buildings
4. Frontinus Gate
5. Frontinus Street
6. Latrine
7. "Tomba Bella"
8. Agora
9. Suburban Theatre
10. North Byzantine Gate
11. Byzantine Walls
12. Nymphaeum of the Tritons
13. Byzantine Baths
14. Travertine Podium
15. Cathedral Church
16. Temple Nymphaeum
17. Temple of Apollo
18. Plutonium
19. House of the Ionic Capitals
20. Theatre
21. Church above the Theatre
22. Castellum Aquae (public reservoir)
23. Octagonal Martyrion of St. Philip
24. Eastern Necropolis
25. Large Baths
26. Medieval Castle
27. Pier Church
28. Gymnasium
29. South Byzantine Gate
30. South Frontinus Gate (?)
31. Southern Necropolis
32. Archaeological Museum

N

0   100   200 M

(L) Tumuli from the Hellenistic era in the north necropolis
(R) Sepulchers and sarcophagi of local travertine

make a scenic backdrop; on the other the rich Lykos valley spreads out below. On clear days Mount Kadmos, 30 km. to the south, makes an inspiring sight.

The North Necropolis of Hierapolis (1) is one of the largest and best preserved in Anatolia. The citizens who could afford it expressed their status through impressive tombs. In the Hellenistic period, burials of important people took place in circular tumuli covered by earth domes and surrounded by stone walls. Their central vaulted chambers approached by a passage, held several sarcophagi for subsequent interments. They were usually topped by a stone phallus for good fortune. In

(L) Tomb 162. The sepulcher of Marcus Aurelius Ammianus Menandrianus, who was affiliated with the Association of Linen Workers. It consisted of two chambers. (R) Tomb 114 of Aelius Apollinarius. An earthquake has dislodged a few stones and broken the sarcophagus on the roof into two.

the Roman era, wealthy families built sepulchers of travertine, some of which resembled small temples or houses. They were usually set within a fenced enclosure that was planted with flowers and used for memorial gatherings. Additional sarcophagi clustered around many of them and in several cases were piled on the roof, with the idea that raising them up high, would glorify the memory of the deceased. Not all sarcophagi were associated with sepulchers; some stood on their own. The poor were simply placed in rock cut graves in the ground.

Archaeologists have identified about 1200 tombs many of them with inscriptions identifying the owners and stating their achievements. Many included warnings against defiling the tombs, and threatening large fines for doing so. One, on a tomb known as the "tomb of the curse" threatened that anyone who removed the inscription "should not enjoy the comfort of offspring or life. Neither land nor sea should welcome him. He should die without children and suffer every misadventure." Since the words remain incised in the stone, we can assume that they achieved their purpose.

The Roman Baths converted to a Christian Basilica (2)

Just outside the North Gate of Hierapolis stood the Roman Baths that served the northern district and allowed travelers to refresh themselves before entering the city. To judge by the size of the calidarium, which is all that remains, this must have been an enormous complex. Excavation in the future may reveal the plan, but nothing else rises above the ground today. Stone from the other rooms was probably removed during the Christian era for other building projects. Like most Roman thermae, its walls were made immensely strong to support vaults, but these had already collapsed by the time it was converted into a church in the sixth century. At that time, square piers were built in the nave to carry new vaults with a shorter span or possibly three domes on pendentives like the church of St John at Ephesus. An atrium added at the north end, and an apse extending the space to the south, gave the church a traditionally Christian character. Christian symbols were carved into the keystones of some of the arches. Large cracks in the north wall, and the dangerous leaning of the west wall show earthquake damage, but the huge travertine blocks of the side facing the road have barely budged.

The Calidarium of the Roman bath outside the Frontinus gate, third century CE. It was transformed into a church in the sixth century

Set between two round towers, a well-proportioned three-arched gate, known as **Frontinus Gate (4)** marks the entry to the city. The central arch rises slightly higher than those on either side and opens a little wider, but the emphasis is subtle. The gate was dedicated to the emperor Domitian in about 84 CE by Sextus Julius Frontinus, the Roman governor of Asia Minor. Frontinus, the son of the general and statesman Publius Scipio, had already distinguished himself as governor of Britain in 75 CE. In that role, as part of a strategy to subdue Welsh tribes, he built a network of forts. He was also involved in hydraulic engineering at a gold mine in Wales. With that experience, he must have been ready to meet the challenges of exploiting the hot springs and supplying drinking water in Hierapolis. He not only built the gate, but also **Frontinus Street (5)**, which leads from it to the far end of the city. He installed a cloaca (sewer) under its centre, covered with stone slabs, to receive sewage and wastewater. It is not surprising that he was later appointed to oversee

Frontinus Gate, leading to Frontinus Street, the principal artery of Hierapolis

the aqueducts of Rome, on which he wrote a well-known treatise *De Aquaeductu.*

Immediately inside the eastern arch of the gate, somewhat obstructing the path are the lower walls of the **Small Church**, probably built in the fifth century CE. The altar was supported on a reused Corinthian capital, and a piece of carved marble screen indicates the ornamentation of the interior. This building appears like a minor victory of religion over civic management: The opportunity to stop and pray on entering the city trumped the flow of traffic. In the Byzantine era the street was also narrowed by a row of houses built a little further south on the other side.

The Latrine, the first building on the east side of the street, concealed behind a fine Doric colonnade, was built in the late first century CE. It was an example of high quality services for the public good. A row of columns divided it longitudinally into two aisles; a row of marble seats ran along the two outer walls; water channels beneath them carried waste to the cloaca a few meters away under the street; fresh water for washing flowed in another channel. The Doric columns, echoed on the other side of the street, continued as far as the next gate. Behind them on the east side was the Agora.

The east side of Frontinus Street. The Doric colonnade at the far end fronts the Latrine

The Agora

After a severe earthquake in 60 CE, during the reign of Nero, when reconstruction was taking place throughout the city, the opportunity arose to build a new Agora on a grand scale, 280 m. long and 170 m. wide. Stoas in the Ionic order lined three sides, while a monumental Basilica in the Corinthian style, raised on a tall flight of steps stretched out along the third. It rose to two stories, the lower one fronted by an arcade.

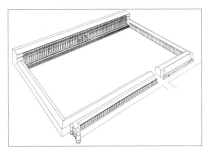

Reconstructions of the Agora. (L) Frontinus Gate can be seen lower left corner. On the east side the Doric colonnade faces Frontinus Street; to its right is the Nymphaeum of the Tritons. The Basilica occupied the entire east side (R) A detail of the Basilica.

Capitals from the Basilica (L) a sphinx (R) a man's head, flanked by lions attacking bulls.

The off-centre entrance, with a distinctly Baroque character offered relief from the repetition of the architectural elements. One section of the steps survives and has been partly restored. This grand edifice, damaged earlier by an earthquake was partly demolished in the fourth century, while the rest collapsed later. Fortunately some unique figural capitals survived and are now in the local museum. They give us an idea of the originality lavished on the decoration of this building.

The Byzantine Gate (10) and Walls (11)

In the Hellenistic and Roman periods Hierapolis was not protected by walls, but in the late fourth century Emperor Theodosius ordered the construction of gates about two hundred meters inside those built by Frontinus, as well as walls and towers surrounding the city. The gates, flanked by square towers had huge stone lintels over the openings, with relieving arches above them to reduce the weight. Despite this precaution, the lintel of the North Gate cracked and was repaired by inserting steel rods into it. It is interesting to compare this construction with the system of small voussoirs forming the graceful arches of the Frontinus Gate. It appears that the walls were hastily built; they include blocks of stone from the shattered Basilica, as well as stone quarried from the **Suburban Theatre (9)**, which filled a natural bowl in the hillside 150 meters east of the Agora.

The Nymphaeum of the Tritons offered visual delight and refreshment to all, who walked through the city gate and continued south on Frontinus Street. Like the grandiose nymphaea in Miletus and Ephesus,

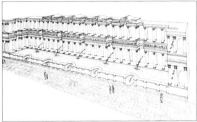

(L) Nymphaeum of the Tritons on the right with the Byzantine Gate in in the background.
(R) Reconstruction of the Nymphaeum

it celebrated the supply of fresh water to the city, brought by aqueducts from distant springs. In a playful manner, the sculptors, depicted tritons blowing their trumpets, as well as bearded men and young women, reclining on rocks, pouring water from large vessels. At their feet, erotes rode on the backs of plump fishes and water splashed into pools where the public could fill their amphorae. Large niches in the wings stepping forward at both ends also displayed statues. An inscription on the architrave of the lower story dedicates it to Good Fortune, to Apollo Archegetes and to the Emperor Alexander Severus, whose reign (222-235 CE) was a period of growth for the city. Excavation of the nymphaeum began in 1993. The archaeologists found many identifiable fragments of sculpture, including a series of spirited marble reliefs of the Amazonomachy, the battle between the Greeks and the Amazons.

One block behind the south end of the nymphaeum are the lower walls of the **Byzantine Baths**, dating from the fifth or sixth century CE. Built on a much smaller scale than the Roman Baths, whose vaults had collapsed, they were composed of rubble from buildings destroyed by an earthquake. They only survived until the seventh century when they succumbed to an earthquake.

The Cathedral, built in the sixth century CE, followed a basilican plan like Early Christian and Byzantine churches in Rome and Ravenna. It was entered through an atrium, which has disappeared and a narthex; two aisles flanked the nave; an apse terminated the interior at the east end. In most churches of this type, clerestory windows in the walls above the nave arcades illuminated the central space directly. In contrast,

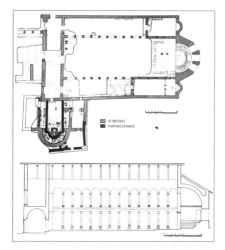

The Cathedral, plan and section

this church included galleries above the aisles where the women worshipped; the upper windows opened through the outer walls of these galleries, creating a more subdued light. But the rows of twelve white marble columns in two tiers, rising to a height of ten meters, and carrying graceful arches, must have been spectacular.

This cathedral, with a nave 50 m. long, is little more than half the length of St. John's church in Ephesus. It is also different in character. In a typically Byzantine manner, St. John's was divided into a series of compartments each covered by a dome; here the lofty interior space was defined by evenly spaced columns running continuously from the west wall towards the apse. The tiers of curved steps in the apse, known as the *synthronon*, provided seats for the clergy.

While, in many cases, elements of buildings destroyed by earthquakes served as materials for new architecture, the builders of this cathedral did not accept old capitals from pagan structures. They chose to carve new

(L) A fallen capital.
(R) The Cathedral from the northwest. The apse with the *synthronon* is clearly visible

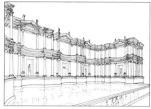

(L) The Temple Nymphaeum. Only the back wall and its projecting wings survive
(R) Reconstruction of the Temple Nymphaeum

ones in the Byzantine manner. A few of them can be seen on the ground. A baptistery with a font sunk in the floor for total immersion opened off the southwest corner of the cathedral. After an earthquake in the seventh century, when the cathedral was in bad repair, two smaller churches were hastily built at the east ends of the two aisles.

Further south along Frontinus street on the right hand side another church, known as the **Pier Church (27)** was built a little later in the sixth century. It has not been fully excavated, but the massive travertine piers that give the structure its name suggest that it was designed to carry heavy vaults. Its spatial character must have been entirely different from the cathedral with its delicate white marble columns. Surprisingly, it was larger than the cathedral: It has been suggested that it was the church of a popular sect named the Montanists that originated in Phrygia, and was later banned by the emperor Justinian.

The back walls and wings of the **Temple Nymphaeum (16)** present a huge mass, which blocks the view of the Temple of Apollo as you approach from the west. But the original edifice, articulated with seventy columns standing in front of those walls, appeared light and decorative. In this U-shaped arrangement, three niches in the back wall and one on each of the wings were framed by groups of columns standing forward in the sunlight and casting shadows behind them. On the lower story, the architraves above the niches curved dramatically forwards to rest on the columns. In contrast, on the upper story, the architraves turned forward at right angles, leaving room for a pediment above each niche. This design created alternating rhythms and gave the nymphaeum a lively skyline. Busts of Artemis, Apollo, Selene, Jupiter and Juno, the gods held most sacred in Hierapolis, emblazoned the centre of each of the five pediments. The statues in the niches have not been recovered from the ruins, but details of an Amazonomachy and erotes riding on sea monsters have been found among the fallen fragments of stone. The nymphaeum was built in the third century CE.

The Temple of Apollo (17) was built in the Corinthian order, in the third century CE, on the site of an earlier Ionic temple with the same dedication. It stood within an existing temenos 70 m. long, surrounded by Doric stoas that dated to the first century. With six columns on the front and only seven on the sides, it was comparatively small, but it made up for its size in its triumphal character. The Corinthian capitals, raised up, today, a little above the stylobate, and pieces of the entablature lying on the ground, convey an idea of its former magnificence.

Since the temple rested on bedrock with noxious fumes emanating from clefts, the original construction and recent excavation were perilous

The Temple of Apollo. A fallen section of the cornice and the Corinthian capitals hint at its architectural character

The Plutonium. The mouth of the cave believed to lead to Hades

undertakings. Gaps deliberately left between the travertine blocks of the stylobate allowed the gases to escape and disperse into the air, but they corroded some of the remains of the temple. Attached to the south side of the temple, the **Plutonium (18)** stands over the cave believed to be the opening to the underworld kingdom of Pluto. The first century geographer Strabo observed the phenomenon that led to that belief. Birds that he threw into the opening died and he reported that bulls for sacrifice were killed by being led into the opening. Strabo wrote that eunuchs, i.e. priests of Cybele, were able to enter because they were immune to the toxic vapors. Since some people were recently killed while investigating it, the opening has been closed in.

On the way from the Temple of Apollo to the theatre you will pass, on your left, the **House of the Ionic Capitals (19)**. This is one of few houses excavated and it is the best preserved. The eight Ionic columns, mostly complete with capitals, arranged around a square atrium, show the elegance of an aristocratic house. In addition to these columns of a pale red marble, shorter columns of onyx give evidence of a second story. They show that wealthy citizens were willing to import luxurious building materials at great expense. It is hoped that other houses, still buried, can soon be excavated, to yield more evidence of domestic life in Hierapolis.

The Theatre, (20) was begun in the late first century BCE with travertine seats, and enriched in the third century CE with marble seats, a larger stage, and an elaborate *scenae frons* (stage building). The three-story stage building had five doors, instead of the usual three, and between them aedicules framed by columns, surmounted by alternately round and triangular pediments. In the fourth century the orchestra was made deeper, so that it could be used for aquatic performances. It attained a capacity of at least 10,000 spectators.

The seats that reposed on the hillside remain virtually intact, but the outer sections that were supported on walls and vaults collapsed in the Middle Ages as did the stage building. Since 1992, the Italian mission has undertaken an impressive restoration of the cavea and the stage building. Fortunately, ninety percent of the architectural and sculptural elements of the stage building retained sufficient integrity to make reconstruction possible. When I last visited in the spring of 2013, I witnessed the enormous progress they had made. The first story above the stage was almost

The Theatre from the southwest. It is partially sunk into the slope of the hill, but raised up on the sides by walls and vaults

The Theatre. The cavea is virtually restored and anastylosis of the *scenae frons* is in progress.

Visualization of the Theatre when the anastylosis (reconstruction) of the scenae frons is complete

complete. Information boards displayed at the top of the theatre give an account of the restoration process and explain its aims.

They also found several inscriptions, including one dedicating the theatre to Emperor Septimus Severus, to his wife Julia Domna and to their sons Caracalla and Geta. Subsequently Geta's name was removed at the insistence of his brother.

A very exciting archaeological discovery revealed a series of reliefs on the plinths of the aedicules between the five doors, depicting the legendary lives of Apollo and his sister Artemis, the deities most revered in Hierapolis. The archaeologists left the panels in place that were still attached to the walls and put the others in the museum. They then installed replicas in the original positions in the theatre. When the restoration work is complete, this will be the most complete theatre in the region.

From the theatre, a short but steep path up the hill to the northeast, ending with a grand flight of steps, leads to the **Martyrium of St Philip (24)**. Since the first century, Christians in Hierapolis claimed that the Apostle Philip had faced martyrdom in their city and was buried there. It appears that he spoke Greek and took the responsibility of preaching in Greece, Anatolia and Syria. He was closely associated with St John. One version of the story of his death is that he converted the wife of a Roman proconsul in Hierapolis, who had witnessed his miraculous healings. The outraged proconsul tortured him and crucified him upside down. The fervent veneration of St. Philip and the desire to build a martyrium in his memory seems to have led to support from Constantinople in the fifth century CE. The inventiveness and sophistication of the plan could only have been conceived by architects of the Byzantine court.

As the plan reveals, the martyrium, a marvel of geometrical order, consisted of an octagon within a 60 m. square. Thirty small rooms with low roofs, that may have accommodated pilgrims, lined the perimeter of

(L) The martyrium of St. Philip,
(R) Plan early fifth century CE

the square. At its centre stood a high octagonal dome just over 20 m. in diameter, supported by eight massive piers. In front of these, stood slender columns linked by arcades of three arches. The central space, opened, on all eight axes, through the arcades into barrel-vaulted rooms with mosaic floors. In the octagon, the columns and arches, concealing the heavy structure behind them, created an illusion of lightness. The marble capitals of the columns, ornamented with acanthus leaves, conformed to a Byzantine type. A *synthronon* on the east side under the dome provided seats for clergy. Except for a few capitals, nothing of the delicate inner structure exists; today, we only see the mighty stone piers that buttressed the dome and some low walls of the small rooms. One detail to notice is that the piers were hollow. They may have contained mausoleums or small chapels.

The martyrium of St. Philip is unique. I am tempted to believe that its remarkable central space may have inspired the design of the iconic octagonal church of San Vitale built by Emperor Justinian in Ravenna, Italy. The martyrium was destroyed by fire in the sixth or seventh century. In 2011 Francesco D'Andria found evidence in a nearby tomb that the remains of St. Philip had been reinterred there.

The Large Baths (25) were built on the second century CE during a period of intense growth. They consisted of the usual rooms at different temperatures, served by the water from the hot springs. In addition, hypocausts under the floors kept the whole establishment warm. After the city declined, water laden with calcium bicarbonate flowed, uncontrolled, across the site towards the travertine terraces, depositing a layer of limestone 4 m. deep in and around the baths, diminishing their height. As a result, the interiors lack the soaring spaces that we expect in Roman Baths. **The Archaeological Museum (32)** has been installed in the Large Baths. The original barrel vaults cover two rooms and others have been restored with new roofs. The Turkish General Directorate of Cultural Heritage and Museums intends to cut away the stone that has

The first hall of the Pamukkale Archaeological Museum with it barrel vault intact, but a raised floor level

(L) Part of a case of ceramics from the Early Bronze Age (R) A priestess of Isis

accumulated to expose the original floors. Therefore some of the rooms in the museum may be closed while work is in progress. When that process is complete visitors will be able to see rare examples of large Roman interiors with their barrel vaults intact, rising to their full height.

The museum displays an impressive collection of sculpture and artifacts from the Bronze Age to the Late Byzantine period. They include sculpture from the nymphaea and the theatre. Among the most captivating are the series of low relief panels from the theatre showing more than twenty scenes illustrating the mythical lives of Apollo and Artemis.

We can learn a lot about the self-image of eminent Romans by examining their sarcophagi. Euthios Pyrrnon, the Archon of Asia, a high official in Hierapolis employed a sculptor to present the phases of his life from youthful heroism to the wisdom of old age. On one end, he and his

The sarcophagus of Euthios Pyrrnon

wife perform a religious duty. They flank the doorway of a pedimented temple, or perhaps a tomb, in which incense burns on a table. On one of the long sides, we see Euthios riding on horseback, as he wards off an attack by a lion. Presumably his missing hand once held a precisely aimed javelin. At the centre of the other side he is seated as a bearded philosopher. Above these animated and dignified scenes, Euthios and his wife recline above the fray as if presiding at a symposium. A series of ornate columns orders the composition, but the gestures and the drapery of the figures overlap the columns, making the composition less rigid.

Unless you go on to the southern gates, the final sight at Hierapolis is the "Antique pool", where it is possible to relax in a café, shop, swim or dangle your feet in water to be nuzzled by small fishes.

Temenos of Temple A

LAODICEA ON THE LYCUS

Laodicea occupies a broad plateau overlooking the fertile valley of the River Lycus (Greek: Lykos) tributary of the Maeander. Lying far inland from the major archaeological sites on the Aegean coast, it has emerged only in the last decade as the second largest Roman city in Anatolia, exceeded only by Ephesus. Dormant since it was abandoned in the late Middle Ages, it was known mainly through biblical and literary sources. Since 1993 archaeologists have discovered new evidence of a thriving metropolis. In ten years they have revealed the Hippodamian grid plan and so much remarkable architecture that UNESCO has placed the site on the World Heritage Temporary List. As excavation and restoration continue, visitors will experience even more evidence of this prosperous metropolis. It is 16 km. from the World Heritage Site of Hierapolis (Pamukkale) and about the same distance from the important classical city of Colossae where almost nothing remains.

Re-erection of a colonnade to the west of temple A in May 2013

History

Abundant pottery and obsidian blades prove that the area was inhabited as early as the fourth millennium BCE. Long before any urban development, indigenous people farmed the rich agricultural land; they produced ample crops and grew prosperous raising sheep. The soft, raven-black wool that they produced was prized for its fine quality. At an unknown date the city of Diospolis, dedicated to Zeus, was established on the site. In the middle of the third century BCE Antiochos II Theos (280-261 BCE), the grandson of Seleucus (one of the Diadochi) founded the new city of Laodicea (or Laodikeia) on the same site, naming it after his wife Laodice. It was one of five cities he named in her honour.

Antiochos spent much of his reign at war with Ptolemy II of Egypt, in a struggle for control of territory in the eastern Aegean. He also devoted time to the founding of several cities, always giving careful thought to their siting. In the case of Laodicea, the combination of fertile land and the crossing of major highways made the location an excellent choice. The trade route running east from Ephesus up the Maeander valley came to this place known as the Gates of Phrygia, where the river flowed through a dangerous, narrow gorge. This geological obstacle forced the highway to divert through Laodicea, entering through the Ephesian Gate and leaving by the Syrian Gate. It then continued east into central Anatolia and southeast to the Euphrates. The busy road from Sardis leading south to the Mediterranean coast crossed it not far outside the city.

The intersection of these two important routes proved crucial for promoting trade. Laodicea not only developed a reputation for wool and garments manufactured in the city, it also became a great financial centre. In 252 BCE Antiochos swelled the population of Laodicea when he moved about two thousand Jewish families from Mesopotamia to Phrygia; many of them settled in the new city. Eventually, in 261 BCE he made peace with Ptolemy, divorced Laodice and married Ptolemy's daughter Berenice. However, the name of Laodicea remained unchanged.

In 188 BCE this city, like most others in the region, came under the rule of Pergamon and, on the death the last Pergamene king Attalos III in 133 BCE, was absorbed into the Roman Empire. This change brought new opportunities and, despite occasional involvement in wars, Laodicea thrived under Roman administration. It soon became the principal banking centre in Roman Asia. Taxes from as far away as Syria and Palestine were brought here to be transmitted to Rome.

In 50 BCE the Roman scholar of Greek philosophy and statesman Cicero came to Laodicea for a few months as a judge and rectified injustices perpetrated by a tyrannical predecessor. Amazingly he took advantage of the advanced banking system to cash letters of credit there. Shortly after his visit, the city was caught up in the conflict between Caesar and Pompey, but quickly recovered. A devastating earthquake in 60 CE caused severe damage but according to the Roman historian Tacitus, the Laodiceans displayed their wealth and independence by rejecting help from Rome for the rebuilding. When Emperor Hadrian visited the city in 129 CE, he would have found it at the height of its architectural splendor.

Despite Laodicea's position between two small rivers, the Asopus and the Caprus, which flowed into the Lycus, the ground yielded insufficient water to support the population. In fact, these rivers dried up in the summer. The Romans demonstrated their engineering talents by building an aqueduct and laying travertine pipes from a spring 8 km. to the south, near present-day Denizli. It flowed, under pressure, to a water tower on the south side of the city just east to the stadium and from there was distributed through underground pipes. With typical Roman ostentation, they celebrated its abundance by building four nymphaia where it splashed into pools for public enjoyment. The calcium in the water quickly clogged the pipes, so they made openings in them with removable stone caps to give access for cleaning. Many pipes discovered on the site are almost entirely closed by white mineral deposits.

Laodicea also gained fame for its medical school, originally at the nearby temple of the Anatolian moon god Men. Its teachers followed the scientific method of Herophilos of Alexandria (born in Chalcedon), the author of nine important medical texts. Galen, the famous physician of Pergamon praised the school and gave special mention to an eye salve made there from 'Phrygian powder' (finely ground stone) and oil, as well as a remedy for diseases of the ears. During the reign of Augustus the doctors Alexander Philaletas and Xeuxis were so well respected that their name appeared on coins with the staff of Hermes, a symbol of healing, and the head of Augustus on the other side.

Jewish and Christian Laodicea

The strength of the Jewish population in Laodicea can be calculated by the amount of gold that its members collected in 62 BCE for the rebuilding of the temple in Jerusalem. Since Jews were taxed for this purpose at a rate of a half shekel per person, the population appears to have included about 7,500 men as well as women and children. Although the Roman authorities generally awarded rights to Jews, the proconsul Flaccus confiscated the gold, on the grounds that it should not leave the country. In contrast, Augustus issued a decree in about 2 CE enforcing Jewish rights in Asia.

The presence of so many Jews made the populace of Laodicea relatively receptive to Christianity. St. Paul never visited the city but during his time in Ephesus around 54 BCE he was in contact with church leaders there. By the time that St. John the Divine wrote the New Testament book the *Revelation* (ca. 70 to 90 CE), the congregation must have been considerable. John named Laodicea as one of the seven churches of Asia. Scholars have debated the interpretation of his forthright words addressed to the Christians there

> I know thy works, that thou art neither cold nor hot: I would that thou wert cold or hot. So because thou art lukewarm, and neither cold nor hot, I will spew thee out of my mouth. Because thou sayest, "I am rich, and impressed with goods, and have need of nothing"; and knowest not that thou art wretched, and miserable, and poor, and blind, and naked: I counsel thee, to buy of me gold tried in the fire, that thou mayest be rich; and white raiment, that thou mayest be clothed, and that the shame of thy nakedness do not appear; and anoint your eyes with eye salve, that thou mayest see. As many as I love, I rebuke and chasten: be zealous therefore and repent. (Revelation 3:15-19)

It is clear that John knew of the hot water of Hierapolis, the refreshingly cold water of Colossae and the water that reached Laodicea lukewarm via the aqueduct, as well as the riches of the city, acquired partly through the production of black woven clothing and eye salve. It seems that he wrote metaphorically employing this knowledge to condemn the Laodicean Christians for their self-satisfaction.

In about 363 CE, four decades after Emperor Constantine convened the Council of Nicea, the bishops of Roman Asia were summoned to the Synod of Laodicea. Its purpose was to develop rules or canons for the conduct of the church. They dealt with such issues as modest behavior, liturgical practices, and the observance of Lent. One decision was to forbid the practice of astrology which had not previously been proscribed by church authorities. In the early centuries after the time of Christ many Christians attended synagogues but a significant canon delivered by the synod created a distance between Jews and Christians by forbidding Christians from observing the Jewish Sabbath.

The principal church of Laodicea, probably constructed soon after 413 CE, when the practice of Christianity became legal in in the Roman Empire, is believed to be the seventh oldest in the world. Its site has not yet been identified with certainty, but a large basilican church between the two theatres and a cruciform church a little west of the Agora provide examples of church building activity in the Byzantine era. Other places of Christian worship are likely to emerge as excavations proceed.

Emperor Theodosius (378-395 CE) bolstered the defenses by surrounding the urban area with walls and building new fortified gates on the four main highways leading out of the urban area. But earthquakes presented a greater threat than invaders. The citizens rebuilt many times after seismic damage, but this great metropolis never recovered from an earthquake in the early seventh century that also wreaked havoc in Aphrodisias and Hierapolis. The water supply system was damaged; most of the inhabitants moved to a nearby town. When Seljuk and Turcoman invaders came to the region in the early twelfth century, the Byzantine Empire was already declining and little remained to defend.

Rediscovery and archaeology

Richard Chandler, who visited many classical sites in the region came to Laodicea in 1764, found little to inspire him. He wrote: "All was silence and solitude. Several strings of camels passed eastwards over the hill; but a fox, which first we discovered by its ears peeping over a brow, was the only inhabitant of Laodicea." The fallen buildings served as sources of stone and lime for centuries, but enough ancient stones remained visible to mark the location of the city. Biblical scholars and Classical historians understood its significance but large-scale excavation only began recently.

The steel and glass platform of Temple A

A Canadian team from Laval University, Quebec under Jean de Gagniers unearthed the nymphaeum from 1961 to 1963 but, after that, the site was neglected for forty years. In 2003 archaeologists from Pamukkale University led by Celal Şimşek began a vigorous archaeological campaign that brought to light the second largest Roman city in Asia. Within one decade they have excavated two theatres, three temples, an Agora with a Basilica, four churches, six bath complexes, and the largest stadium in Anatolia. They exposed 260 m. of Syria Street that stretches through the city from the Syrian Gate in the centre. As their excavation progressed, the archaeologists succeeded in re-erecting many fallen columns. Thanks to their efforts, Syria Street, with much of its original paving in place, makes an impressive entry to the city. Their partial restoration of temple A respects the principle that new replacements should be distinguishable from original elements. Finding that the platform of the temple had collapsed beneath vaults that supported it, they stabilized the remnants of the vaults and placed a floor of steel and glass over them. This allows us to see the unusual construction below our feet. The four columns of the temple front and a few columns of the surrounding stoas now convey the spatial quality of the sacred precinct. In January 2011 the archaeologists used radar to discover the fourth century church and baptistery that they had sought for a long time. They are hoping to find the evidence of textile workshops, so that we can learn more about weaving techniques of the time.

While the archaeological work at many sites in Turkey is financed and organized by foreign archaeological institutes in collaboration with the Turkish Ministry of Culture and Tourism, the project at Laodicea is supported locally. The governor and provincial government of Denizli sponsor the project; local businessmen and industrialists have donated funds; the Municipality of Denizli is actually in charge of it and provides financial assistance. The joint efforts of the University of Pamukkale, the local authorities and community leaders encouraged UNESCO to take the first step in designating Laodicea as a World Heritage Site.

Visiting Laodicea

It is easy to combine visits to Aphrodisias, Hierapolis and Laodicea in two days. Since each place has its own character, the three complement each other. The site of Laodicea on high ground with distant views is exhilarating. On clear days the majestic Mount Kadmos (Honaz Dağ) to the southeast and Mount Salbakos (Babadağ) to the west dominate the skyline. The well-signposted entry from the east approaches the city through the Syrian Gate, leading onto Syria Street. I have described the sights in a sequence that begins with Roman buildings and finishes with those from the Byzantine era.

Little remains of the **Syrian Gate (23)**, which was the original entry to Laodicea for traffic from the east, but the remains of the **East Byzantine Gate (30)** still exist 500 m. west of it. Emperor Theodosius II built new walls around the city of Constantinople, also protecting the central part of Laodicea with **walls (29)**, using recycled stone from Roman buildings. At the same time he constructed this inner gate with a wide arched opening for wheeled vehicles and a narrower one for foot traffic. Reinforced with square towers on both sides, it was similar to the gate he built at Hierapolis. In both cities his strategy was to reduce the time and materials needed for the construction by only surrounding the central part of the city.

Syria Street (11), running right through the city from east to west is the best-preserved Roman street in Anatolia after Curetes Street in Ephesus. Shady stoas with shops behind them lined it on both sides, allowing plenty

(L) The Byzantine Gate opening through the Theodosian walls
(R) Syria Street a short way inside the Byzantine Gate

N

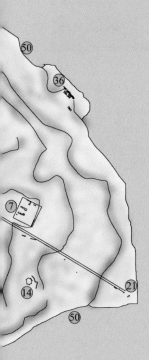

LAODICEA SITE PLAN

1. Council Chamber
   (Bouleuterion)
2. South Baths Complex
3. Water Distribution
   Terminal I
4. Stadium
5. Central Baths
6. West Baths
7. East Baths
8. North Theatre
9. West Theatre
10. Caracalla's Nymphaeum
11. Syrian Street
12. Temple A
13. Round (Rotunda)
    Byzantine Building
14. Octagonal East Byzantine
    Building
15. Corinthian Temple and
    North Basilica
16. Southwest Basilica
17. Northwest Basilica
18. Cruciform Byzantine
    Church
19. Ephesian Gate and
    Byzantine Gate
20. Hierapolitan Gate
21. Syrian Gate
22. Aphrodisian and South
    Byzantine Gate
23. West Agora
24. Round Building (Macellum)
    in Ephesian Street
25. Roman Bridge on Asopos

26. Water Distribution
    Terminal II
27. Propylon I
28. Central Agora
29. Early Byzantine Walls
30. East Byzantine Gate
31. East Byzantine
    Nymphaeum
32. Nymphaeum A
    (Fountain of S. Severus)
33. Ephesian Street
34. South Agora
35. South Roman Villa
36. North Workshop
37. Southwest Temple
38. Room with Pithos
39. Water Distribution Centre
    for Streets
40. Round Building
    (Prytaneum?)
41. Building south of the West
    Theatre
42. Temple?
43. Temple?
44. Temple?
45. Monumentel Pasage
46. Portico
47. South Nymphaeum?
48. West Nymphaeum
49. Northwest Byzantine Gate
50. Necropolis areas

Temple A standing at the north end of its symmetrically planned temenos

of space for commerce. With goods arriving on this street from east and west, and exports flowing out, it must have been a busy artery. A sewer, accessible under removable stone slabs ran down the middle of the street.

The restoration of the unidentified temple known as **Temple A (12)** offers visitors a chance to visualize the architectural space of a Roman temple precinct. The Greeks usually created an organic connection between their architecture and the landscape. They often approached their temples obliquely, linking them to the ground, which sometimes sloped, with steps on all four sides. In contrast, the Romans enclosed their temples within level rectangular spaces surrounded by colonnades. They generally raised their temples on high podiums with steps only at the front. Four columns of this prostyle temple stand above a flight of steps in a way that emphasizes a frontal approach. The entry to the temenos on the central axis and the stoas enclosing the marble paved court respect absolute symmetry.

To recreate the open space of the court, the archaeologists cleared the debris of a later chapel, as well as a baker's oven and some pools. The stoas were originally fronted with fifty-four columns, but the nineteen standing columns of both the temple and the stoas are sufficient, today, to establish the proportions and the sense of order inherent in the design. The re-erected, spirally fluted columns, the restored cella wall and door frame as well as the capital of the anta on the west side, reveal more details of the architecture. Fragments of the frieze, which has not been restored, were beautifully carved with foliage as well as roosters, cornucopias and fish. Niches in the back walls of the stoas probably contained statues

The anastylosis (rebuilding) carried out by Celal Şimşek is controversial. Some archaeologists and connoisseurs of ancient architecture would prefer to see classical ruins excavated and recorded without any reconstruction. Others will agree with my opinion is that these archaeologists have brought this piece of Laodicea to life in an appropriate manner. As I mentioned above, in the section on the archaeology, they have carefully distinguished between original stone and replacements. I appreciate the way that they have provided the cella with a glass floor so that we can look down on the vaults beneath it. We do not know the dedication of this temple. Since Zeus and Athena were the gods most revered in Laodicea, it seems likely that a temple in such a prominent position was consecrated to one of them. However, it has been suggested that it was a *sebasteion*, a temple for the imperial cult. It was built in the second century CE and renovated in the reign of Diocletian (284-305 CE). The vaulted space beneath it served as a treasury for gifts to the temple, but after Christianity supplanted the pagan religion, it became an archive.

The Nymphaeum of Septimius Severus (32) occupies one block on the north side of Syria Street, just beyond Temple A. An inscription on

(L) Nymphaeum A, a place where Laodiceans celebrated the arrival of water in their city
(R) The menorah and cross on a column of the Nymphaeum

the architrave shows that it was dedicated to Emperor Septimius Severus. Since it stood directly opposite the central Agora it was clearly intended as a civic ornament displaying the abundant fresh water brought from a distant spring. Marble statues of Athena, Tyche and other deities stood in niches in the two story walls on three sides of a rectangular pool. The walls were ornamented with columns in the Composite order on the lower level and Corinthian columns above. Water from the pool overflowed into three circular basins and the surplus ran into the sewer system.

After the earthquake of 494 CE the space occupied by the pool appears to have been enclosed to make an interior space, possibly for religious use by Christians. A menorah, a seven branch candlestick, has been incised on the shaft one column, with a cross, resting on a globe above it. It appears that the cross, superimposed on the sacred Jewish symbol, implies Christian dominance over Judaism, but it may speak of accommodation between the two religious communities.

Opposite the nymphaeum the **Central Agora (28)** has been cleared so that we can appreciate its large scale. The steps around the perimeter show where the surrounding stoas stood. To the west of the Agora another civic fountain, the **Nymphaeum of Caracalla (10)**, was built to celebrate the visit of the emperor Caracalla to Laodicea. It was enclosed with two story walls ornamented with columns in the Corinthian order. Many fragments of the cornice and other architectural details lie on the ground. Reliefs on a parapet depicting dramatic mythological scenes: the abduction of Ganymede by Zeus in the form of an eagle, Theseus slaying the Minotaur and the labors of Hercules. These have been removed to the museum in Denizli.

South of the Agora, the **Central Baths (5)** built in the second century CE show the monumentality of Roman bath complexes. Many walls and arches built of massive travertine blocks are still standing, but all the original vaults have collapsed. Continuing south about 400 m. you will come to the **South Agora (34)**. Since it has not been excavated there is little of interest to see, but in the middle of its north side the semi-circular bowl of the **Bouleuterion (1)** can easily be recognized. This building, dated to the reign of Hadrian (117-138) served as an Odeon for musical performances and for orations as well as the council house of Laodicea. Seating 5,000 to 6,000 participants, it was probably covered with a wooden roof. Unfortunately, few of its stone seats have survived.

Travertine arcade of the South Bath Complex   The water tower.

The muscular piers and arches of the **South Bath Complex (2)** immediately south of the Agora show the resistance to earthquakes of this type of construction. Some of the huge voussoirs have shifted a little, but the arches remain intact.

A strange looking outcropping of stone standing 7 m. tall to the west of these baths is the **Water Distribution Terminal (3)**, a water tower to which water under pressure flowed from a distant spring. A close examination of it shows many clay pipes embedded in the stonework, indicating that the water was separated into different streams even before it left the tower.

The Stadium (4), 280 m. long, immediately to the south of the South Baths is the largest in Anatolia. Most of the marble seating has been carted away, but the deep, elongated bowl is impressive. With 25 rows of seats, it held 20-25,000 spectators at athletic events and gladiatorial contests. According to an inscription, Nikostratos a citizen of Laodicea built it at his own expense in honour of Emperor Titus (79-81). He was clearly an exceptionally wealthy man.

A path from the west end of Syria Street leads north to the **West Theatre (9)**, which dates from the Hellenistic period. In many of the cities in this region the theatres rise up from the ground level of the civic spaces into tiers of seats recessed in the sides of hills so that they overlook the urban centre. In Laodicea, the opposite is true. Here, patrons descend from street level into the cavea of the theatre and have a view of the

(L) The Stadium, the largest in Anatolia
(R) The west theatre, facing west to catch the afternoon breezes

landscape beyond. This was the first theatre to be built here. It held about 8,000 spectators. Its westerly prospect enabled it to catch the afternoon breezes, but ensured that the spectators would have the afternoon sun in their eyes. The upper tiers of seats remain in good condition.

During the Roman Imperial era the larger **North Theatre (8)** was carved out of the north-facing slope. When we look at it today with few of the seats in place it is hard to imagine its magnificence in Roman Imperial times. Built entirely of marble, it seated twelve thousand spectators and is believed to have been used for aquatic spectacles as well as the performance of plays. The elaborate *frons scenae* (stage building) rose to the full height of the cavea, enclosing it entirely. If the reconstruction drawing is accurate, a huge arch filled the centre of the wall behind the stage, flanked by four aedicules three stories high covered by broken pediments. Over thirty sculptures, framed by columns and surmounting the pediments adorned the façade. As on so many other sites most of these ended up in limekilns. The lower tiers were divided into 9 sections of 18 rows, expanding into 18 sections of 27 rows above. Adding to the monumentality of the theatre, vaults sheltered the diazoma at the top. A canvas canopy supported on poles protected spectators from the sun. This theatre continued in use up to the seventh century CE.

On the high ground overlooking the valley, between the two theatres stood a **Corinthian Temple (15)** with inscriptions from the first and second centuries CE. After the earthquake of 494, the **North Basilica (15)** was built with its narthex slightly overlapping the foundations of the temple. This three-aisled basilica, with apses at the east ends of both side aisles, as well as the nave, was a substantial building 60.8 m. long

(L) North theatre from below. The spoil from the excavation has left a slight mound on which grass and poppies grow (R) The street leading south from the north theatre towards the fourth century church. The travertine terraces below Hierapolis make the white streak on the distant hills

including the narthex. It was about the same size as the cathedral in Hierapolis, but because farmers cleared the site of stone, the details of its construction are unknown.

Early in 2011 the archaeologists, using radar, finally located a structure that they believe to be the **Fourth Century Church** built not long after Emperor Constantine legalized the practice of Christianity in the Roman Empire. Strong pillars that supported the roof are still standing and the mosaics on the floor, in surprisingly good condition, are undergoing restoration. The church is not open to visitors at the time of writing. A small rectangular baptistery with an apse contains an excellent example of a baptismal pool for baptism by immersion, typical practice in the early centuries of Christianity for it was mainly adults who were baptized.

As you leave by the East Byzantine Gate you can see the remains of **East Byzantine Fountain (31)**, which dates from the fifth century CE. Built of brick and river rocks, it lacked the triumphal and decorative qualities of the Nymphaea of Septimius Severus and Caracalla but it demonstrates an interest in water as an element of civic design in the Byzantine era.

The fourth-century church in the process of excavation and restoration

Tetrapylon

APHRODISIAS

Lying 150 km. inland from Ephesus, in the upper Maeander valley, Aphrodisias differs in its historical roots from the Greek and Roman cities on the coast. As early as the Stone Age, inhabitants may have worshipped the Sumerian goddess of love and fertility Ishtar, known to the Assyrians as Nina. An Assyrian trading post, established there in the fourth millennium BCE, sustained links with Mesopotamia. Later, Carians who settled on the site, named the place Ninoë after its legendary founder Ninos. The cult of Aphrodite, so central to this city, evolved from the veneration of Ishtar. By classical times Greeks throughout the Hellenic world revered Aphrodite as an omnipotent fertility goddess who retained the attributes of Ishtar.

The cult Image of Aphrodite

An imposing cult image of Aphrodite stood for centuries in her temple at Aphrodisias. Although defaced and buried by Christians when they converted the temple into a cathedral, it still expresses her power. Scholars regard it as the "canonical image" that inspired many copies in the Greco-Roman world. With the help of the other almost identical versions, they have analyzed the iconography and established its meaning. Compared with well-known, sensual, nude or semi-nude depictions of the goddess of love by Hellenistic and Roman sculptors, this fully clothed figure appears rigid. Covered in a solid tunic, she stands stiffly with her arms pulled into her sides and hands pointing forward in the manner of ancient Anatolian goddesses. Aphrodite wears a crown on her head resembling a crenellated turret of a city wall, obviously a symbol of protection. Below it a band of myrtle, a plant associated with her, adorns her brow. A garland of flowers encircles her neck and a pendant hangs between her breasts. The tunic, or *ependites*, divided into four horizontal bands, proclaims her important attributes. In the middle of the upper zone, the three Graces,

The Hellenistic cult
image of Aphrodite
from the Bouleuterion
(Aphrodisias Museum)

the beautiful handmaidens of Aphrodite, dance in a customary pose with the central one turning her back while the others face forward. According to Lisa Brody, two busts flanking them represent the earth goddess Ge and the sky god Uranos. In the second zone, busts of the sun god Helios, with rays of light streaming from his head, and the moon goddess Selene, sitting on a crescent moon, represent the heavenly bodies. Beneath them, in the third band, a half nude female figure, clearly a personification of Aphrodite, rides on Capricornus, a marine creature with the tail of a fish and the fore-quarters of a goat. The lowest band no longer exists, but, with the evidence of many copies, such as the one shown here, it can be reconstructed. Three winged Erotes playfully dominate the scene as they perform rituals in her honour. Together, these images affirm Aphrodite not only as the goddess of love and desire, but also as one who holds dominion over all living things of the earth the sea and the sky.

Hellenistic and Roman Aphrodisias

In Hellenistic times, the Seleucids, who succeeded Alexander the Great as rulers in this region, founded several small towns in the fertile, well-watered region. They gave farmland there, as a reward, to Macedonian soldiers, who had fought for them. They also fortified the towns to secure the important highways that led east to Syria, north to Sardis and down the Maeander valley to the coast. Aphrodisias, as the centre of the Panhellenic cult of Aphrodite, eclipsed the others in importance.

In the late second century BCE the city sought alliances with the Romans, and soon came into their orbit. In 85 BCE the Aphrodisians took Rome's side in a war against Mithridates VI of Pontus, in which they suffered devastating losses but gained Roman favour. It seems that the Aphrodisians remained culturally independent after they cast their lot with the empire. We do not know the extent of Roman influence on the planning and administration of the growing city. The grid plan with irregular edges, as opposed to one confined within a rectangle, appears more Greek than Roman.

The Romans knew Aphrodite as Venus and worshipped her as an ancestor; therefore they honoured Aphrodisias with special favours. Emperors Julius Caesar and Tiberius both issued decrees recognizing the city's sacred nature and demanding respect for it as a place of sanctuary. Later emperors renewed these privileges. Excellent marble quarries, only two kilometers away, provided the finest possible material for sculpture and architecture. Good potter's earth – clay without impurities such as iron – helped to promote the ceramics industry, and some iron ore was available. The site is level, making building easy, but one distinct hill offered a suitable place for the theatre. Furthermore, nearby Mount Salbakos (Baba Dağ) graced the city with its inspiring presence.

In the first century CE Aphrodisias entered a period of great prosperity and launched ambitious building programs. It was then that the Theatre, the Agora, the Temple of Aphrodite and several other civic buildings were erected and adorned with lavish sculptural ornament. The city continued to flourish in the Byzantine era, but was slow to embrace Christianity. The civic leaders were so devoted to their patron goddess and other Olympian gods that the pagan religions persisted long after other Roman populations had converted. Aphrodisias became the seat of a bishop in the early fourth century and, in the mid-fifth century the temple was converted into a church. A serious earthquake in the early seventh century caused major damage that was not repaired. As the Byzantine Empire became less secure, civic leaders placed priority on defense, and built a citadel above the theatre out of rubble from fallen buildings. The dwindling population abandoned parts of Aphrodisias and it divided into two communities, one huddled around the theatre, the other centred on the cathedral. Four centuries later Seljuk Turks attacked Aphrodisias.

Architecture and sculpture and its patronage

Only fragments of Hellenistic architecture survive. The buildings we see demonstrate the city's illustrious role as a leading metropolis in the Roman Province of Asia and later as the capital of Caria. They also display the prodigious patronage of leading citizens. Wealthy individuals asserted their own status as well as their dedication to the empire by donating ambitious works of architecture to the city. The most notable benefactor, C. Julius Zoilos, born in Aphrodisias, had served both Julius Caesar and Octavian as a slave, but returned to his birthplace a wealthy freedman. He became a priest of Aphrodite and donated funds for a new temple dedicated to her. He also paid for a stage building for the theatre and the North Stoa of a new agora. Other members of the local aristocracy commissioned works of architecture such as the sebasteion, a building honouring both Aphrodite and the imperial rulers.

A walk through Aphrodisias in the late Roman era, before earthquakes wreaked their havoc, would have been a joyful experience of architecture enlivened with copious sculpture. Playful and sensual images complemented heroic depictions of deities, emperors and prominent citizens. Reading the complex iconography, a scholarly visitor would perceive the efforts of the city's benefactors to portray Aphrodisias as a place favoured both by gods and benevolent rulers. The passion for architectural sculpture in the city, as well as the export trade, kept the sculptors exceptionally busy. They gained such renown that their work was in demand in Rome and far-flung parts of the empire. Examples have been found as far away as Leptis Magna in North Africa and Hadrian's villa at Tivoli. Many are even signed with the names of their creators, followed by Aphrideus confirming their place of origin. It is likely that some of the sculptors had migrated there from Pergamon, a city famous for its sculpture, when commissions dwindled after the Attalid dynasty came to an end in 133 BCE.

Literature and Philosophy

Alexander of Aphrodisias who lived in the third century BCE moved to Athens, where he became famous for his commentaries on Aristotle. He headed the school of Peripatetic Philosophy, so named because of Aristotle's habit of walking around with his students as he expounded his theories. Several of his writings survive, including his treatises *On Fate* and *On the Soul*. The Aphrodisian author Chariton is believed to have written the first Greek love novel *Chaereas and Callirhoe*. In this exciting story of passion and jealousy; the heroine, Callirhoe, believed to be dead, is entombed alive, discovered by pirates robbing the tomb, kidnapped, rescued and, after many adventures, finally reunited with her lover. The narrative ranges from Syracuse in Sicily to Miletus in Ionia and includes historical figures such as the Persian King Artaxerxes. Probably written in the first century CE, it has been hailed as the first European novel.

Rediscovery and excavation

The distinguished French archaeologist Charles Texier visited the site in 1835 and a French engineer Paul Gaudin began excavations there in 1904. Focusing his efforts on the Temple of Aphrodite and Baths of Hadrian, he discovered significant sculpture. The most thorough archaeological study was begun in 1961 by a Turkish scholar Kenan T. Erim under the sponsorship of the Institute of Fine Arts at New York University, which still continues the endeavor under the direction of C. Ratté and R. R. R. Smith. Erim's early seasons of excavation produced a series of exciting revelations. A generous grant from the National Geographic Society made it possible to move the inhabited village of Geyre, which covered the top of the hill described as the Acropolis. This allowed the archaeologists to expose the well-preserved theatre built into its eastern side and also to make a fascinating discovery. The hill was not a natural rise in the land, but a höyük or tell - a mound built up over millennia, of mud brick houses gradually superimposed on each other. The ancient objects found within it confirmed that the site of Aphrodisias had been inhabited since the Chalcolithic Age. They dated it to 5,800 BCE.

Plan of Aphrodisias including walls and Stadium

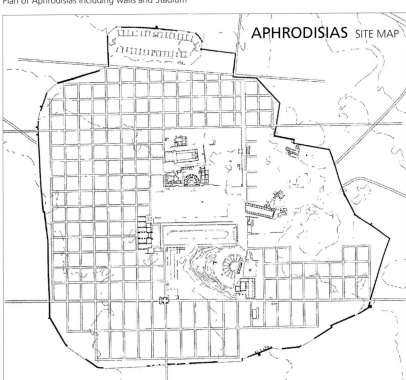

APHRODISIAS SITE MAP

Erin made further discoveries in other parts of the site, and unearthed an astonishing trove of sculpture from the Sebasteion and the Basilica. Before his untimely death in 1991 he began brilliant restorations of buildings that had been completely reduced to ruins. Since then, work has continued with dramatic results. For example, in the last decade, archaeologists have rebuilt a substantial part of the Sebasteion; its vast array of sculpture is now exhibited in a specially constructed hall in the museum. Erin's simple tomb lies on the site.

Visiting Aphrodisias

When I first explored Aphrodisias, I was beguiled by the sensual character of the place. I found it particularly beautiful in the spring, when the scent of the flowers still perfumed the air and the slender white columns rose among tall vegetation. As soon as I arrived, I walked through the museum just to receive an impression of the sculpture that once adorned the buildings I would see. Then I looked at the Sebasteion, a unique building that offers a key to Aphrodisias and lies on the way to my next goal, the theatre. Later, after I had discovered as much as I could of the architecture,

The Tetrastoon from the top of the Theatre. In the centre are columns of the Basilica; the Theatre Baths are on the right against the Theatre

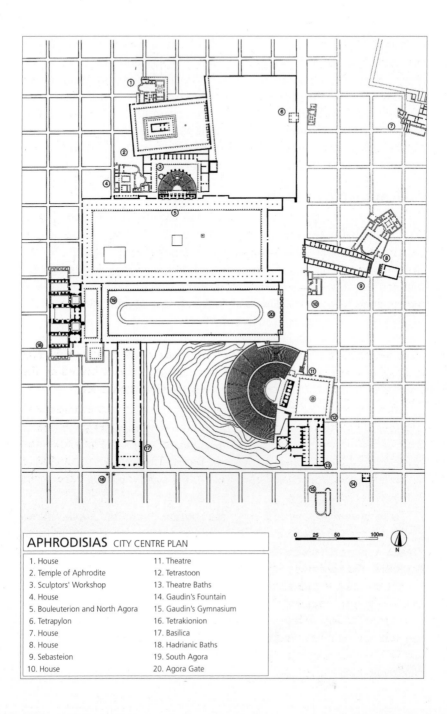

APHRODISIAS CITY CENTRE PLAN

0   25   50   100m

N

1. House
2. Temple of Aphrodite
3. Sculptors' Workshop
4. House
5. Bouleuterion and North Agora
6. Tetrapylon
7. House
8. House
9. Sebasteion
10. House
11. Theatre
12. Tetrastoon
13. Theatre Baths
14. Gaudin's Fountain
15. Gaudin's Gymnasium
16. Tetrakionion
17. Basilica
18. Hadrianic Baths
19. South Agora
20. Agora Gate

View from the Theatre across the North and South Agoras to the distant Temple of Aphrodite.

I returned to the museum to look at the sculpture in much more detail and to imagine where it had once stood. This experience was helped by the clear identification of the items displayed on well-written labels.

After a quick museum visit, I suggest that you stop at the Sebasteion, and then climb to the top of the theatre so that you can command a good view of the site. Looking southeast you will see the Tetrastoon and beyond it the Basilica and the Theatre Baths. The elegant colonnade of the Small Basilica contrasts with the heavy masonry supporting the vaults of the rooms for bathing.

To the northwest you can see across both the North and South Agoras to the Temple of Aphrodite, whose columns stand tall in the distance. Beyond it, almost twice as far away as the temple, and invisible from the Acropolis, the enormous Stadium stretches out on an east-west axis. To the left, past the Western Stoa of the South Agora, you will just be able to identify the heavy masonry of the Baths of Hadrian. Since certain areas are closed to sightseers, and some places are waterlogged in winter and spring, you will not be able to walk as freely as you wish, but, having oriented yourself, you can begin at the Sebasteion, Tetrastoon and Baths and then follow the path leading to the north toward most of the major buildings.

The Sebasteion

The Sebasteion was dedicated to the imperial cult. Built to honour both Aphrodite and the Julio-Claudian emperors who ruled after the assassination of Julius Caesar, its name derives from the Greek word sebastos the equivalent of the Latin title augustus. Two aristocratic families donated it to the city. Tiberius Claudius Diogenes commissioned the south portico, while Menander and his brother Eusebes donated the north portico. This unprecedented monument, richly adorned with sculpture offers vivid insights into the Roman imperial psyche. It proclaims the glory of emperors, raising them to the level of gods, and shows the loyalty of their subjects, who helped the empire to flourish. The sculpture also expresses the deep Roman association with Greek mythology. We can imagine the excitement when the Sebasteion was first excavated by Kenan Erim in 1979 and the astonishing marble reliefs emerged, many of them intact, from the heaps in which they had lain since an earthquake in the seventh century. Thanks to expert restoration work, we can see the best-preserved panels of sculpture in the museum where they reveal the expressive quality of Aphrodisian sculpture. At the same time, replicas placed on the partially reconstructed building help us to visualize the original architecture.

The partially reconstructed Sebasteion from the East

(L) The sacred way running through the Sebasteion. (R) Plan of the Sebasteion showing how its outline was adapted to fit between existing buildings on the east side and the city grid on the west

The Sebasteion enclosed a paved sacred way 80 m. long leading towards a small temple. The narrow buildings on either side were adorned with large panels of high relief sculpture. Doric colonnades on the lower level opened into stoas, which offered shaded viewpoints from which the public could admire the sculpture on both sides. Above them, Ionic columns on the second level and Corinthian columns on the third, framed large carved panels 1.3 m. wide. The public entered this unusual work of architecture from the city centre through a propylon, a ceremonial gateway incorporating statues of Augustus in the role of Zeus and his wife Livia as Hera, the wife of Zeus. Steps at the east end led up to a temple dedicated to Aphrodite as well as to Tiberius and Livia.

Building the Sebasteion began in in 20 CE during the reign of Tiberius, continued while Caligula and Claudius ruled, and finished in 60 CE, soon after Nero became emperor. For several centuries it stood as an emblem of Roman civilization. In the Byzantine era the stoas were filled in for commercial use; then after almost six hundred years it collapsed. The recent opening of a new hall for the display of the sculpture from the Sebasteion culminates years of work. While it is necessary to travel to Istanbul, Berlin, Paris and London to see the sculpture of most of the cities in this book, we can see the majority of the Aphrodisian discoveries on the site.

The panel honouring "Claudius, Master of Land and Sea" vividly affirms the agenda of this sculptural series. Claudius, his muscular body idealized in the manner of gods and heroes, strides forth energetically, while receiving on one side a cornucopia signifying the bounties of the earth and on the other, the steering oar of a ship from a female triton. It proclaims the emperor's divine role as universal protector of his subjects. A pleated cloth billows around his head, almost forming a halo, and flows with a whiplash curve above the head of the triton. This characteristic device in Aphrodisian sculpture increases the sense of motion animating the scenes.

One dramatic panel depicts "Claudius defeating Britannia." He stands with one arm raised while the other bears down on her head as she cowers, disheveled, on the ground. Those familiar with images of Britannia, triumphantly enthroned with trident and shield, will see the dramatic contrast in her ignominious downfall. Other panels represent mythological subjects such as "Leda and the Swan" or "Poseidon and his wife Amphitrite." A dramatic scene, relating to the Trojan War, shows Achilles, overcome with love for the Amazon queen Penthesilea, whom he mortally wounded, holding her in his arms as she dies. In another the Three Graces dance in an often-quoted pose identical to the one on the front of Aphrodite's cult statue that stood in her temple.

In the cult statue found in the great temple and described above, Aphrodite appears as a powerful figure enclosed in a solid, protective tunic. However, a low relief panel from the Sebasteion portrays her as a

Claudius master of land and sea   Claudius defeats Britannia

Anchises and Aphrodite   Bellerophon and the winged horse Pegasus

graceful, desirable woman showing the son she had borne to the handsome, young Anchises. The Romans had good reason to depict the goddess of love with this mortal man. According to legend, Aphrodite fell desperately in love with Anchises, a prince of Troy, and, without divulging her identity, enjoyed two passionate weeks with him. She conceived a boy, and revealed herself to him when their son Aeneas was born. Later, Anchises, bragging about his liaison with Aphrodite, enraged Zeus who hurled a thunderbolt at him, making him lame. In the *Aeneid* Virgil tells of Aeneas carrying his old father Anchises from the burning city of Troy and of his long journey, which ended with his founding of Rome. Julius Caesar, and all the Julio-Claudian emperors believed that they were descended through Romulus from Aeneas. So this romantic scene, with its erotic overtones, leads the Romans directly to their divine ancestor Aphrodite, whom they named Venus.

Another low relief on the Sebasteion brings to life the legend of Bellerophon, who, in the manner of Hercules with his seven labors, performed dangerous and seemingly impossible tasks with the help of the winged horse Pegasus. One of his missions was to slay the chimera (or chimaera), a terrifying creature with the head of a lion, the body of a goat and the tail of a snake. He stands calmly, spear in hand, while his steed, impatiently raising one hoof, appears eager to fly off on the next adventure. In addition to the themes mentioned above, a series of panels shows the extent and diversity of the Roman provinces with scenes characterizing the racially different peoples of Africa, Europe and Asia. These images seem similar in their intent to the sculpture at the base of the Albert Memorial in London, which represents the multi-ethnic peoples of the British Empire under Queen Victoria. The almost two hundred panels of sculpture on the Sebasteion, with life-sized figures carved in exceptionally high relief, must have challenged the workshops of Aphrodisias. Although not as well known as the sculpture in Rome of the Ara Pacis (13-9 BCE), the Arch of Titus (81 CE) or the Trajan Column (early second century CE) they make a powerful statement about the character and history of the empire in the first century CE. While some pieces were obviously carved by less skilled craftsmen, much of it is of excellent quality.

The Theatre

The theatre was first carved out of the east side of the 'Acropolis' in the late Hellenistic period; at this time the cavea was probably not yet lined with tiers of marble seats. Soon after G. Julius Zoilos arrived in Aphrodisias in 38 BCE, he built at least the lower tiers with prohedria, the marble seats for dignitaries, and constructed the monumental stage building. An inscription states that he dedicated the theatre to Aphrodite and the *demos* – the people. The Doric columns that supported the stage have been re-erected. Two more tiers in the Ionic and Corinthian order displayed statues that can now be seen in the museum. These include a bust of Aphrodite, and statues of Nike, captured in dramatic motion, Melpomene, the muse of tragedy and a handsome young man representing the demos. In addition, a muscular athlete appears to be based on a statue by Polykleitos, the famous classical sculptor from Argos on the Greek mainland. A few statues represented local dignitaries.

Improvements to the theatre in the reigns of Claudius and Nero (40-68 CE) included the addition of side entrances and marble seating rising higher up the hillside to accommodate 8,000 spectators. In the second century, when gladiatorial contests and blood sports with wild animals attracted the public, the orchestra was enlarged by eliminating the two or three

The Theatre, improved between 38 and 28 BCE with the Doric lower tier of the stage building.

lowest rows of seats and protecting the audience with a railing. A flight of new steps leading to a marble throne in the middle of the first row allowed victorious gladiators and athletes to receive honours from the presiding luminary. At this time, a central archway opened from the Theatre to the Tetrastoon outside, so an orator speaking to a packed auditorium could occasionally turn and address the crowd outside. Compared with the vast theatres at Ephesus and Miletus, this one possesses an intimate character that must have been ideal for the performance of classical drama.

The Tetrastoon

To reach the Tetrastoon and the Baths, go down to the orchestra and through the Doric colonnade of the stage building. You can then pass through the central arch and into the Tetrastoon. Antonius Tatianus, governor of Caria, built this urban square in the fourth century CE after an earthquake had caused flooding in the Agora. Placed on higher ground, it served the same purpose as a civic and commercial space. Since not all the Corinthian columns of the surrounding stoas were identical, it appears that some came from existing buildings. A circular base about six meters in diameter at the centre of this elegant urban space probably surrounded

(L) The nave of the Basilica, with a carved pier on the left
(R) Detail of Erotes on the pier

Flavius Palmatus

a fountain. South of the Tetrastoon by the Theatre Baths, two rows of Corinthian columns define the central nave of a basilica with aisles on either side, all paved with marble. Two pillars at the entrance are carved with playful scenes of Erotes, birds and animals among lively foliage. Erim believed that a statue of the emperor stood in a recess at the end of this important civic space. Along the sides of the aisles, low walls separated small shops.

A statue of the stern looking Flavius Palmatus, governor of the Province of Asia in the mid-fifth century CE, was found near a pedestal stone base about 6 m. in diameter at of the centre of the Tetrastoon probably with an inscription describing him as a "benefactor to all Caria." He wears a full toga and carries a scepter in his left hand and an insignia of rank in the right; his hairstyle is in the latest fashion. As with many Roman portraits his facial expression reveals his individuality in stone.

The Theatre Baths

The Theatre Baths served a large residential district on the southern side of the city. Unlike the Baths of Hadrian, this establishment did not include a palaestra for athletic pursuits, but only bathing facilities. Like most Roman *thermae* it consisted of vaulted spaces serving as the usual *frigidarium*, *tepidarium* and *calidarium*. A dome covered the impressive circular calidarium but we do not know how light entered. The large

The Calidarium of
the Theatre Baths

Two panels from the gateway to the South Agora represent the Gigantomachy, the battle between the gods and the giants. Athena is shown fighting the giants whose legs are snake-like coils covered in scales, similarly to those of tritons (Istanbul Archaeological Museums)

niches at its four cardinal points, and smaller ones between them create an alternating rhythm and emphasize the massive structure. These recesses, once lined with marble, provided entrances or contained basins of hot water. A furnace and a hypocaust under the floor brought radiant heat to the interior. The baths continued to be used in Byzantine times when some alterations were made. Then, after the decline of the classical city, the marble facings would have been the first elements removed by people scavenging for building materials.

The South Agora

On the path leading north from the theatre you will come to the eastern end of the Agora where a propylon or gateway stood until it was toppled by an earthquake. The most notable ornament from this structure was a low relief depiction of the Gigantomachy, now in Istanbul. After an earthquake caused floods in the Agora, this monumental edifice was transformed, as if to turn a disaster into an opportunity, into a nymphaeum, a fountain-like structure alive with playful water nymphs. The South Agora, 212 m. long, was surrounded by stoas lined with small shops. A large pool ran down the centre – a delightful feature in the manner of one at Hadrian's villa at Tivoli, near Rome. If you walk along the south side, you will reach the entrance to a large Civic Basilica on the left. Beyond it, closing the west end of the Agora stood the **Portico of Tiberius** leading through to Hadrian's Baths, whose water system was connected to the pool.

(L) View from the Baths of Hadrian through the Portico of Tiberius into the South Agora and to Mount Salbakos. (R) Ionic columns of the Portico of Tiberius

The Civic Basilica

The Aphrodisians built their Civic Basilica late in the first century CE as a majestic space for important ceremonies; it also served as a roofed street in which moneychangers, legal advisors and scribes offered their services. In addition it provided a covered link between the civic centre and the southern districts of the city. With its length of 108 m. it was the largest interior space in the city, exceeding most provincial basilicas in the Roman Empire. Although little of it remains standing, archaeologists have been able to reconstruct it in drawings and understand its iconography. The façade facing the Agora, proclaimed the importance of this building. Like the Library of Celsus in Ephesus and the market gate of Miletus, columns standing forward from the walls gave it a sense of depth. The public entered through a central arch, and passed through a grand vestibule before reaching the long hall. To fit in with the architectural context, a frieze of masks and garlands running above the entablature of the adjacent Portico of Tiberius continues across the façade of the Basilica and along its entire interior. Two tiers of 39 columns on both sides supported the upper walls and separated the central space from the broad aisles beyond. Large clerestory windows illuminated the interior.

An elaborate program of sculpture ornamented the balustrade panels between the columns of the upper tier. While floral designs and acanthus leaves decorated many of these panels, others celebrated the city's ancient origin with mythological scenes, deities and legendary figures.

Sections of mask-and-garland frieze from the Portico of Tiberius and the Basilica stacked near the sebasteion

Byzantine monogram capital

In the centre of the hall, on a series of panels known as the 'founders reliefs,' Ninos the founder of the Bronze Age city of Ninoë and his wife Semiramis took a place of prominence with Aphrodite, Dionysus, Zeus, Apollo, Gordios, king of Phrygia, and the hero Bellerophon with his winged steed Pegasus.

In the north end of the space, archaeologists found a powerful, life-size sculpture in dark blue-grey marble of a cantering horse, with only a single thigh of a white marble rider. Nearby lay the enormous, draped, but headless figure of a woman. Both sculptures, probably dating from the fourth century CE can be seen in the museum.

Little remains to show the architecture of the Basilica, and today it is often waterlogged.

There is no evidence that the Basilica was ever converted to a church as sometimes happened in Christianizing Roman cities. However, just outside its south entrance Christians built a small church in the Middle Byzantine era. Because of its three apses it is described as the **Triconch Church**. Its lower walls and some unusual capitals displaying monograms survive.

The Baths of Hadrian

Passing through the Portico of Tiberius, you will see the massive masonry piers that supported vaults over the customary bathing spaces. In the foreground lies the palaestra, the place for exercise and athletic contests, so important in Greek cities and frequently combined with baths in Roman ones. In addition to the hot, cold and tepid rooms there appears to have been a sudatorium or sweat room recognizable by the close spacing of flues from the furnace on the walls of one space. As in most important Roman thermae, heroic sculpture adorned the Baths of Hadrian. Splendid heads of Aphrodite and Apollo emerged from the rubble of collapsed vaults, as well as the head of a second-century nobleman with the diadem of a priest.

A pool in the complex of the Hadrian Baths

The North Agora

Fewer columns of the North Agora remain and poplar trees cover part of the site, but just beyond it you will find the Bouleuterion, which opened directly off is north side as well as the house of a wealthy individual, which later became the bishop's palace.

The Bouleuterion

The Bouleuterion, the council chamber of Aphrodisias, built in the late second century CE, opened off the North Agora. With its stage building adorned with statuary and upper tiers of seating supported on vaults, it resembled a miniature Roman theatre. Originally roofed, it also served as an indoor performance space for music as well as drama. The upper rows of seats have collapsed, revealing passages and staircases that led to them from the doors in the back wall, similarly to those found in the much larger theatre at Miletus. The ten surviving tiers define a space that served as the political meeting place and entertainment hall of the Aphrodisians. Not surprisingly, guides take advantage of it today to address

Bouleuterion interior, with pedestals for sculpture

tour groups. A geometric pattern with dark blue and white marble as well as red slate covered the semi-circular orchestra of the Bouleuterion. These are presently in storage.

Today, only the pedestals of the principal statues on the lower level survive, but the statuary shown in the museum representing local dignitaries and deities convey an idea of their dignity and authority. One of the simple represents the demos, the people.

The Bishop's Palace

This building, identified as the bishop's palace, served earlier as the residence of a wealthy aristocrat; possibly even of the governor. Arranged around an elegant peristyle court and provided with large reception rooms, it is of a type found in many parts of the empire. Built at a time when wealthy citizens were more interested in embellishing their own houses than on funding public buildings, it aimed to impress visitors with symbols of wealth and status. On the north side, approached by an anteroom, but not open to the peristyle, was a large room with an apsidal

Frons scenae (stage building) of
the Bouleuterion restored.

The *demos* from the
frons scenae

end, where the owner might have sat to receive people in a manner that would demonstrate his power. Evidence suggests that a large statue of Aphrodite stood in the apse.

Other rooms appear to have been intended for entertaining in a lavish but less formal way. Archaeologists have recorded many changes, including turning some of the rooms on the south side into a bath. Behind marble wall-facings they found incomplete paintings representing the Three Graces and winged Nike. Traces of painting also appeared in other areas. It seems that, after the earthquake in the seventh century, this townhouse was abandoned for a time; then in the ninth century when Aphrodisias was becoming prosperous again, it became the bishop's palace. At this time the new triconch room, so named because of the three apses opening off it, added to its splendor. Although it was similar in form to the church south of the Basilica, and may appear ecclesiastical, the triconch shape was occasionally used in the houses of important Romans. This patrician residence, conveniently close to the cathedral reinforced the bishop's status. The discovery of fragments of Christian imagery, and a lead seal of 'the Metropolitan Bishop of Caria' leave little doubt that this was the residence of the bishop. Today only the lower walls survive, but we can imagine the grandeur of the reception rooms as well as the beauty of the court.

The Bishop's Palace, atrium

Sculpture workshop

In the building directly north of the Bouleuterion, just outside the precinct of the Temple of Aphrodite, many marble chippings as well as some unfinished works uncovered suggest that sculptors worked here. The abandoned pieces include a statue of Hercules as an adolescent youth, the Rape of Europa and a marvelously expressive head of a bearded philosopher

The Temple of Aphrodite

Fourteen Ionic columns of the Temple of Aphrodite still stand, conveying an idea of both its scale and elegance. With eight columns across the front and thirteen on the sides, it almost equaled the renowned Temple of Artemis at Ephesus. The orientation eastwards towards the striking form of Mount Salbakos diverged slightly from the city's planning grid; it probably followed the alignment of an earlier temple that respected the sacred nature of the mountain. Archaeologists found evidence of two earlier temples beneath the foundations of this one. Similarly to the beautiful temples designed by Hermogenes at Teos and Magnesia on the Maeander, this temple conformed to the *pseudo-dipteral* style. This means that the broad roof overhang projected far beyond the walls of the

The Temple of Aphrodite, first century BCE. Column bases in the foreground belong to stoas that enclosed the sacred precinct during the reign of Hadrian. Some walls remain from the apse of the Christian church

cella. It was probably built in the first century BCE. During the reign of Hadrian, early in the second century CE, the sacred precinct assumed a more Roman character when it was surrounded by colonnades.

A new, grandiose gateway, the Tetrapylon built in about 200 CE celebrated the entrance to an enlarged enclosure. Although the worship of Aphrodite continued in Aphrodisias long after pagan religions declined on the coast, Christians finally claimed the temple and converted it, with ambitious structural alterations, into a large church dedicated to St. Michael. To give it the plan of a Christian Basilica, they took down the walls of the cella and re-erected them around the outer columns of the temple. These columns, augmented by others taken from the ends of the temple, then separated the aisles from a nave 20 m. wide. A courtyard and a narthex made a traditional western entrance and an apse, containing a *synthronon* (curved, stepped seating for the clergy), extended the interior to the east. This radical transformation into a basilican structure probably occurred in the reign of the Byzantine Emperor Theodosius II who visited the city in 443. These alterations as well as archaeological efforts in the nineteenth century have confused the evidence available to modern archaeologists, making dating and complete understanding of

The north temenos house with the columns of the Temple of Aphrodite in the background

the original design difficult. It appears that, when the temple was converted to a church, the cult statue of Aphrodite in the cella was mutilated and buried nearby.

North Temenos House also called the **'School of Philosophy'**

The remains of a large house just to the north of the temple also give an idea of the luxury enjoyed by wealthy Aphrodisians. It possessed two courtyards, one of them with a pool surrounded with blue-grey marble columns. One large hall was furnished with an apse. Its unusual plan, lacking customary domestic spaces, has suggested to some scholars that it was a school of philosophy.

The Tetrapylon

The Tetrapylon, so named because of consists of four rows of gateways, still makes an imposing entrance to the sanctuary. Approached from the east, it presents an unusual façade with four spirally fluted columns and a central arch rising into the pediment. The broken pediment of an equally distinctive west side, facing the temple, helps to identify

The Tetrapylon,
east side

this as one of the Roman buildings with "baroque" characteristics. Low reliefs on the inner surfaces of the broken pediment represent a playful scene of Nikes and Erotes hunting wild boar among a profusion of acanthus leaves. A central gap between two of the four rows of columns allowed a passage through the Tetrapylon at right angles to the main axis to accommodate an ancient north-south road. When we see this unique work of architecture today, it stands alone, seemingly far from the Temple of Aphrodite. We need to imagine the walls that connected it to the temple precinct whose second entrance stood 100 m. away.

The Stadium

The spectacular, well-preserved Stadium, built in the first or second centuries CE to hold 30,000 spectators, lies to the north of the Temple of Aphrodite. Rounded at both ends, 262 m. long and 59 m. wide, with thirty tiers of seats, it is the largest and most complete in

The Stadium seating 30,000 spectators is the most complete and one of the largest in the classical world

the Greco-Roman world. While its main purpose was for athletic contests like the Pythian Games at Delphi and the Olympic Games at Olympia, it also served as a place for festivals or public meetings. It widens slightly in the middle to make it easier for spectators to see the whole length of the space. In the Byzantine era, perhaps after an earthquake damaged the theatre, the east end was converted into a small arena, closed off by a curved wall. At the same time a wall was built to protect spectators from wild animals.

The City Walls

Aphrodisias was not fortified in Hellenistic or Early Roman Imperial times. The walls, running 3.5 km. around the city, were built in the fourth century CE mostly out of stone recycled from other structures. This might lead us to think that the citizens erected them hastily at a time when invasions were anticipated and feared. But actually they first encircled the city during a period of prosperity and peace, when Aphrodisias was the thriving imperial capital of the province of Caria. Inscriptions on gates announce that imperial governors ordered their construction; we can assume that their objective was to convey an impression of strength. This was a time of active civic improvements, including repairs to damage from an earthquake in 359. Some of the stones may have come from buildings that had collapsed. However, archaeologists have discovered that most of it was gathered from tombs that lined highways leading into the city and filled necropoleis on its edge. This would explain why scarcely any tombs have been found in and around Aphrodisias, a city obsessed with conferring honour and creating memorials. Most tombs were plain cubic structures 4 or 5 m. square and about the same height, made of marble blocks of various standard sizes. Inscriptions identifying citizens interred in demolished tombs are found in the walls, though often turned inwards so as not to be visible.

The walls did not exactly align with the grid plan, but the 8 or 9 gates opened on the axis of streets; the principal ones stood at cardinal points. In addition to the gates 27 towers completed the fortifications. Surviving sections of the wall remain in many places, but since they are some distance from the civic centre, the best place to see them is where they come close to the Stadium.

The Museum

In the mid-1960s the archaeologists considered converting the Baths of Hadrian into a museum, but for philosophical and practical reasons they abandoned that plan in favour of a new building near the entrance to the site. The subsequent discovery of a large quantity of sculpture has vindicated that decision. With the help of funds from the National Geographic Society, the new museum of brick and travertine, opened in 1979; recently a splendid new hall for the sculpture from the Sebasteion was added. It is now the finest museum of Greco-Roman art devoted to a single archaeological site. Since I have mentioned some sculpture in relation to their architectural settings, and the items are identified by well-written labels, I do not describe the contents of the museum; there are plenty of explanations in English. You will see evidence for Erim's belief that Aphrodisian sculptors excelled in portraiture and produced 'penetrating character studies;' he admired their imaginative approach to decorative work; he saw clear evidence of their familiarity with the work of great classical masters but, at the same time their originality.

(L) The cult figure of Aphrodite found buried near the temple.
(R) The 'blue horse' found in the Basilica on display at the Sebasteion Gallery

After years of discovery and restoration work, Erim perceived a vigorous school of sculpture in which artists developed their individuality, while expressing a common spirit.

Zoilos Tomb

One group of sculpture that stands out for special mention is the so-called 'Zoilos Frieze' that belonged to an elaborate tomb for the city's benefactor C. Julius Zoilos. We have no idea where the tomb stood, but enough is known about his fascinating life give the tomb its historical context. Born in Aphrodisias, Zoilos was taken captive either by pirates or in war and sold as a slave to Julius Caesar. He was passed to Octavian (later known as Augustus), who esteemed him highly. He rose to become a trusted envoy for Octavian and returned to Aphrodisias as a freedman. His homecoming in 40 BCE as a rich man is probably explained by an opportunity to gain prodigious war booty while fighting in the service of Octavian. He not only became a priest of Aphrodite, but also commissioned a new temple dedicated to her. His patronage of lavish architecture in the stage building of the North Stoa of the Agora, added to his status; at least two public statues were erected in his honour. The tomb appears to have been square with 5 m. of sculpture almost 2 m. high on each side. The low relief panels that survive in the museum show Zoilos's place of honour even with the gods, who associate with him. On the left of this sequence, Zoilos, now headless, receives a shield and a helmet from Andreia (out of the picture) who stands for honour. To

The Zoilos Frieze, left, Zoilos, (headless, left)

his right Timé representing virtue, places a crown on his head. Further to
the right, Zoilos appears again while two figures look at him admiringly;
the bearded man facing him is Demos (the people); to the far right, Polis
(the city state), appears as alluring as Aphrodite herself. Her cloak, flowing above her shoulder brings the sculpture to life in a quintessentially
Aphrodisian manner.

The Library of Celsus seen through
the South Gate of the Agora

EPHESUS

Of all the cities in this guide, Ephesus, with its inspiring vistas along colonnaded streets, possesses the strongest Roman character. The ruins allow us to visualize the grandeur and vitality of this vibrant metropolis; they show the wealth of the citizens and convey imperial ideals. Arches, which played no role in Greek architecture, span generous openings. Ornate and symbolic sculpture enriches many surfaces to proclaim Ephesian values and desires. Moreover, you can actually pass through the opulent interiors of patrician houses adorned with frescoes and mosaics. If as you explore the city you feel oppressed by the throngs of tourists, consider how busy and crowded this centre of government, trade and culture must have been in its heyday. Tragically, one vital element is missing: The Temple of Artemis, one of the Seven Wonders of the World, has vanished, leaving only one column to show where it stood.

The Neolithic Era and the Bronze Age Ephesus lies only 500 m. outside the eastern walls of the city. The recently excavated tell of Çukuriçi Höyük dates back to the seventh millennium BCE. Austrian archaeologists have established at least five levels of permanent habitations built one upon another in this humanly made mound. Their excavations have revealed artifacts fashioned of obsidian that verify habitation in the Neolithic era. Sophisticated ceramic wares and objects manufactured from copper, as well as foundations of multi-roomed dwellings, show that this proto-city flourished in the Chalcolithic Age. It was destroyed in the sixth millennium BCE, rebuilt 1,500 years later and reduced to ruins again in the middle of the third millennium BCE. The site is not accessible to tourists.

In the fifteenth century BCE the fertile land near the mouth of the Kaystros River, on the western edge of the Hittite Empire, attracted Minoan and Mycenean colonists. The Myceneans left evidence of their Bronze Age occupation on Ayasoluk Hill, to the north of the classical city. Following the collapse of both the Hittite and Mycenean cultures in about 1200 BCE, people named by Strabo as Carians and Lelegians lived in the area. They worshipped the Anatolian fertility goddess Cybele at a shrine close to the same hill. In the tenth century BCE, according to ancient accounts Androklos, the son of King Kodros of Athens, crossed the Aegean, under the guidance of an oracle, to found the city of Ephesus. The Ionians who followed him joined the indigenous people in the worship of Cybele, but they endowed her with the identity of their own goddess Artemis, the daughter of Zeus and Leto, and twin sister of Apollo.

The Homeric Hymn to Artemis begins: "I sing of Artemis, whose shafts are of gold, who cheers on the hounds, the pure maiden, shooter of stags, who delights in archery, own sister to Apollo with the golden sword." She appeared in many representations as a graceful huntress wielding her bow. However, the cult statue of Artemis at Ephesus, known throughout the classical world in many replicas, proclaims her role as a great mother-goddess and protector of animals. Wearing a high cylindrical crown and a tight garment tapering to her feet, she is adorned with potent symbols. Perceived generally as many-breasted, she is, more likely, garlanded with bulls' testicles, emblems of the sacrifices offered to her at her temple. Below her waist, in five rows, images of animals show her, in Homer's words, as "mistress of animals." Her stance, similar to that of Aphrodite at Aphrodisias with arms held tightly at her side and hands pointing forward suggests an Anatolian origin.

The Archaic Era

In about 650 BCE Cimmerians, attacked several Greek cities. The Ephesian poet Kallinos, recognized as the first Greek elegiac poet, composed a patriotic elegy exhorting his people to fight the invaders: "It is honourable to fight for city and family, death finds everyone... For there is a longing among the entire people when the strong-hearted man dies, and while alive he is worthy of demigods." The invaders razed Ephesus and desecrated the Temple of Artemis but were eventually driven out. Warriors then took control and ruled the city as tyrants. After a period of oppression the citizens revolted and set up a council named the Kuretes, thus initiating a more democratic system of government. For a few decades the Ephesians lived in peace as leading members of the Ionian League; their commercial and cultural life thrived.

In addition to Kallinos, whose verse radiates nobility and bears similarities to the language of Homer, they produced the iambic poet Hipponax, famous for his biting satire and exposure of vulgarity in Ionian life. Another famous Ephesian, Heraclitus (or Herakleitos, ca. 535-475) made significant contributions to Greek philosophy. He lived after Thales of Miletus but before Socrates. Although regarded as obscure and pessimistic he is best known for his belief in the inevitability of change in the universe: "Everything changes and nothing remains still ... and ... you cannot step twice into the same stream." His theory of the unity of opposites, and his thesis that all entities come to be in accordance with the *logos* have led to interpretations by many philosophers.

Roman copy of archaic Artemis of Ephesus

When Croesus of Lydia invaded Ephesus in 585 BCE, he destroyed the city and forced the citizens to move inland. Nevertheless, he admired the Greeks and revered the Olympian gods. He supported the transformation of Cybele into Artemis and promoted her worship. With her new Hellenic identity she became the emblem of Ephesus and brought renown to the city. Croesus, fabulously rich in gold, provided the funds to rebuild the Temple of Artemis on a grand scale. It stood only for two centuries but fell prey to arson. Croesus's rule came decisively to an end when Cyrus the Great defeated him. The Persian King took Ephesus in 546 BCE and insisted on relocating it again.

The Classical and Hellenistic Eras

In 336 BCE Macedonian forces threatened Persian hegemony. Philip II of Macedon sent his general Parmenio to conquer Ionian cities including Ephesus. The populace, anticipating his arrival, had overthrown the Persian satrap and Parmenio was able to take the city. He set up a statue of Philip in the partially rebuilt temple giving him equal status as Artemis. However, the Persians soon recovered Ephesus and destroyed the statue.

When Philip's son Alexander the Great arrived at Ephesus in 333, it was the largest and most powerful city in Anatolia. Mercenaries guarding it had learned of Alexander's triumph in the battle of Granicus and fled leaving the citizens to welcome him.

Finding a new temple to Artemis under construction, Alexander offered to pay for its completion, but the Ephesians, troubled by his desire to dedicate it to himself, employed flattery to dissuade him. They said it was improper for a god to make offerings to a god. While in Ephesus, Alexander made a momentous change in his policy. Emissaries from nearby Magnesia and Tralles told him that their cities had thrown off the Persian yoke and established democracies. Their message proved persuasive. From that pivotal moment, he favoured independence and self-government for Greek cities.

Alexander's successor, Lysimachus, moved Ephesus to its present position. To achieve this relocation against the will of the residents, he resorted to blocking drains after a violent rainstorm in order to flood them out of their houses. He also forced the inhabitants of Teos, Colophon and Lebedos to join them on the new site to create a larger metropolis. The city then developed along a road winding down a narrow valley between the mountains Koressos (Bülbül Dağ) and Pion (Panayır Dağ) and spread out on more level ground by the harbour. In this more salubrious position away from the marshes Ephesus thrived. Although the city flourished, it suffered bloody episodes, as a series of rulers fought over it. In 188 BCE after the battle of Magnesia, in which Rome and Pergamon opposed the Seleucid ruler Antiochos III, King Eumenes of Pergamon took Ephesus.

Roman and Early Christian Ephesus

After death of the Pergamene King Attalos III, who willed his empire to Rome, membership in the Roman Empire brought peace. Under Augustus (63-14 BCE) Ephesus entered a Golden Age; it became the capital of the Roman Province of Asia and the second largest city in the Empire. An invasion of Asia by the Pontic King Mithridates completed in 88 BCE briefly interrupted Roman control, but the Roman General Sulla drove him out and restored Roman rule. By the year 100 CE the population reached at least 200,000. The fame and status of the rebuilt Temple of Artemis increased, enriching the silversmiths who produced and exported effigies of the goddess. The well-placed harbour and the Royal Road, built by the Persians to the Anatolian interior, encouraged trade, not only in goods but also in slaves. Indeed Ephesus became the slave trade capital of the Mediterranean as well as the banking centre of Asia. Citizens amassed wealth and displayed it by building grandiose structures in honour of emperors. Even former slaves with talent and enterprise could excel there. For example two freedmen Mazaeus and Mithridates built the impressive gateway beside the Library of Celsus in honour of Augustus and Agrippa.

Since the early days of Greek settlement, the temenos (sanctuary) of Artemis gave the right of sanctuary to any who took refuge within its boundaries. Alexander extended the area to a distance of one *stade* (a little under 200 m.) from the temple. Mark Antony enlarged it further to include part of the city, but Augustus, responding to complaints about the miscreants causing trouble under this protection, reduced it again. Cleopatra's half-sister Arsinoë was one of those, who took refuge in the temple after Julius Caesar had exiled her to Ephesus. Nonetheless, Cleopatra persuaded Mark Anthony to order her murder.

In the late first century CE a distinguished Ephesian physician, Soranos made significant strides in medicine. His writings, including his treatise on gynecology and his book *On Acute and Chronic Diseases*, which still survive, offered a deep analysis of biological functions. Only Galen, the Pergamene physician who lived after Soranos's death, surpassed him.

Ephesus played an important role in the development of Christianity in Anatolia. Since the cult of Artemis remained popular and received imperial support, Christians encountered fervent opposition. St. Paul came there in 58 CE and met with a small Christian community, including Timothy, whom he chose as companion on several journeys. They made the city their base for missions in Asia and to Corinth. In 65 CE Paul consecrated Timothy as Bishop of Ephesus, a position he held until 97 CE when an angry mob beat him to death for trying to stop a procession honouring Artemis. Earlier, Paul himself barely escaped martyrdom when, after preaching against idolatry, he inflamed the silversmiths by denouncing their trade in figurines of Artemis. Only the prudent words of a city official calmed the angry crowd that gathered in the theatre. In the fourth century CE, under Constantine, who legalized Christianity, and Theodosius I, who mandated the Christian faith as the sole religion of his empire, Ephesus became a Christian city.

Many believe that the Virgin Mary ended her days in Ephesus. Since Jesus, on the cross, charged the apostle John with the care of his mother (*John* 19:26-27) and John is thought to have written his version of the gospel in Ephesus, the story seems reasonable. On the other hand a competing tradition places her death in Jerusalem. The house identified as the House of the Virgin Mary could possibly be the site of her last dwelling, though it is of Byzantine construction. The main testimony that she lived there came in visions experienced by a Bavarian nun, who provided convincing descriptions of the place. Popes Paul VI, John Paul II and Benedict XVI have all given credence to the story by celebrating mass there.

In 431 about two hundred bishops attended the third Ecumenical Council of the Early Christian Church in Ephesus to resolve the heated argument between Nestorius, Patriarch of Constantinople, and Cyril, Patriarch of Alexandria over the divine and human natures of Christ. Nestorius believed his two natures to be distinct and asserted that the Virgin Mary could be called the Mother of Christ but not the Mother of God. To great rejoicing of Ephesian Christians, Nestorius was defeated. The council took place in the Church of the Virgin Mary, an immense building created out of a ruined basilica and altered several times since. Early in the fifth century Christians built a vast cruciform church almost 80 m. long over the tomb of St. John on Ayasoluk Hill.

Meanwhile the relentless action of the Kaystros River impeded navigation by silting up the harbour. Nero ordered an ambitious dredging project and, after the attempt failed, Hadrian diverted the course of the river. But imperial decrees could not overcome the forces of nature; by the third century the harbour lay three miles from the sea and malarial swamps threatened the health of the population. In 359 CE an earthquake caused serious damage in the city, for example destroying the upper cavea of the theatre. In the late Roman period, as Ephesus declined, political strife prevailed.

Byzantine and Muslim Ephesus

Under Emperor Justinian Ephesus entered a third Golden Age. The Artemision, the greatest Ionic temple of the classical world, became a stone quarry for a new church of St. John that rose above the ruins of the first one on Ayasoluk Hill. This five domed, cruciform church, based on the design of the Church of the Holy Apostles in Constantinople, became the emperor's most ambitious church outside Constantinople. Justinian also enlarged the castle, begun in the Late Roman era, on the crown of the hill. With its fifteen towers and two gates it remains an impressive sight today. As Byzantine power waned, Arab fleets assaulted Ephesus from the sea in 655 and 717, carrying away all the booty they could obtain. The Seljuk Turks captured it in 1090 and around 1300 it fell to the Aydınoğlu dynasty of Seljuks, who restored some of the former prestige of the city. By the mid-fourteenth century they had converted the church of St. John into a mosque and, shortly after, began construction of the new Isa Bey mosque. The Ottoman Turks took Ephesus in early in the fifteenth century, but in 1402, during the reign of the Ottoman Sultan Bayezid I, the Mongol ruler Timur ravaged it. The Ottomans continued to reinforce the castle on Ayasoluk Hill but the great classical city had been reduced to a pitiful state.

Rediscovery and archaeology

In the mid-fifteenth century, when the classical city lay in ruins, the Italian merchant and humanist scholar Ciriaco de' Pizzicolli visited Ephesus and noted some inscriptions. Ciriaco, who represented the business interests of his family in Ancona, possessed a passion for antiquity; he travelled throughout the Eastern Mediterranean recording his discoveries in his *Commentaria*. For his acute observations in Rome, Athens, Constantinople, Anatolia and Egypt he has been named the "father of archaeology." Significant excavations began when John Turtle Wood, an English architect, began work in Ephesus. Contracted by the Ottoman authorities in 1858 to design railway stations on the line from Smyrna to Aydın he became obsessed by the search for the famed temple of Diana. Rather like Heinrich Schliemann in his quest for Troy on the basis of his reading of the *Odyssey*, Wood took his cue from the verse in the *Acts of the Apostles* describing St. Paul threatened by the hostile crowd in the theatre shouting "Great is Diana of the Ephesians." Determined to find the Temple of Artemis (named Diana by the Romans) he gave up his architectural work, obtained a small grant from the British Museum, and in 1869, after two years' work, discovered the pitiful remains of the temple buried under 6 m. of sand. Among the debris left by the builders of the church of St. John and the Isa Bey mosque, who had used it as a quarry, he found some broken sculpture and architectural elements, which he shipped to the British Museum. Returning to England, suffering the effects of malaria and various injuries, he devoted the following years to publishing *Discoveries at Ephesus* (1877) and lectured on his findings.

Since the late nineteenth century the Austrian Archaeological Institute has been responsible for the archaeology at Ephesus. In the late nineteenth century Sultan Abdul Hamid II donated several works of sculpture from Ephesus to the Austrian Emperor Franz Josef I. Recent ambitious projects including the reconstruction of the Library of Celsus in the 1970s by F. Hüber and the protection, under a roof, of the terraced houses have helped to bring the city to life. The Institute has produced a series of fine publications on their work.

VISITING EPHESUS

The site at Ephesus is so large that you should allow at least a full day there. I recommend going to the Basilica of St. John when it first opens in the morning to enjoy early sunlight and avoid crowds. The classical city, thronged with tour groups in the mornings, generally clears at lunchtime so, unless you want to avoid the mid-day sun, you could go to the museum first. The remains of the Artemision look best in the early evening. I propose visiting the main site in a sequence beginning at the east entry. If you go in through the main entrance on the northwest side, you will need to return there to your car or bus at the end of your visit. I therefore suggest you begin by walking past the theatre and the Library of Celsus and up Kuretes Street to get oriented to the site. Then, after going to the farthest point inside the East Gate, follow the itinerary back to the car park. I include one main map and three more detailed ones. Some of the places shown on the maps and discussed in the text may not be accessible because of archaeological work or for protection; others, outside the site boundary, are not open to visitors.

THE TEMPLE OF ARTEMIS

Between the Archaic and Hellenistic eras, the Ephesians built at least five successive temples for their patron goddess Artemis. In about 700 BCE they replaced an open-air sacrificial altar with a naiskos, a roofed shrine protecting the cult image of the goddess. A second, similar structure, perhaps of more elaborate design, followed it but was damaged by a flood. Then, as the city grew, the priests demanded a more worthy temple. In about 570 BCE, determined not to be outshone by the vast temple of Hera under construction on the nearby island of Samos, they commissioned a Cretan architect, Chersiphron of Knossos, and his son Metagenes to design a comparable one. They also sent for Theodoros, one of the architects building the rival Temple of Hera to assist in their project. The temples on Samos and at Ephesus were not only larger than any previous temples, but also revolutionary in design.

They were the first dipteral temples to be built; in other words two rows of columns surrounded them. This scheme enhanced the three-dimensional quality of the architecture and conveyed a powerful sense of depth. The impact must have appeared particularly strong where the columns continued into the deep pronaos. These temples also exhibited the first use of the Ionic order.

The architects may have seen Egyptian temples with their multiplicity of columns and desired to achieve the same effect. Many Greek merchants travelled to Egypt, particularly to Naukratis on the Nile Delta, where a Greek community built temples to their own gods. Architects there could have developed a proto-Ionic capital, based on an Egyptian lotus motif. Although archaeologists have not discovered anything to substantiate such a theory, it offers a plausible solution to the origin of the Ionic order. Virtually nothing remains of the Heraion of Samos, but sufficient fragments of the archaic Artemision have survived to make

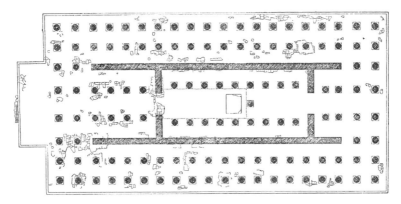

The archaic Temple of Artemis, Plan. The double row of columns makes it dipteral

ANCIENT
HARBOUR

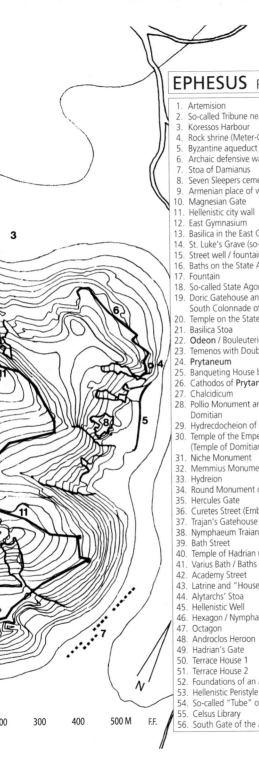

EPHESUS PLAN OF THE RUINS

1. Artemision
2. So-called Tribune near the Artemision
3. Koressos Harbour
4. Rock shrine (Meter-Cybele shrine)
5. Byzantine aqueduct
6. Archaic defensive wall (Koressos)
7. Stoa of Damianus
8. Seven Sleepers cemetery
9. Armenian place of worship
10. Magnesian Gate
11. Hellenistic city wall
12. East Gymnasium
13. Basilica in the East Gymnasium
14. St. Luke's Grave (so-called)
15. Street well / fountain
16. Baths on the State Agora
17. Fountain
18. So-called State Agora
19. Doric Gatehouse and South Colonnade of State Agora
20. Temple on the State Agora
21. Basilica Stoa
22. **Odeon** / Bouleuterion
23. Temenos with Double Monument
24. **Prytaneum**
25. Banqueting House by the **Prytaneum**
26. Cathodos of **Prytaneum** with Embasis
27. Chalcidicum
28. Pollio Monument and Fountain of Domitian
29. Hydrecdocheion of Laecanius Bassus
30. Temple of the Emperors (Temple of Domitian)
31. Niche Monument
32. Memmius Monument
33. Hydreion
34. Round Monument on the Panayırdağ
35. Hercules Gate
36. Curetes Street (Embolos)
37. Trajan's Gatehouse
38. Nymphaeum Traiani
39. Bath Street
40. Temple of Hadrian (Embolos)
41. Varius Bath / Baths of Scholasticia
42. Academy Street
43. Latrine and "House of Pleasure"
44. Alytarchs' Stoa
45. Hellenistic Well
46. Hexagon / Nymphaeum
47. Octagon
48. Androclos Heroon
49. Hadrian's Gate
50. Terrace House 1
51. Terrace House 2
52. Foundations of an Altar
53. Hellenistic Peristyle House
54. So-called "Tube" or Culvert Gate
55. Celsus Library
56. South Gate of the Agora
57. Grave of Dionysius Rhetor
58. Brick vault (Embolos)
59. Circular Monument with Fountain
60. Marble Street
61. Tetragonos Agora (Commercial Market)
62. Hall of Nero
63. West Gate of the Agora
64. North Gate of the Agora
65. West Road
66. Medusa Gate
67. Temple precinct (Serapeion)
70. Round Monument on the Bülbüldağ
71. St. Paul's Grotto (so-called)
72. Theatre Place with fountain
73. Arcadiane east gate
74. Hellenistic Well House (Theatre)
75. Theatre
76. Byzantine Banqueting House (Panayırdağ)
77. Byzantine city wall
78. Theatre Street (Plateia in Koressos)
79. Theatre Gymnasium
80. Apsidal building
81. Byzantine Palace (Sarhoş Hamam)
82. Arcadiane
83. Arcadiane with adjacent Colonnades
84. Four-Column Monument
85. Church on the southern Arcadiane
86. Exedra
87. Middle Harbour Gate
88. Southern Harbour Gate
89. Northern Harbour Gate
90. Market buildings at the Harbour
91. Atrium Thermarum
92. Harbour Baths
93. Harbour Gymnasium
94. Xystoi / Halls of Verulanus
95. Church of Mary
96. Baptistery of the Church of Mary
97. Episcopium of the Church of Mary
98. Olympieion
99. Acropolis
100. Macellum (so-called)
101. Byzantine Well House
102. Late antique Peristyle House / Hellenistic Fortification
103. Crevice Temple
104. Stadium
105. Church in the Stadium
106. Vedius Gymnasium
107. Coressian Gate
110. South Road from the Magnesian Gate
115. Upper Entrance to Ephesus
116. Lower Entrance to Ephesus

3

1

200   300   400   500 M   F.F.

N

reconstruction drawings possible. While most of the capitals showed traditional volutes, some of them substituted rosette designs, one of which is in the British Museum. We can look to Ephesus as a primary source of the Ionic architecture that flourished both in Anatolia and in Athens. On the Athenian Acropolis, the Erechtheion, as well as the interiors of the propylons and the treasury of the Parthenon achieved a high point in the evolution of the Ionic order. These buildings also illustrate the duality of the Doric and Ionic modes, standing side by side.

The Archaic Artemision completed in about 550 BCE is known as the Croesus Temple because the wealthy Lydian King, even before his conquest of Ephesus, donated several unique columns and may have financed much of the construction. The bases of the columns he presented added to the originality of the architectural conception. While the traditional Doric column stands directly on the stylobate, the Ionic one rests on a molded base. At Ephesus, as the Ionic style emerged, the columns rose from square plinths on which four rings of molding created a strong effect of light and shade. Above these elements, low relief sculpture ornamented the lowest drums of the columns, which were almost twice as high as the others. These *columnae calatae* stood two rows deep in front of the temple and continued into the pronaos, but the remaining columns were plain.

The temple was 115.14 m. long and 55.10 m. wide; 127 columns supported its roof, but the height of the columns is unknown. Because of the difficulty of roofing such a large temple the central part took the form of a court; the original naiskos still occupied its centre.

The archaic temple stood for two centuries. It escaped damage by the Persians when they invaded Ephesus, but in 356 BCE, on the night when Alexander the Great was born in far-away Macedon, a madman named Herostratos set fire to it. It was said that Artemis was too busy presiding over the birth of Alexander to watch over her temple. Fragments of one column base, now in the British Museum survived with the highly significant inscription "Presented by King Kroisos (Croesus)". Construction of the Hellenistic Temple of Artemis began soon after the destruction of the earlier one. It followed an almost identical design with the same number of columns and similarly carved bases for those across the front. According to Pliny, both Praxiteles and Skopas, two of the greatest sculptors of the era, contributed to the sculpture.

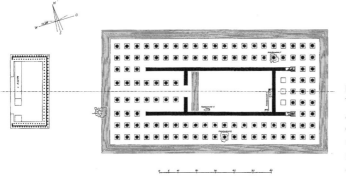

Hellenistic Temple of Artemis in the dipteral style, reconstructed plan with the altar

Column base 6' high from the fourth century temple, representing a draped woman between Thanatos (death) and Hermes (British Museum)

Since the previous temple, built on marshy ground, barely rose above the water table, the architect raised the stylobate of the new one 2.68 m. higher and built 13 steps on all four sides. Thus he elevated the exquisite work of architecture on a graceful pedestal. By all accounts the perfect proportions and sheer beauty of the ornament qualified the Artemision as one the Seven Wonders of the World. The idea of listing the greatest monuments can be traced back to Herodotus, who never saw the Artemision, but the first to name actually the seven was the poet Antipater of Sidon who, having described the six others, wrote "But when I saw the sacred house of

Artemis that towers to the clouds, the others were placed in the shade, for the sun itself has never looked upon its equal outside Olympus."

Completion of the temple took a further two centuries, but it contributed to the glory and fame of Ephesus during the golden age of the Pax Romana and beyond. After destruction by the Goths it was reduced to a sorry state on swampy ground. Today a single, incomplete column, assembled from fragments, stands beside a stagnant pool of water. This last Temple of Artemis maintained its full glory during the Early Christian Era.

THE ADMINISTRATIVE DISTRICT

The Magnesian Gate (10) built by Emperor Vespasian in 69-79 CE marked the entrance to Ephesus from Magnesia, as well as a ceremonial route from the Artemision. John Wood, while searching for the remains of the temple, found an inscription about processions from the temple to the Magnesian gate. With this important clue, he identified the gate and unearthed a paved road, which showed him the way to the place where the temple lay buried. Today its sparse remains lie in a hollow on the south side of the road 350 m. outside the east entrance. It opened originally to a small paved square and, on the same axis, to the street leading to the State Agora. A stretch of the city wall, no longer attached to the gate, can

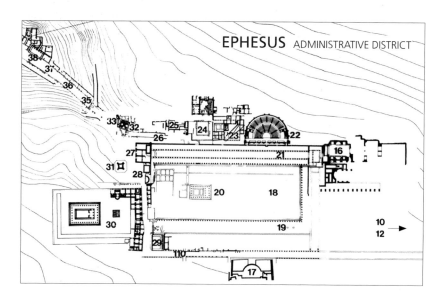

EPHESUS ADMINISTRATIVE DISTRICT

(L) The ruins of the baths, behind a fence
(R) East Gymnasium and Baths. The palaestra lies in the centre, in front of the baths. A long gallery runs around the outside of the bathing rooms

be seen nearby on Mount Pion to the north. About 500 m. further to the southeast lie the remains of the Bronze Age *tell* of Çukuriçi Höyük that are not accessible to the public.

On the north side of the road stood the **East Gymnasium (12)**. Little remains of the Long Stoa, with a pedimented portico, that formed its stately front, but the massive walls beyond it belong to the baths that served the gymnasium. To reach the usual hot, tepid and cold rooms, the public passed through the palaestra flanked by a lecture room and a space identified as the Emperor's Hall. An unusual element of the design, a long, vaulted gallery with large windows opening to the landscape, ran around three sides of the rooms for bathing. Archaeologists found a statue of Asklepios, the god of healing in the Emperor's Hall, emphasizing the connection between athletics, bathing and good health. Weary travelers entering Ephesus could refresh themselves here before reaching their destination. In the southeast corner of the complex behind the stoa, a small church with a nave and aisles was added in the Byzantine era. The foundations of its apse have disappeared beneath the new asphalt road. If you want to see the baths and the gate, you can ask the guard at the exit to let you go out for a few minutes and return on your original ticket, but visiting these buildings may not be worth the extra time.

The street aligned with the Magnesian Gate leads to the south side of the **State Agora (18)** built on level ground between Mount Pion and Mount Koressos. While the Agora near the harbour served as a commercial market, this more dignified space with a temple at its centre served as the political and ceremonial meeting place for governmental functions and

The central aisle of the Basilica Stoa of the State Agora, looking west

political activities. The **temple (20)**, once thought to have been dedicated to Isis, was more likely consecrated to Divine Caesar and Dea Roma (the goddess Rome). Augustus promoted the cult of the deified Julius Caesar after his murder. Ephesus was one of the few cities awarded the honour of building a temple for his worship; nothing remains of it today. Since Christians found the imperial cult particularly distasteful and materials were needed for earthquake repairs, they demolished it in the Byzantine era.

On the north side of the Agora, a splendid, three-aisled basilica, known as the **Basilica Stoa (21)**, 160 m. long and two stories high, built in 11 CE, functioned as a court of law and offered a setting for

(L) Bulls head capitals from the Basilica (R) Augustus and his wife Livia seated (Selçuk Museum)

(L) Cult statue of Artemis found buried in the **Prytaneum**
(R) The **Prytaneum**, Doric columns of the entrance

ceremonial events. The widely spaced interior columns of the central aisle carried bulls' heads that projected from the Ionic capitals to reduce the spans of the architraves. However, an earthquake 12 years later caused serious damage. After that event, intermediate Corinthian columns were inserted to help support the roof. **A Chalcidicum (27)** (committee room), at each end of the Basilica added to its immense length. Some remains of the one at the west end, built by Nero, survive. The one to the east, altered in Byzantine times, probably held the seated statues of Augustus and Livia now in the Selçuk Museum.

Two important civic buildings, the Prytaneum and the Odeon opened off the North Stoa. **The Prytaneum (24)**, the city hall, rebuilt under Augustus, contained the perpetually burning flame on the altar of Hestia that had protected the city in the Hellenistic period. The altar occupied a room beyond the peristyle court while a spacious banqueting room opened to the left. Inscriptions on the Doric columns of the entrance court list many names of those who served the goddess Hestia. In 1956 excavators discovered a well-preserved statue of Artemis from the second century CE buried in soil beneath the court of the Prytaneum. They concluded that faithful supporters of Artemis, after official denunciation of the old religion, had carefully interred the precious relic to save it from the Christians.

The Odeon **(22)**, which also served as the Bouleuterion, the council house of Ephesus seated 1500 people. It was built in the second century CE

(L) The Odeon can be seen beyond the Basilica (R) The Upper Gymnasium Baths

both for meetings of the boule and for musical performances. Only a few rows of the marble seating are original; the upper part has been restored with concrete. Like the Odeon at Aphrodisias, the theatre-like cavea faced an elaborate stage building ornamented with columns and sculpture; only fragments of this feature remain. A building that was clearly a sacred sanctuary between the Odeon and the Prytaneum remains unidentified.

Directly east of the Basilica Stoa three strong stone arches and massive brickwork once supported the vaults of the caldarium in **Upper Baths (16)**. This complex, which has not been fully excavated, probably

Sculpture from the Hydrodocheion: Two Goddesses? (left) A triton, (right) (Selçuk Museum)

included a palaestra. The water for these baths and other outlets in the city came from two structures to the south of the State Agora. Although little remains of them, they once demonstrated the Romans' artistic response to a function as mundane as water distribution. The **Nymphaeum (17)** on the colonnaded street from the Magnesian Gate stood at the point where water brought by a system of aqueducts and underground conduits from the rivers Marnas and Klaseas entered the city to be distributed through pipes. This was an installation of the late first century, made more elaborate with a central basin and two side wings. Some sections of the aqueducts, restored in Byzantine times, can be seen on the northwestern slope of Mt Pion. The **Hydrodocheion (29)**, a water reservoir, was adorned with sculpture on a two-storied façade. It was built by the Roman Governor C. Laecanius Bassus in 80-82 CE.

Domitian Street, running along the west side of the State Agora, separated it from the **Temple of Domitian (30)** and led north to the **Pollio Monument and Fountain of Domitian (28)**. This emperor, who possessed a reputation as a tyrant, reigned for 15 years from 81 to 96 CE. Devoting himself to reinforcing control of the empire, he believed strongly in the imperial cult. He demanded to be addressed as *dominus et deus* (lord

Temple of Domitian. One bay of the façade stands before the vaults of the undercroft

Head and forearm of the colossal seated cult statue of Domitian in the Selçuk Museum

and god) and has been accused of persecuting Christians. During his reign the Ephesians gained the title of temple-wardens *(neokoros)* and thus had the right to erect an imperial temple to him. This honour may explain their effort to design one that would dominate the city. It stood on a high terrace over a vaulted substructure fronted with a grandiose façade. A broad flight of steps, entered through an arch, led up to the terrace where worshippers encountered an open-air altar and a colossal seated statue of Domitian in front of the octastyle portico of the temple. Despite its eight columns on the front and thirteen on the sides, it was only 34 meters long, making it a small scale version of the Temple of Artemis. Today part of the altar is on display at the Selçuk Museum and the temple was dismantled down to its foundations in the Christian era. We only see two reerected columns from the façade of the lower structure against a background of decaying vaults. On

(L) The reconstructed arch at the entry of the Domitian Fountain
(R) The Late Hellenistic sculpture of Odysseus and Polyphemus, which stood in a half circle around the pool (Selçuk Museum)

their upper tier, above two Doric columns, male and female figures probably represent captured Barbarians. Reviled at the time of his assassination by a servant, Domitian's name was removed from the temple; the citizens rededicated it to his father Vespasian, so that they could maintain their rights as temple-wardens.

They smashed Domitian's statue and hurled it into one of the vaults below where archaeologists discovered the vast head and forearm. They can be seen in the Selçuk Museum. An inscription museum occupies the vaults beneath the temple, which originally served as storerooms. On the east side a row of small taverns faced Domitian Street.

The **Pollio Monument (28)**, built in 93 CE, stands against the west wall of the State Agora facing Domitian Street. It honoured C. Sextilius Pollio, who donated the Basilica in the State Agora and an aqueduct to the city. This rectangular structure, originally faced with marble, was a rare example of a tomb inside the city walls. The **Domitian Fountain (28A)** erected in 97 CE immediately south of the Pollio Monument, consisted of a semi-circular enclosure with water flowing into a pool through the apse. An arch across its entrance, reconstructed of fallen voussoirs, gives an idea of the scale of the composition, but little evidence remains of the three fountains that adorned it. Behind the pool, a group of Late Hellenistic sculpture, moved from another site represented the dramatic scene in Homer's *Odyssey* where Odysseus is preparing to blind the giant cyclops Polyphemus, who has trapped him and his men in the cave. The sculptor showed Greeks bringing wine to Polyphemus, seated in the centre, to get him drunk while Odysseus sharpens a stake. Two Greeks slain by the giant lie on the floor. We do not know where this sculpture stood originally; one theory is that it came from the pediment of the temple of Isis. Its presence in the fountain of the first century CE shows the significance the Romans attached to Greek mythology.

FROM CURETES STREET TO THE AGORA

Near the top of Curetes Street on the north side of Domitian square, the Late Hellenistic **Memmius Monument (22)** stands out as one of the most striking sculptural elements of Ephesus. What we see today is nothing like the original structure. Drawings that suggest alternative reconstructions are only conjectural. Much of the monument is missing; the

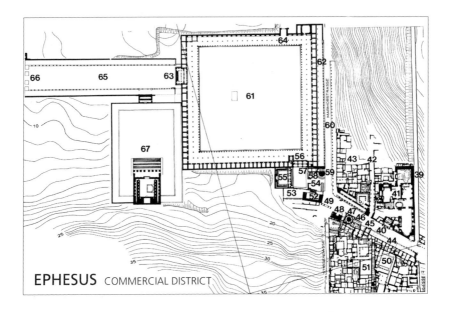

EPHESUS COMMERCIAL DISTRICT

archaeologists have assembled what remains so that it can be appreciated on its original site. Memmius was the grandson of the Roman dictator Sulla, who defeated the Pontic King Mithridates VI and expelled him from Ephesus. The figures probably represent members of Memmius's family. The **Hydreion** (33) added to the west side of the Memmius monument was yet another fountain. Little remains of it.

The Memmius monument

The Gate of Hercules built in the late fifth century CE, narrowed the upper end of Curetes Street to exclude wheeled vehicles. We do not know its original form, but it is clear that the pillars bearing low relief images of Hercules on their west side came from an earlier, unidentified architectural setting. They carried an arch, possible with the image of Nike in the spandrel to its left. Hercules is the Roman version of the Greek hero Herakles.

(L) The gate of Hercules from the west with low relief figures of the Greek hero bearing the pelt of the Nemean lion that he slew as one of his seven labors
(R) Nike, the flying goddess of victory bearing a palm branch, possibly in a spandrel of the arch over the gate

Nymphaeum Traiani (38) presents a further example of the Romans' obsession with water sculpture. They glorified emperors while dramatizing the delivery of precious water to their cities. The Asiarch (priest of the imperial cult) Tiberius Claudius Aristion erected this monumental fountain in honour of the emperor Trajan before 114 CE. Taking a similar form to the stage building of Roman theatres, it offered a precedent for the nymphaeum on the sacred way in Miletus. In the usual manner of such buildings two tiers of columns stood in front of the walls, framing statues of gods and heroes. Rounded pediments on the side wings flanked a triangular one in the centre; entablatures stepped forward and back while water

(L) Marble statue of Dionysus from the Nymphaeum (Selçuk Museum)
(C) Nymphaeum Traiani, partially reconstructed on site Nymphaeum Traiani
(R) Reconstruction drawing

The Temple of Hadrian *ca.* 118 CE.

poured into a rectangular basin below. Sculpture from the Nymphaeum Traiani in the Selçuk Museum include a nude statue of Dionysus and a figure tentatively identified as Androklos, the legendary founder of the city. At the centre stood a colossal statue of Trajan of which only one foot remains.

Continuing down Curetes Street, you will pass a street leading up to the right, lined with mostly residential buildings that have not been excavated. In the middle of the next block, the partially restored **Temple of Hadrian (40)**, on the north side, presents a memorable façade to the street. It was built by P. Vedius Antoninus Sabinus and dedicated in 118 CE to Hadrian, Artemis and the people of Ephesus. To give it a prominent place on the busy street he constructed it on space borrowed from the Varius Baths. Compensating

Androklos discovering the boar that, according to the oracle, showed him where he should found the city

for the small cella, he lavished ornament on the street façade and the pronaos. The square corner piers, the central arch and the wide spacing of the columns are unusual; the ornament in the frieze, which lifts in a graceful semicircle over the central opening, comes to life with intricate foliage. Tyche, protector of Ephesus, ornaments the keystone of the arch while a naked female figure rising from vegetal scrolls commands the tympanum over the inner door. A statue of Hadrian probably stood in the cella, easily visible through the door. Hadrian travelled throughout the Empire and came to Ephesus more than once. He admired Greek culture and took a pride in speaking and writing Greek. He not only commissioned the Pantheon in Rome, but also encouraged architecture in the provinces.

Around 300 CE, statues of the tetrarchs Diocletian, Constantius, Maximus Galerius and Maximian were placed on pedestals that still stand in front of the temple. Later, an image of Theodosius I (379-395), the last emperor to rule both the eastern and western empires and a great supporter of Christianity, replaced that of the despised Maximian.

After the temple suffered damage in an earthquake in the fourth century, those who restored it added four recently carved low relief panels that they had taken from another building in the corners of the pronaos. The one on the west side of the pronaos concerns the founding of the city by Androklos, the son of King Kodros of Athens. According to legend he arrived with a band of Ionians from Attica and settled on an island where they lived for twenty years. Finding the place unsuitable they sent for guidance from the Delphic oracle, which prophesied that a fish and a boar would reveal the ideal site. While some fishermen were preparing their lunch, a fish they were grilling leapt out of the fire with glowing charcoal attached to it and set the grass on fire, revealing a wild boar hiding in a thicket. Androklos killed it with a spear and declared that they had found the place to build their city. The panel shows Androklos on horseback throwing his spear at the boar running up a hillside. The panel on the right hand side also reveals Ephesian beliefs of the time. It shows the emperor Theodosius and his family standing with Artemis in the company of Athena and six other Greek gods and goddesses. This work of art shows the continued homage to the Olympian gods in Ephesus, even while Christianity prevailed in the Empire. The Austrian Institute of Archaeology reconstructed the temple, as far as was feasible, in the 1950s.

(L) The apodyterium of the Scholastica Baths
(R) The marble seats of the latrines around the court

Behind the Temple of Hadrian, with an entrance just to its right, you can find the **Varius Baths (41)**, also named the Scholastica Baths. A Christian woman named Scholastica refurbished these thermae in the fourth century CE after a severe earthquake. Her statue surveys the premises from a niche affirming that Christians had not yet repudiated the joy of luxuriating in hot water. The tall Corinthian columns in the apodyterium (changing room) convey the ostentatious character of the interior. A hypocaust under the marble floors kept the rooms warm; large windows in the apse admitted sunlight from the south. While the patrons, relaxed, socialized and gossiped in rooms lined with white marble, unseen slaves stoked the furnaces underneath. Across the street just west of the baths, flowing water passed under the marble seats of the **Latrine (43)**, which was arranged around a small court like the peristyle of a patrician Roman house; a separate channel brought clean water for washing. The restored seats show the typical arrangement for Roman sanitation. An adjoining set of rooms, previously identified as a brothel probably served another purpose.

Bath Street (39) running onto the slope of Mt Pion to the east of the baths was lined with buildings that all remain unexcavated except for a palatial Byzantine building which stood immediately above the theatre and afforded a fine view over the lower city and the harbour. This probably served as the Proconsul's Palace or a **Banqueting Hall (76)**. This area is not open to the public.

Alytarchus Stoa (44) offered shelter to pedestrians on the south side of the street opposite Hadrian's temple. Along its back wall, between small shops and taverns, discreet entries gave access to some of the terraced houses behind it. Geometric mosaics, with a few flowers and birds, ornamented its pavement, adding distinction to the area. At the western end of the Stoa stood a well house from which water flowed through lions' heads.

The **Octagon (47)** to the west of the Alytarchus Stoa has been identified as the tomb of the Ptolemaic Queen Cleopatra's half-sister Arsinoë IV. She was murdered in Ephesus in 41 BCE; a skeleton found in the tomb belonged to a young woman and Egyptian motifs were discovered on the sarcophagus.

The Terrace Houses (50 & 51)

The excavation, scholarly analysis and conservation of the terrace houses on the hillside opposite the Temple of Hadrian, directed by H. Vetters followed by Friedrich Krinzinger of the Austrian Archaeological Institute, is an outstanding achievement. The complex organization of the houses, the fragility of their fabric and the throngs of tourists visiting them posed severe challenges. Teams of archaeologists, scientists and other professionals responded with great expertise. They covered an area of 7,000 sq. m. with a translucent roof without damaging the structures underneath. To allow the public to move through the site while the archaeologists continue their work, they devised and installed elegant stainless steel and glass catwalks. **Terrace Houses 2 (51)** are now open to visitors with an additional fee.

Protective roof over the Terrace Houses   Glass and stainless steel catwalk for visitors

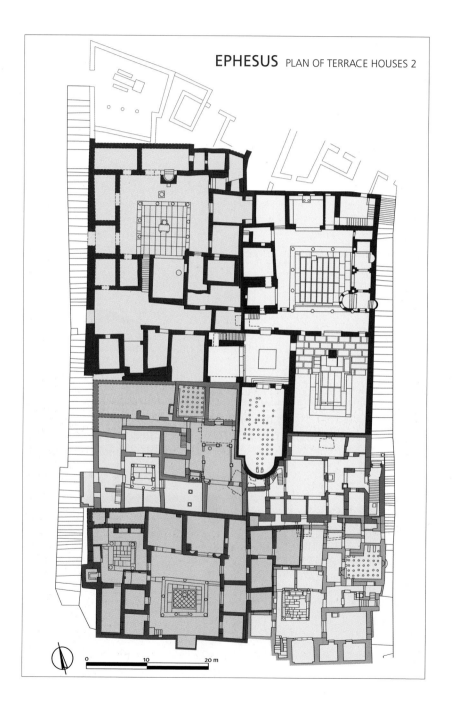

EPHESUS PLAN OF TERRACE HOUSES 2

0   10   20 m

The layout of the houses appears chaotic; however, with some understanding of the context it is possible to make sense of it. The plans conformed originally to the Hippodamian grid on which the city was based but since Curetes Street, from which the southernmost houses are entered, diverges from the grid, the *insulae* (blocks) are not rectangular. Steep, stepped alleys ascended the lower slope of Mt Koressos between *insulae*, reaching a second street that conforms to the grid. The archaeologists have named this Hanghausstrasse (Terrace House Street). Some houses opened off the alleys and others from the upper street; thus the *insulae* are penetrated from all four sides. Their designs followed familiar traditions of Hellenistic and Roman domestic architecture. The Greeks and Romans tended to live privately. They preferred not to proclaim their wealth by building imposing façades. Entrances generally led into a vestibule and then an atrium open to the sky, off which the rooms open. Many houses included a few surprisingly large rooms for entertaining and ceremonial use, but most were small. Over the centuries some houses expanded into spaces taken from others and, responding to changing styles and the desires of owners, many were remodeled. The largest atrium, in the southwest

Lion mosaic

View down into an arcade around an atrium

(L) Wall decorations (R) Atrium floor decorated with contrasting marble squares

corner of the plan above belongs to a house with a large reception room with an apse (shown near the centre of the plan). This was probably an addition. The houses were served with piped water and drains under the floors for domestic water and sewage. The sewers ran deep in the ground under the alleys and joined the main ones under the street below. After the decline of Rome, it would be centuries before any system as advanced as this would appear in Europe.

Although the houses remained isolated from the life of the city behind enclosing walls, the mosaics and wall decorations evoked a wider world. They not only introduced colour and variety but also illustrated scenes from mythology, literature and nature. Light from the sky filled the atriums, but the smaller rooms, often windowless, must have been dark and airless. Lit only by oil lamps and mostly unheated in winter except by charcoal braziers, they cannot have been pleasant places, even with their painted wall decorations.

It is beyond the scope of this book to offer a detailed guide to the terraced houses. When you go through them you will find helpful explanations posted on signboards and you will be able to witness the work in progress by the archaeologists, who are painstakingly sorting fragments of painted plaster, analyzing their discoveries and continuing restoration.

Hadrian's Gate (49) stands tall at the foot of Curetes Street on the south side just beyond the terrace houses. It combines with the **Library of Celsus (55)** and the South Gate of the Agora to define a significant urban space. Like most Roman triumphal arches it was designed in a tripartite manner with the widest opening in the centre. The pairs of tall, fluted Corinthian columns on either side originally supported a high

Hadrian's Gate (L) *ca.* 117 CE, Celsus Library (C), 117 CE and the South Gate of the Agora (R) 3 BCE

central arch. A superstructure with columns and statuary included a central image of Artemis, which Christians hurled down and replaced with a cross in the fourth century CE. The light structure and emphasis on height gave Hadrian's Gate a different character from the massive Agora gate, opposite it on the north side of the library.

The Library of Celsus, the third largest library in the classical world, after Alexandria and Pergamon, held 12,000 scrolls. Its powerful architectural form on a pivotal site at the foot of Curetes Street gave prominence to culture and learning in this commercial metropolis. It also demonstrated the homage paid to an illustrious man, who governed the city. Gaius Julius Aquila erected the library in 117 CE in honour of his father Gaius Julius Celsus Ptolemaeanus, a consul in Rome at the time of Trajan, who in 106-107 served in Ephesus as governor of Asia. This splendid edifice made an appropriate mausoleum for this official, who had also been in charge of all public buildings in Rome. It possessed the virtue of benefiting the living residents of Ephesus as well. His lead coffin, which has never been opened, lay within a marble sarcophagus in a vaulted chamber here.

The east-facing façade shows the ingenuity of the architect, who endowed it with an alternating rhythm and brought it to life with light and shade. On the lower story, four aedicules, each with an entablature

APETH (Virtue) ΣΟΦΙΑ (wisdom) Two of the four copies of statues representing ideals on the Library of Celsus façade. The originals are in the Ephesus Museum, Vienna

supported on two Ionic columns, frame niches for sculpture. Between them three doors open to the interior. On the upper story, three wider aedicules in the Corinthian order straddle gaps in the entablature below them; they rise to carry alternating triangular and curved pediments. Their broad openings allow light to enter through large windows. Single columns at the ends and the widening of the central openings add further complexity to the rhythm of the façade. The four niches held statues representing APETH (Virtue), ΣΟΦΙΑ (wisdom), ENNOIA (intelligence), and EΠIΣTHME (knowledge). These are copies of the originals preserved in the Ephesus Museum in Vienna. Statues of Gaius Julius Celsus Ptolemaeanus stood on pedestals flanking the steps; inscriptions on them can still be read. The façade of the library finally collapsed in another earthquake during the middle ages.

In the vast interior, thirty niches, arranged on three levels, contained the scrolls. Staircases and passages concealed in the thickness of the walls reached the two upper galleries. The voids in the walls surrounding the central space, visible in the plan, also helped to protect the precious scrolls from dampness. A colossal statue of Celsus, proclaiming his virtue, occupied the tall apse in the west wall, directly above his tomb chamber.

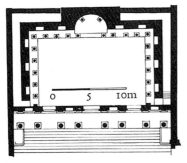

Celsus Library, plan

Interior, restoration

In 269 Goths attacking Ephesus set fire to it and destroyed the interior and the precious scrolls. Losing its purpose as a library, the area in front of the façade became a fountain with huge basins adorned with high relief sculpture from the Parthian Altar that stood elsewhere in the city. They represent, in a heroic manner, the campaign in Mesopotamia in 165 CE under Lucius Verus (co-emperor with Marcus Aurelius). The most striking panel represents the apotheosis of Lucius Verus in the chariot of the sun god Helios. Since in the same war he sacked the city of Ctesiphon after its mostly Greek inhabitants had surrendered, his welcome by the gods on Mount Olympus seems dubious. This panel, and many others are displayed in the Kunsthistorisches Museum in Vienna, but a few that were discovered later can be seen in the Selçuk Museum.

The South Gate of the Agora (63)

Immediately to the north of the library stands the monumental arch built in 3 BCE, more than a century before the library, by two former slaves who had gained their freedom and amassed riches. Also re-erected by the Austrian archaeologists, it helps to define the impressive urban space before the library.

To the east of the arch a flight of steps, partly missing today, led up to the austere Doric façade of the Hall of Nero. According to inscriptions, this two-aisled basilica was dedicated to Artemis, the emperor Nero and the citizens of Ephesus. It served as a court of law and for ceremonial purposes. Widely spaced doors opened into its two aisles. The interior space, divided longitudinally in two by a row of columns, lacked the spacious quality of

(L) Hall of Nero, reconstructed south façade and the circular monument (R) The steps of the circular monument and the base of the Hall of Nero, with the Agora Gate and Celsus Library to the left

the Basilica Stoa (21). In front of it, rising on a plinth from the steps is a circular structure that may have performed as a fountain or a water clock. Sections of its roof helped archaeologists to visualize its appearance.

The Tetragonos Agora

The principal Agora of Ephesus, the largest and best preserved in Anatolia, remained in use for almost 900 years. Originally surrounded by about 75 shops and a few civic offices, it once teemed with the commercial activity of Roman Asia's capital city. Lysimachus sited it on the flat coastal plain between the harbour and the city centre, when, in the third century BCE, he moved Ephesus inland from its previous position. During the reign of Augustus in the first century BCE, it was raised up about 3 m. and rebuilt on a larger scale with stoas 112 m. long on each side. After an earthquake 200 years later it was restored and finally, in the late fourth century CE, the Christian emperor Theodosius reconstructed it, using architectural elements from several pagan buildings. It continued in use until the seventh century. Many of the columns, capitals and sections of entablature that we see today came from the temple of Domitian, the Vedius Baths and the Harbour Baths. Although nothing remains of the second story, a large number of the central colonnades that divided the two aisled stoas, as well as those that fronted it, still stand to their full height, enabling us imagine the spatial quality and scale of this vast civic space. Many honourific statues stood in the Agora, but only their bases remain.

The Tetragonos Agora looking south towards the South Gate and the Library of Celsus

The Serapeion (67)

The magnificence of the temple of Serapis attests to the strength of the Egyptian community in Ephesus. An earthquake caused its collapse and much stone has been removed. While the back of the temple was excavated into the steep slope of Mt Koressos, a flight of steps approached the front. With eight monolithic Corinthian columns 14 m. high carrying a broad pediment, the facade dominated the sacred precinct. In a type of construction rare in Roman temples, a barrel vault supported on heavy stone walls gave the interior a cave-like quality. Fragments of a cult figure carved of Egyptian granite and inscriptions pertaining to an Egyptian cult confirm the purpose of the temple. In the reign of Theodosius I it was converted into a place of Christian worship.

The West Gate (63), West Road (65), the Medusa Gate (66) and the Harbour Plain

From the Ionic west gate of the Agora, ten steps led down to the west road connecting the harbour with the Agora. Heads of Medusa, found on the ground at the foot of the street, probably crowned the pillars of another gate, named by the archaeologists as the Medusa gate. Inscriptions and other evidence suggest that this area included a West Agora, a fishery customs house, a meeting hall for merchants from Rhodes, a shrine to a mystery cult from the island of Samothrace, and a shrine of the Egyptian Gods.

Marble Street (60)

Running between the library plaza and the theatre, this broad, straight boulevard paved with white marble served as the principal street of Ephesus and continued north to the Temple of Artemis. The massive lower wall of the Hall of Nero defines its west side; a colonnade along its east side gave access to shops and the houses stepping up the slope of Panayır Dağ behind them. The residential district to which they belonged has not been excavated, but archaeologists believe its houses were smaller than those built on terraces south of Curetes Street.

THE HARBOUR PLAIN AND NORTHWEST DISTRICT

The Theatre

While many of the cities of Asia Minor built large theatres in Hellenistic times, the Ephesians did not construct theirs until the first century BCE. Carved into the lower slope of Mount Pion, this vast structure dominated the intersection between Marble Street and Arcadian Street. It offered a crucial stopping place for processions on the Sacred Way, which led north to the Temple of Artemis. Citizens assembled here for major civic events as well as theatrical performances. It was in this theatre that

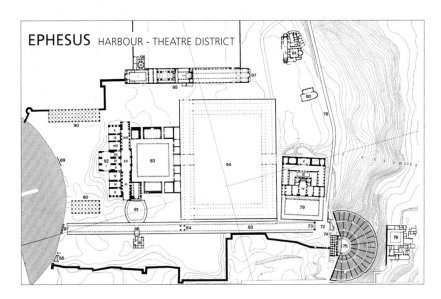

EPHESUS HARBOUR - THEATRE DISTRICT

The Theatre seating 24,000 spectators, dated from the first century BCE. Arcadian Street, in the distance leads towards the Harbour

the silversmith Demetrius roused the anger of a crowd in response to St. Paul's preaching against the worship of Artemis.

At first, following the tradition of Greek theatres the stage remained narrow, but in the first century CE, since the action in Roman drama took place on the stage rather than the orchestra, it was extended forward and also lengthened. Between 87 and 92 CE, an elaborate façade with sculpture in many aedicules and niches was built behind the stage. While today we can look out to the slope of Mount Koressos and along Arcadian Street towards the site of the harbour, spectators in classical times were enclosed by this elaborate architectural feature that paid homage to gods and heroes. As the population grew, the theatre gradually expanded up the slope. The first tier with 19 rows of seats was arranged in 11 segments separated by narrow staircases. The second tier of 20 rows, divided into 21 segments was supported on vaults. A third tier, added later with 21 rows, increased the capacity to 25,000. In the second century CE a vast awning stretched over the cavea protected spectators from the sun. A final change, allowing aquatic performances, eliminated the first six rows of seats and enclosed the orchestra with a wall so that it could be flooded.

Earthquakes in the third and fourth centuries caused extensive damage. By the eighth century, when Byzantine Ephesus feared raids by Arabs, the theatre was converted to a fortification.

(L) Reconstruction of Arcadian Street. (R) Arcadian Street today. One column of the four-column monument is visible in front of the distant hill

Arcadian Street (82)

After the earthquake of 359 CE, Emperor Arcadius (408-450 CE), the son of Theodosius I, restored the grand colonnaded street leading from the harbour to the theatre. It had existed since Hellenistic times, but now bears his name. Lined with shops and provided with fifty street lights as well as sewer and water pipes beneath the marble paving slabs, it showed the progressive spirit of Ephesian planning. Two centuries later, in the Justinian Age, the Christians of Ephesus transformed it again by building four columns on elaborate bases, probably carrying statues of the four evangelists. The **Four-Columned Monument** (84) proclaimed the Christian nature of the city to all who entered this way. The street terminated at the harbour with the monumental Middle Harbour Gate, a variant, in the Ionic style, of the Roman triumphal arch.

Buildings North of Arcadian Street

Immediately to the northwest of the theatre, on the north side of Arcadian Street, the **Theatre Gymnasium (79)** occupied an important position in the city centre. Its palaestra, just across the north end of Marble Street from the theatre, made a neat rectangle surrounded by stoas with mosaic floors. Along its north side a tribune (four rows of stepped seats), still visible today, provided for spectators at athletic contests and lectures. Behind it, a bath building included a swimming pool and the usual hot, tepid and cold rooms. The heavy stone walls that rise a few meters high supported the vaults over the rooms for bathing. These have not yet been excavated, but it is possible that beautiful mosaic floors and marble wall panels still lie beneath the debris.

The stepped seating for spectators in the palaestra with the walls of the baths on the left

Immediately to the west of the Theatre Gymnasium lie the remains of two much larger complexes built during the reign of Emperor Domitian (81-96 CE), the **Harbour Baths (93)** and an enormous palaestra known as the **Halls of Verulanus (94)**. Their original size and architectural grandeur show the importance of bathing, athletics and the education of epheboi (young men). The palaestra occupying an area 240 x 200 m. consisted of an open space far larger than the nearby Agora, surrounded on four sides by exceptionally wide three-aisled stoas. These spaces, also known as xystoi, served as covered running tracks. During the reign of Hadrian (117-138), the chief priest of Asia Claudius Verulanus bequeathed funds to cover the walls of the xystoi with marble of many colours, thus giving his name to the complex.

The plan of the Harbour Baths is unusual. It consists of a small palaestra with halls about twice the size of the Library of Celsus opening onto its north and south sides. The one to the south served as a lecture room; the other, resplendent with coloured marble columns and statuary, was clearly designed for important ceremonies. The Austrian archaeologists have named it the Kaisersaal (Emperor's Hall). A bronze sculpture found in this vast room but now in the Ephesus Museum, Vienna, represents an athlete, who once held a strigil, an instrument for scraping dirt and sweat from the body. This Roman copy of a Greek original of ca. 320 BCE, gives us an idea of the artistic quality demanded in this grand architectural setting. Patrons moved through the ends of the West Stoa of the palaestra into changing rooms *(apodyteria)* and from there into the *frigidarium* with a long plunge pool *(natatio)* that lay between them. From there they could pass through smaller rooms for bathing in tepid water, to the *calidarium*, which jutted out westwards towards the harbour. Large windows facing the afternoon sun helped to warm this space; a hypocaust beneath the floor produced radiant heat to bring comfort to the naked bathers. The brick columns supporting the floor are now exposed allowing us to see how the hypocaust worked. The hot gases that passed between them moved up through flues in the walls, warming them also. Vegetation obscures the ruins.

Church of the Virgin Mary (95)

A path leading north across the palaestra of the Harbour Baths, just to the left of the exit from the site, leads to the church of the Virgin Mary, also described as the Church of the Councils. Like many churches in the Early Christian era it was converted to religious use from an existing Roman structure of the basilican type. Bean describes it as a hall of muses, containing statues of the seven muses and therefore known as a

Church of the Virgin Mary, the nave looking east, the apse

Baptistery with sunken pool

"museum". However, Akurgal suggests that since Ephesus was the main centre for banking and commerce for the Roman province of Asia, this building close to the harbour and the Agora was a money and grain exchange. The original Roman edifice dating from the second century CE was 260 meters long with an apse at each end. Many bankers and brokers may have worked in offices in the aisles, while magistrates presided over legal proceedings in the apses.

This Roman building was probably converted to Christian use after damage by fire during a period of economic decline in the mid-fourth century CE. An alternative theory suggests that Christians first acquired it at the time of the third Ecumenical Council, a pivotal event in the history of Christianity, which took place there in 431. It became the cathedral of Ephesus and served as a model for other churches in the region. Worshippers entered through a spacious atrium at the west end, and passed through a narthex paved with mosaics into a three-aisled nave with a roof supported by 40 columns. At a later stage it was divided into three smaller churches, one of them the domain of the bishop. An octagonal domed baptistery surrounded by a square ambulatory opens off the north side of the atrium; it still contains the sunken pool for total immersion of candidates for baptism. Marble lined its walls, making it almost as splendid as a Roman bath.

To the north of the church of the Virgin Mary, the **Temple of Hadrian Zeus Olympios (98)** stood in a huge temenos surrounded by stoas. Built in the triumphal Corinthian style, this was the largest temple in the city after the Temple of Artemis. It measured 85x57 m. and rose to a height of 25 m. but it was razed in the Christian era leaving no trace. On the small hill west of the Stadium, stood the **Macellum (100)**, the meat market.

The Stadium (104)

Little of the Stadium has been excavated, but much can be imagined. In Hellenistic times animated spectators watched athletic competitions in honour of the Greek gods. Under the Romans the Stadium flowed with blood as gladiatorial contests drew raucous crowds to witness mortal combat. The first appearance of gladiators in Ephesus took place in 69 BCE under Lucullus, the commander-in-chief of the army. During the reign of Nero (54-68 CE) several wealthy Ephesians, including the freed-man C. Stertinius Orpex donated money to increase the capacity of the Stadium to 25,000. Additional tiers of seating were raised over vaulted passages whose arched entrances can be seen today. In the third century CE, when gladitorial combat reached a height of popularity, the eastern end of the Stadium was enclosed to create an elliptical arena half the size of the Colosseum of Rome. The chief priest of the imperial cult organized these contests, which proclaimed the strength of the Empire while providing popular entertainment. When gladiators died they were carried to their own cemetery, which lay only about 300 m. to the east. Inscriptions on some of their sarcophagi mentioned highlights of their careers and bones revealed the evidence of their wounds. This burial ground, discovered in 1993, now lies hidden under an orchard.

The ends of the north and south sides of the Stadium. The vaulted passages supported the tiers of seats.

The Vedius Gymnasium (106)

Just beyond of the Stadium, the processional route from the city centre ran eastwards towards the Artemision. Along its north side a stoa 136 m. long fronted the monumental Vedius gymnasium, the best preserved building of its type in the city. A wealthy and influential citizen of Ephesus, Publius Vedius Antoninus, erected this lavish bath and gymnasium complex in about 150 CE in honour of the goddess Artemis and his patron, the emperor Antoninus Pius. The first entrance from the colonnaded stoa lined with shops led directly into the **apodyterium** (changing room) from which bathers could pass into the thermae; a second entrance led to a spacious latrine. A more formal portal to the complex took the form of a propylon ornamented with statues. This gave access to a large palaestra surrounded by stoas. On its west side, between rooms for education, a large hall for ceremonial purposes opened on one side to the stoa. The main focus of the hall, a statue presumably representing the emperor, stood in a niche on the long wall facing the palaestra; only its base survives. When ceremonies took place, teachers and *epheboi* or officials made offerings at altar in front of the statue.

The architect planned this complex, like most Roman *thermae*, symmetrically with identical spaces on either side of a central axis, but he devised a unique plan in which a hall for a variety of sports stretched the full width of the building and expanded it into cross wings at both ends, giving it an I-shape. Beyond it the *natatio* (swimming pool), fitted into the space beside the shaft of the I, opposite the imperial hall. From there patrons could proceed on the central axis through the *frigidarium* and the small *tepidarium* into the calidarium, which in five different compartments occupied the entire west end of the building. The various rooms probably offered different temperatures to suit the desires of patrons. Underground furnaces on either side of the tepidarium heated the water and

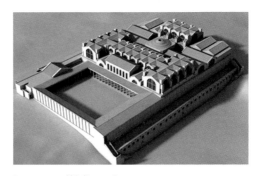

Reconstructed bird's eye view

generated hot gases to circulate under the floor of the *tepidarium* and rise through clay pipes embedded in the walls. Slaves carried the vast quantity of fuel needed to keep the fires burning through an underground passage. Large west facing windows brought evening sun into all five rooms. No doubt the walls were embellished with floor mosaics, coloured marble and sculpture. A river god, carved in stone, who once reclined above a pool in the *frigidarium* and poured water from an amphora, survives in the museum at Izmir, but most vestiges of decorative materials have disappeared.

Defensive Walls

Some stretches of Hellenistic walls constructed by Lysimachus, with their postern gates and towers on Mount Koressos, are still standing. According to the Austrian archaeologist Franz Miltner, it took 200,000 cubic meters of stone to build the walls, not including the towers. Where the wall descends from the hill towards the old harbour, a well-preserved tower has, for some obscure reason, been named St. Paul's prison. Another stretch of the walls runs from the north side of the harbour to the ridge of Mount Pion. In Byzantine times new walls were built around the northwest district of the city to enclose a smaller area.

The Cave of the Seven Sleepers

Cave of the Seven Sleepers

A signposted turning off the road back to Selçuk leads in about 550 m. to the cave on Mount Pion where, according legend, seven young Christian men fleeing persecution under Emperor Decius (249-251 CE) took shelter. The story relates that they went to sleep and awoke 200 years later in the age of the Christian emperor Theodosius. Two churches and several tombs have been excavated there. The impressive vaults of the larger church show the veneration for this site. A Muslim version of the story of these young men sleeping 300 years also survives.

AYASOLUK HILL

East of classical Ephesus, between Selçuk and the Artemision the walls of a fortress crown the top of Ayasoluk Hill. In the fifth century CE Christians built a church with a wooden roof over the grave of St John and dedicated it to him. By the time of Justinian, this structure became dilapidated, and a great new domed church supplanted it. The fortifications, covering an area about 500x180 m. begun in the Early Christian era, were strengthened by the Byzantines and further reinforced by the Seljuks after their conquest in 1090 CE. These were built of stone taken from the classical city, particularly the Temple of Artemis and the Stadium. With 20 towers and four gates this citadel remains an impressive sight, a medieval counterpart to classical Ephesus. Water reached it from springs at Belevi 14 km. northwest by means of an aqueduct that traversed the site of present-day Selçuk. Visitors enter the fortified area from the town of Selçuk through the impressive Gate of Persecution at the south end of the hill. After visiting the church, it is worth climbing up the terrace above the church to enjoy views over the town and the archaeological site. The fortress is currently under excavation by Mustafa Büyükkolancı of Pamukkale University and not open to public.

The single column of the Artemision assembled from fragments of different columns stands in the foreground. On Ayasoluk Hill, the Basilica of St John can be seen directly behind the column and towering above it, are the walls of the Byzantine fortress. The mosque of Aydınoğlu Isa Bey lies below it

The Basilica of St John

The emperor Justinian (527-565) built the Basilica of St John on the site of the saint's fourth century church and tomb. With a cruciform plan and six domes extending 110 m. long, it was his grandest creation outside Constantinople. It conforms to a splendid architectural type first developed under Constantine I in the church of the Holy Apostles in Constantinople. Following Early Christian and Byzantine tradition, the worshippers passed through an atrium and a narthex before entering the nave. This space consisted of two lofty domed compartments with aisles and galleries on the north and south sides. Beyond the nave four more domes covered the crossing, the transepts and the sanctuary; the dome over the crossing rose higher than the others and admitted light through openings in its drum. Windows in walls above the galleries illuminated the nave. The same architectural scheme was adopted centuries later in the five-domed church of St. Mark's Venice (1063-1094).

The lower five or six meters of the massive stone piers that supported the domes still stand; they vividly convey an idea of the weight they carried. In several areas the row of four columns between the piers are still in place and, in a few bays, the arcades and upper columns have been restored so that we can imagine looking through to the aisles and upper galleries that surrounded the nave and transepts. The simple capitals of the unfluted columns, far less ornate than those in Justinian's masterpiece Hagia Sophia, carry stylized foliage and Christian symbols. Four columns in the crossing indicate the bema, the sacred place over the tomb of

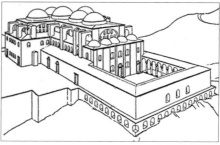

The St John's Basilica, built by Byzantine Emperor Justinian
(L) The tomb of St John
(R) Exterior perspective

St. John. Archaeologists found four sarcophagi in this place, one of them larger than the others and presumed to belong to John. However, they were all empty.

The **Mosque of Aydınoğlu Isa Bey (170)**, built in 1375, represents the transition from Seljuk to Ottoman traditions. Designed by Ali, an architect from Damascus, it shows influence from the Great Mosque in Damascus. The skilled Syrian artisans who built it used materials from the ruined Basilica of St John as well as the Temple of Artemis; indeed the decaying classical city provided plentiful antique marble to adorn its walls.

Mosque of Aydınoğlu Isa Bey, 1375.

However, avoiding any show of Roman ornament, the details are entirely Islamic. It was the first mosque in Turkey with a courtyard.

The House of the Virgin Mary

The belief that Mary, the mother of Jesus, came to Ephesus with St John is credible, but the building named as the House of the Virgin Mary on the slope of Mount Koressos is a small Byzantine chapel probably dating from the thirteenth century. The conviction that Mary lived and died on this site is based solely on the visions, in the nineteenth century, of the German nun Anna Katerina Emmerich. The Catholic Church has not made any pronouncement on the authenticity of the claim, but several popes have visited the site and given papal apostolic blessings there. Visitors witness the peaceful, spiritual quality of the place as well as the devotion of many pilgrims.

SELÇUK ARCHAEOLOGICAL MUSEUM

Many of the archaeological discoveries from Ephesus can be seen in this well designed and organized museum. It includes the iconic figure of Artemis and other sculpture shown in this chapter. I have illustrated several of them with the buildings they originally adorned. Since the items on display are identified with labels, I have not listed or discussed them in this book.

Stoa of the Agora

MAGNESIA ON THE MAEANDER

At first sight Magnesia, lying on flat ground far from the sea, shows little promise. The famous Temple of Artemis is scarcely more than a pile of rubble, but the recent discovery of the best-preserved Stadium in Anatolia makes a visit worthwhile. The city was founded in the tenth century BCE by Aeolian colonists from Magnesia in Northern Greece, who chose a place that had long been sacred to the Anatolian mother goddess Cybele. Although Magnesia lies in central Ionia, a few kilometers from Ephesus, it was never a member of the Ionian League or the Delian League. During the Archaic Era, Magnesia suffered invasions by aggressive powers: King Gyges of Lydia conquered it and ruled there in the early seventh century; the rapacious Cimmerians after taking the Lydian capital of Sardis, around 650 BCE, looted and destroyed Magnesia. Within twenty years, Alyattes, king of Lydia, drove the Cimmerians out of western Anatolia and regained power. In 546 BCE, when the Persians vanquished his son Croesus and seized the Lydian Empire, Magnesia came under their control.

Ironically, Persian domination led to rule by a Greek statesman. The brilliant Athenian General Themistokles, who fought the Persians at Marathon and led the Greek fleet to victory over them at Salamis, was accused by his countrymen of treachery and exiled. He gained favour with the Persian King Artaxerxes, who appointed him as satrap of Magnesia in 464 BCE. Clearly an opportunist, he lived there in luxury for the last fifteen years of his life and governed the Greeks well. He built a temple to Cybele and appointed his wife and daughter as priestesses. At the age of 65, when ordered to lead an army against Greece, Themistokles decided to end his life by taking poison, or, as the legend goes, drinking bull's blood. Nothing remains of the Magnesia of his era: Like other cities in the region, the changing course of the River Maeander made it necessary to move it to higher ground. The site chosen, by the archaic Temple of Artemis at the small town of Leucophryene (meaning 'Whitebrow'), proved advantageous. The new Magnesia thrived as a religious site dedicated to the popular goddess. When Alexander the Great had gained possession of Ephesus, the Magnesians sent emissaries to submit to him and received his protection. After his death they supported Seleucus and soon came under the rule of the Attalids of Pergamon. They gained favour, both of Eumenes II and the Romans when they joined forces with them to defeat of their enemy Antiochos III in the battle of Magnesia. In reward Magnesia became a free city. During this period of peace and prosperity they built the new Ionic Temple of Artemis Leucophryne, which added to their prestige. In 133 BCE, as the Romans absorbed the Pergamene possessions into their empire, Magnesia became an important city in the Province of Asia.

Magnesia continued to thrive in Byzantine times; it became the seat of a bishop and was enclosed by new walls; but, as the ever-changing River Maeander (Büyükmenderes) turned fertile land into marshes and buried buildings in silt, the city declined and was eventually abandoned.

Rediscovery and archaeology

A French team of archaeologists excavating at Magnesia (1842-3) removed 40 m. of the temple frieze to the Louvre, but did not publish a report on their findings. Half a century later, Osman Hamdi Bey, an important Turkish artist and director of the Ottoman Imperial Museum in Istanbul, took a further 20 m. of the frieze to install there. Surprisingly, Carl Humann, excavating for the German Archaeological Institute (1891-3), was still allowed to carry away more blocks of the frieze for the Pergamon Museum in Berlin. Excavation stopped for many years, but Dr. Orhan Bingöl of the University of Ankara has directed excavations and has published his findings since 1984. He has discovered remarkable Hellenistic sculpture in the Market Basilica that Humann believed to be a Byzantine church. He has also executed some impressive restoration of the previously unexcavated Agora. His most astonishing discovery, has been the Stadium.

Visiting Magnesia on the Maeander

Magnesia lies close to Ephesus, Miletus and Priene. Highway 525 between Selçuk and Söke passes through the forbidding Byzantine walls (3) around the sanctuary of Artemis. You can park close to the temple and Agora. After visiting them you can take a path leading west to the Greek and Roman theatres and to the Stadium.

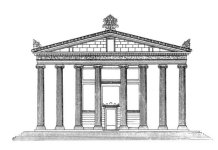
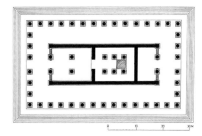

Temple of Artemis Leucophryene, designed by Hermogenes, *ca.* 150 BCE, elevation and plan (After C. Humann and J. Köhte 1904). The pseudo-dipteral design gives a spacious quality

The Temple of Artemis Leucophryne (1)

In the second century BCE the citizens chose Hermogenes of Priene as their architect for a new Temple of Artemis on the site of the archaic one. He had already designed the exquisite Temple of Dionysus at Teos, and had articulated a new theory concerning architectural proportions. The Roman architect and theorist Vitruvius (80–70 BC), admired him greatly, visited his temples and was familiar with the architectural treatises he had written. He based his own influential plans for temples on Hermogenes's principles and followed his interpretation of the Ionic order. Since Vitruvius became a source for classical architecture in the Italian Renaissance and Classical Revivals ever since, the temples at Teos and Magnesia possess a more enduring significance than their ruins suggest. The version of the Ionic order perfected by Hermogenes became ubiquitous.

The new Temple of Artemis Leucophryene, with eight columns on the front and fifteen on the sides, was the fourth largest temple in Anatolia. The Greek geographer Strabo (ca. 63 BCE – 24 CE) considered it more beautifully proportioned than the Temple of Artemis at Ephesus, one of the seven-wonders-of-the-world. But the characters of the two temples

An Ionic capital and part of a column shaft

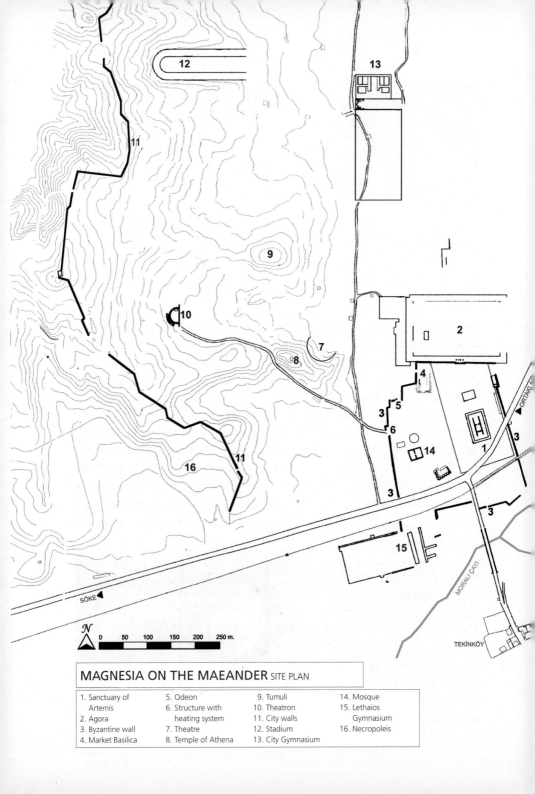

MAGNESIA ON THE MAEANDER SITE PLAN

1. Sanctuary of
   Artemis
2. Agora
3. Byzantine wall
4. Market Basilica
5. Odeon
6. Structure with
   heating system
7. Theatre
8. Temple of Athena
9. Tumuli
10. Theatron
11. City walls
12. Stadium
13. City Gymnasium
14. Mosque
15. Lethaios
    Gymnasium
16. Necropoleis

Panel from the frieze of the Temple of Artemis Leucophryene (İstanbul Archaeological Museums)

differed significantly. While a double row of columns surrounded the Arte-mision at Ephesus (making it dipteral), Hermogenes extended the roof at Magnesia far beyond the walls of the narrow cella, but omitted the inner row of columns. It is, therefore, described as pseudo-dipteral. This may seem like a mere technicality, but the architect created an effect of open space, light and air. The decision to build only the outer peristyle also allowed the citizens of Magnesia to complete their great temple relatively quickly. Akurgal describes it as "one of the most important works in the history of art." He stated: "Its monumental dimensions and magnificent 200 m. long frieze also place it among the major buildings of antiquity."

The frieze represents the Amazonomachy, the battle between Greek warriors and the Amazons, a subject proclaiming Greek superiority and

The ruins of the Temple of Artemis today: (L) Fallen column drums on the stylobate;
(R) The pediment reassembled on the ground

giving sculptors the opportunity to convey muscular bodies in violent action, expressed by strong diagonals. With many capitals stored on the site and the shafts of columns lying on the stylobate, a partial re-erection would be possible, but with the frieze dispersed between Istanbul, Paris and Berlin the opportunities for a full restoration are limited.

The **Altar of Artemis** stood in front of the temple. It followed the model of the altar of Zeus at Pergamon, but on a smaller scale.

The Agora (2)

Hermogenes was probably also the architect of the Ionic Stoa of the Agora. The reerected columns give an idea of the elegant surroundings built for commercial activities. The small prostyle **Temple of Zeus Sosipolis** (Zeus, Savior of the city), which once stood on the west side of the Agora, has also been attributed to Hermogenes. It follows the proportions he advocated: For example, the height of the columns is exactly nine and a half times their lower diameter. A restored version has been placed in the Pergamon Museum in Berlin. Nothing of it remains on site today.

The **Market Basilica (4)** built in the second century CE, with a nave, aisles and apse, became a church in the Byzantine era. Its most intriguing

A reconstructed Ionic Stoa of the Agora reflected in the water of the winter floods

feature is a distinctly pagan pillar capital, one of a series, representing the adventures of Scylla, a beautiful naiad, turned into a monster by a rival in love. In Homer's *Odyssey*, when Odysseus sailed past her cave, he came close enough for her to devour some of his sailors, thus avoiding the worse fate of losing his ship in the whirlpool of Charybdis opposite her abode. The story gave us the epithet for impossible choices: "sailing between Scylla and

Pillar capital illustrating the story of Scylla

Charybdis" This capital combines vigorously curling acanthus leaves with a muscular male and a voluptuous female figure. Recent work in the Agora has included the restoration of a large latrine, with mosaic wall decorations. Leaving the precinct and walking to the west of the temple, you will pass the site of an unexcavated **Hellenistic Theatre (7)** to the north and reach an unfinished **Roman Theatre (10)**. From there, continue north about 500 m. north to the site of the Stadium.

The Stadium (12)

In 2011, the Turkish archaeologist Orhan Bingöl began excavating the Stadium that lies almost a kilometer northwest of the Temple of Artemis. At the time of writing, his team has cleared most of its theatron (the curved end), revealing what promises to be the best-preserved Stadium in Anatolia. While many stadia became convenient stone quarries for future generations, this one has been preserved by the deep deposits of silt from the Maeander River that overwhelmed the classical city. Since the **Hellenistic city walls (11)** pass well beyond this structure, enclosing a much larger area than the Byzantine walls, the potential exists of many more discoveries. If funding is available the whole Stadium and many other buildings can be brought to light.

The west end of the recently discovered Stadium

Athena Temple

PRIENE

As we approach Priene from the flat valley of the Maeander River we see a dark green band of trees on a broad terrace below the craggy cliffs of Mount Mycale. They mark the site of the splendid city that prospered and gradually declined over a period of eight centuries. It sloped gently to the south offering a prospect over fertile land towards its harbour and distant mountains. A spring flowing from the rock behind the city provided copious water. The perimeter was easy to fortify, because the terrace comes to an abrupt edge where walls could be built with steep slopes below them. Above the cliffs, lies a higher plateau, known as Teloneia. This Acropolis, also defended by walls, served as a military garrison and an ultimate refuge from invading enemies. The city whose ruins we see today is not the original Priene, which existed long before the present one, 6 km. to the southwest, near the ancient harbour of Naulochos. Archaeologists have found no evidence of Bronze Age habitation among the remains of the new Priene, or even buildings of the archaic period.

Priene sited on a broad terrace below Mount Mycale. View from the road from Miletus to the southwest

Their absence confirms that the site was unoccupied until the new city appeared there in the fourth century. Equally, no trace of the earlier town has been discovered in the valley below, not even shards of pottery; the constantly shifting silt and waters of the river have obliterated them.

Early history

We know nothing of Priene in the so-called "Dark Age"; Homer never mentions its name. According to Strabo, Priene was originally founded by Athenians and Thebans, who migrated to Ionia in the twelfth century BCE after the Dorians moved into Greece. While we lack clues to the physical form of the first city, documentary evidence reveals its political role in the region, particularly as a leading member of the Ionian League. During the Archaic Era, the city defended itself against a series of invaders and was sometimes subjugated by them. The ambitious kings of Lydia, with their capital at Sardis, sought to bring neighboring Greek cities under its control. King Gyges attacked Priene in the seventh century, but was forced to repel assaults on his own kingdom by Cimmerians, a people from an area south east of the Black Sea. With the help of Assyria he defeated them in 630 but soon died. His son Ardys captured Priene but the city soon regained independence. In the sixth century, Alyattes, the grandson of Gyges, determined to surpass his ancestors, laid siege to Priene. By this time the leader of Priene was Bias, celebrated throughout the Greek world as one of the seven sages. Bias organized the defense and managed to trick the Lydians into believing that his people had enough food to last a long time. Convinced by this ruse, Alyattes called off the siege. The next Lydian king, Croesus, famous for his wealth, came to the throne in 560 and gained control over the Ionian and Aeolian cities. He admired the Greeks; indeed he contributed to the repair of Greek shrines at Didyma and Delphi. He granted some autonomy to his subject cities but he demanded tribute from them.

The next dynasty of aggressive rulers to threaten Priene was Persian. The relative stability and independence that the citizens enjoyed under Croesus came abruptly to an end in 545/544 when the Persian king Cyrus began a campaign to bring the Ionian and Aeolian cities into his empire. His commander Mazares vanquished Priene and took some of the citizens into slavery. The city that had governed itself democratically came under the rule of satraps or governors appointed by the Persians. For half a century the

Prienians, reduced in numbers, languished under the Persian yoke. The Ionian League continued to unite the twelve cities, and, at their assembly in 499, Aristagoras the renegade satrap of Miletus boldly announced a plan to revolt against the Persians. Five years later Priene had gained enough strength to contribute twelve ships to a fleet assembled to engage the Persians in the battle of Lade. This naval battle proved disastrous for the Ionians, particularly for the Milesians whose city was destroyed by Persian forces. Priene did not share the same fate, but continued to suffer under Persian rule.

The Panionion

On the northern slope of Mount Mycale, within the territory of Priene, lay the Panionion, a religious site dedicated to Poseidon Heliconius, and sacred to all the people of Ionia. The history of this sacred place goes back to the seventh century when Carians inhabited the area. The Prienians competed with the Samians for the right

Coin minted in Priene, *ca.* 290-250 BCE with the trident of Poseidon, the city's symbol, enclosed in a "Maeander circle" and the head of Athena, the patron Goddess of the city. (asiaminorcoins.com)

to manage the sanctuary and remained at odds with them for centuries; but generally Priene appointed one of its own citizens as chief priest and organized an annual meeting and festival each year, after the harvest had been gathered in. They built a fine Ionic temple there in about 540 BCE, of which no vestige survives. In honour of Poseidon, coins minted in Priene carried his symbol a trident. The labyrinthine emblem forming a circle around it symbolized the river Maeander.

The new Priene

The Maeander showed little respect for human settlements; by the fifth century BCE its shifting waters seriously eroded the edges of Priene. By the fourth century the citizens found conditions so untenable in that they decided to leave the place where their ancestors had lived for seven hundred years and move to higher ground. Making a virtue of necessity, they set out to build an ideal city on a more favourable site. No account of their deliberations survives, but the results speak for themselves. Priene,

Reconstruction of a fountain below the temple

conceived as a perfect whole, is unique in the Hellenic world: It combined Greek idealism with the most up-to-date planning principles developed by the Milesian city planner Hippodamus a hundred and fifty years earlier. Indeed, Priene comes closer than any other city to Aristotle's description of the ideal polis in his *Politics* written at about the time of Priene's design. Its relatively small size of about 50,000 – 60,000 inhabitants, its self-sufficiency and sense of architectural order, accord with Aristotelian principles.

Maussollos, the Persian Satrap of Halikarnassos, probably played a role in the decision to move Priene and encouraged its citizens to aim for high architectural standards. Pytheos, the architect of the famous Mausoleum of Halikarnassos that commemorated Maussollos at his death in 353 BCE designed the Temple of Athena Polias ("goddess of the city") at Priene. It seems likely that Pytheos also masterminded the planning of the entire city. Artemisia, the widow of King Maussollos and Queen of Caria, wishing to offer support to Priene, may have released Pytheos from her service to work there. The city plan embodies the system of harmonious proportions advocated by the Ionian philosopher Pythagoras and embraced by Pytheos: The dimensions of the residential blocks conformed to a ratio of 3:4; civic buildings employed the ratio 2:3 while, in the temple, the proportion of 1:2 prevails. On this virgin site, no existing structures stood in the way of the plan; only the irregularities of the ground intervened with the designer's ideal conception.

The advanced water supply system at Priene demonstrates superior urban infrastructure. A prolific spring behind the east side of the Acropolis provided all the water the Prienians needed. It ran via an aqueduct into a reservoir and from there in pipes throughout the city. It even flowed from fountains that ornamented public places, a rare luxury in Greek settlements. However, no public latrines or domestic bathrooms have been found.

When Alexander the Great marched into Priene in 334 BCE, while besieging Miletus, he was pleased to be welcomed by the citizens and to discover a fine temple dedicated to Athena Polias under construction. Taking the role of a generous benefactor, he offered to pay for its completion. According to an inscription in the British Museum, he dedicated the temple personally to the goddess. After the death of Alexander, control of the region passed between his feuding successors; Priene suffered attacks by king Ariarathes of Cappodocia and Attalos II of Pergamon, who inflicted damage on the temple. The wars between Mithridates VI of Pontus and the Romans in the first century BCE also impacted Priene. Despite the effects of power struggles caused by outside forces, the urban life of Priene and its architectural development continued. However, the repeated attacks may explain a two hundred year delay in the completion of the temple.

The Roman and Byzantine eras

By the time that Priene passed to the Roman Empire in 133 BCE it had grown into a rich and stately city, but, lacking plentiful goods to trade or a major port, it could not compete in wealth with Ephesus and Miletus. Under Roman rule Priene neither expanded nor received grandiose civic monuments in its centre; it remained intrinsically Greek. The Roman propylons at the entrance to the Temple of Athena Polias made the only exception. The temple, however, was converted to the worship of Augustus as well as Athena.

In the Byzantine era Priene became the seat of a bishop. The Christians built a church in a constricted space on the south side of the theatre; the remains of a synagogue show that a small Jewish community coexisted with them. When Arab raids in the sixth century CE began to threaten Priene, the Byzantine authorities constructed a fortress to the southeast of the Agora but their defenses could not forestall abandonment of the city at the end of the seventh century. Priene revived again in the middle of the tenth century under the new name Samson. When Catholic crusaders in the disastrous Fourth Crusade occupied Constantinople in 1204 they attempted to create a Latin Empire in the formerly Greek Byzantine territories. One of their factions occupied Priene, but failed to hold it for more than a few years. The Turks gained control of the city in 1295, not long before the last citizens migrated to more prosperous places.

Rediscovery of Priene and archaeology

English traders from Smyrna rediscovered Priene in 1673, but almost a century passed before any serious record was made of the ruins. In 1769 the Society of Dilettantes in London sent James Stuart and Nicholas Revett to Ionia to record the remaining architecture of the Greek cities there. They had previously commissioned the two architects to measure and draw the buildings of the Acropolis in Athens bringing about publication of the highly influential *The Antiquities of Athens* in 1762. A second volume entitled *The Antiquities of Ionia* (1769-97) included drawings of Priene. More than a century passed before Carl Humann and Reinhard Kekule von Stradonitz, directors of the Department of Antiquities at the Berlin Museums, began systematic excavations at Priene. In 1896, after Humann's death, Theodor Wiegand assumed the responsibility. He described the city as "the Pompeii of Asia Minor". Little excavation has been carried out recently, but scholarly investigations have continued, notably a study of the sculpture from the Temple of Athena Polias. In 2009 Nadine Burkhardt of Goethe University, Frankfurt am Main and Mark Wilson, director of the Asia Minor Research Centre in Antalya, excavated the house that had been converted for use as a synagogue and gained new knowledge of its history and its form.

The urban form and character of Priene

Priene offers a fascinating dichotomy: The site is far from level, but a rectangular grid imposes a rigorous geometry on it. The design draws richness, like San Francisco, from the conflict between the rational grid and the natural topography. It combines a powerful sense of order with subtle juxtapositions of architectural elements. Rejecting the axial symmetry that governs placement of temples in many Roman cities, the planners carefully disposed the religious and public buildings according to Greek aesthetic principles. They sited the Agora, the Temple of Athena, the sanctuary of Zeus, the Bouleuterion, the theatre and other civic buildings in response to the opportunities of the terrain and the demands of urban life.

The six major streets, about 6 m. wide, ran from east to west; the slope required many of the 15 narrower streets at right angles to them to be stepped, making the passage of carriages impossible. Priene consisted of 80 insulae or blocks, with 8 houses to an insula and public or religious buildings occupying one or two insulae.

Hellenistic Priene. The Lower Gymnasium and Stadium stand close to the walls in the foreground; the Agora occupies the centre; above it, the Temple of Athena commands a prominent site to the left and the theatre is carved into the hillside to the right. The sanctuary of Demeter appears centrally, just below the trees under the cliffs. The grid of streets adapts to the sloping terrain

In the subtle manner typical of the Greeks, the pattern of streets and open spaces encouraged people to approach major buildings obliquely, so that the architecture would be gradually revealed; changes in level added variety to the experience of walking through the urban centre. An east-west road, running almost the whole length of the city, and originally passing through the Agora acted as the major artery. After the addition of the Sacred Stoa to the Agora, traffic no longer passed through it. A north-south street near the eastern end of the Agora led uphill to the theatre.

Visiting Priene

As you approach across the Maeander Plain, from the south west you will enjoy superb views of the ancient city in the distance. If possible, stay overnight in the nearby village of Güllübahçe so that you can walk up to the site early in the morning before any tour bus arrives. Enjoy entering through the walls and go straight to the Temple of Athena Polias, the focal point of the city. From there, following the plan, you can easily find your way, in a few minutes, to the Agora, the theatre and the residential

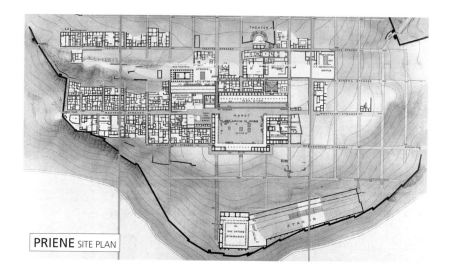

districts. I strongly recommend taking the trail up through the wooded slope to the sanctuary of Demeter where you can sense the sacred character of the place, and also descending by a steep and indistinct path to the Lower Gymnasium and the Stadium. You are likely to be alone in both areas. The original city, built of marble from a nearby quarry, was completely urban and almost devoid of trees. Today pine trees grow throughout most of the site, transforming it into a shady, verdant environment. This makes your visit comfortable even in hot weather.

The city walls

The defensive walls of Priene still stand in several places, though not to their original height. You will walk up steeply beside a well-preserved stretch as you enter the site from Güllübahçe and pass the wall again at the exit, where a drawing shows a reconstruction of the gate flanked with square towers. Powerful remains of the walls can be seen at the end of the street leading west from the Agora, and below the Lower Gymnasium. These walls give a strong impression of their

The city walls

impregnability from the road to the south of the site. Adventurous visitors, willing to climb the steep mountainside can discover impressive remnants of fortifications on the east side of the Acropolis.

The Temple of Athena Polias

Five re-erected columns, standing against a dark cliff, proclaim the former magnificence of the Temple of Athena Polias. But, missing almost a quarter of their original height, they do not show the elegant proportions of the Ionic order. The stylobate, the well-preserved platform on which the temple stood, clearly conveys the siting and original size of the temple. Fragments of carved stone, scattered nearby on the ground, help us to imagine the precisely carved entablature and pediment. However to visualize it completely it is necessary to see elements of it in far-away museums and drawings by those who studied the evidence. The temple was designed in about 350 BCE by Pytheos, the architect of the

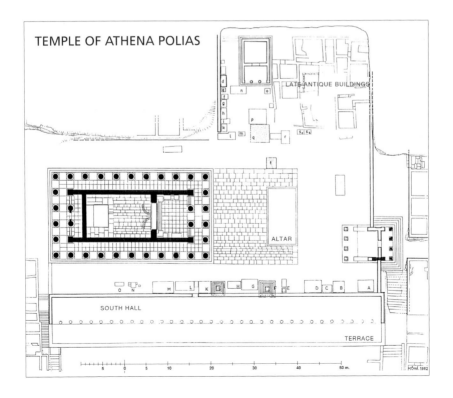

Temple of Athena Polias built in the mid-fourth century by architect Pytheos

Mausoleum at Halikarnassos. He had probably also designed the Temple of Zeus at Labraunda, commissioned by King Maussollos or his brother Idrieus. Skilled in sculpture as well as architecture, he developed a version of the Ionic order that proved highly influential. The first century BCE Roman architect and theorist Vitruvius studied a treatise written by Pytheos that no longer exists and praised his work. Indeed he based his own drawings of the Ionic order in his *Ten Books of Architecture* on designs by Pytheos. He wrote that this treatise, which included material on the education of architects, was in use as a design manual for two centuries. Vitruvius, in turn became an important source for architectural theory in the Italian Renaissance. Thus, details of the Temple of Athena Polias entered the vocabulary of European architecture in the Renaissance and prevailed in the Neoclassical Era. Rigorous proportions guided every aspect of the design. With a perisyle of eleven columns on the long sides and six on the ends, the architect came close to achieving a proportion of two to one in its length and breadth. Multiples of the attic foot (marginally less than the English foot) give order to the dimensions: the centres of the columns were twelve attic feet apart; the shafts of the columns, each with twenty-four flutes and subtle entasis, stood on molded bases resting on square plinths. They rose to the height of twelve times their smallest diameter to support the capitals and entablature. The stylobate was one hundred attic feet long.

Pytheos gave prominence to the temple by bolstering the edge of the terrace on which it stood with a high retaining wall of fine masonry, part

The stylobate of the Temple of Athena Polias from the southwest

of which still survives. Three steps of uniform height raised the stylobate above the terrace. A few fallen capitals with an egg and tongue motif on the echinus between the spiraling volutes, lie nearby; they still show the precision of their carving. The entablature exemplifies Pytheos's subtle manipulation of light and shade, texture and ornament. The architrave, in three plain bands, spans between the widely spaced columns; above it an egg and tongue molding, with a slim bead and reel border, makes the transition to boldly projecting dentils; above which a second egg and tongue molding, to a smaller scale, supports the plain band of the corona. Lions' heads serving as spouts for rainwater thrust out from the cyma (the upper part of the cornice); between them palmettes and lotus flowers decorate the curving surface. This cornice resembles an earlier one with lions' heads by Pytheos on the Mausoleum of Halikarnassos. He may have followed the precedent of a cornice on

The bead and reel border of the egg and tongue molding casts a shadow on the dentils above the architrave.

Recreation of the cult image of Athena Polias (from Carter)

the Artemision at Ephesos, but at Priene he showed a greater freedom in the elaborately swirling pattern.

The peristyle (the linear space between the columns and the cella wall) possessed an unusual feature, first developed by Pytheos in the Mausoleum at Halikarnassos. A series of coffers (recessed squares) containing low relief sculpture, ornamented its ceiling on all four sides. Worshippers, looking up, would have seen a sequence of powerful images, mostly scenes from the gigantomachy, the battle between the gods and the giants. In separate panels Athena, Zeus, Gaia, Hermes, Cybele, Aphrodite, Dionysus and Heracles engaged in struggle with giants. These depictions of violent combat seem to play the same role as the metopes in the frieze of the Parthenon in Athens. A few pieces of the coffer frames can be seen on the site, but the much-damaged sculpture is in the British Museum.

From the exterior, the two ends of the temple appeared similar but at the east end, an unusually deep pronaos with two columns between antae formed an antechamber to the cella. The shallower opisthodomos at the west end did not connect with the cella. Evidence of a bronze grill closing off this space suggests its use as a treasury. The original statue of Athena in the cella, of which no description survives, was replaced, in the second century BCE by a new one donated by Orophernes, king of Capadoccia who had lived in Priene as a youth. Affirming the strong affinity between Priene and Athens the new cult figure of Athena resembled, to a smaller scale, the vast cult statue by Phidias in the Parthenon of Athens. Similarly at Priene, Athena, wearing a helmet, stood with a shield and spear on her left side, holding a small figure, probably the winged victory goddess Nike, on her right arm. Pausanias described it with admiration in the second century CE; British archaeologists in the eighteenth century recovered part of the bronze covering to Nike's wings.

An earthquake destroyed the temple sending column drums rolling in all directions, some of them even as far as the residential street to the west. Other elements fell closer to the stylobate.

The Altar of Athena Polias

While the temple provided a house for Athena and a shelter for her cult image, public rituals of worship took place at an altar just to its east. Pillaged of stone by local people, little trace of it remains today, but artists and archaeologists in the eighteenth and nineteenth centuries found enough evidence to reconstruct its original appearance. They concluded that it resembled, on a smaller scale, the altar of Zeus at Pergamon. A flight of seven steps approached an offering table surrounded on three sides by walls adorned with figures, carved in high relief, framed by Ionic columns carrying a simple entablature. Richard Pullen, who visited the site in 1869, made sketches and employed a grid to locate findings accurately. His work helped Schrader and von Gurkan to make their reconstruction in the twentieth century. They believed that the sculpture on the east side represented a chorus of priestesses and maidens while, on the narrower south side, Apollo, accompanied by muses, played his lyre.

Some panels from a gigantomachy at the lower level survive in the Istanbul Archaeological Museums. The altar was probably built shortly after 158 BCE, long after the death of Pytheos, but Carter suggests the possibility that those who built it followed his design.

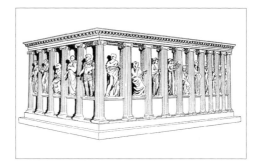

The altar of Athena (from Carter)

The Treasury, Stoa and Propylons in the Sanctuary of Athena

With the erection of additional buildings near the temple, the sanctuary of Athena gradually became more confined. The treasury, similar to ones at Delphi and Olympia, erected to the north of the altar, helped to define space, and in the second century BCE a stoa closed off the south side of the sacred precinct. Later, perhaps at the time when the temple was rededicated to Augustus the entrance from the Agora became formalized by the addition of a propylons aligned with the main street from the east, near the top of a flight of steps from the Agora. The placement of the Doric Stoa on the south side, which blocked the dramatic view of the temple from the Agora and did not open towards the temple, seems hard to explain. Perhaps its purpose was to offer a gathering place with a panoramic view to the south over the city. It may also have been built to provide a blank wall as a background to the many votive statues standing along the southern edge of the precinct.

The Agora

While the religious buildings in Priene commanded their own sacred precincts isolated from civic functions; the Agora served a mainly political function; it expressed the ideals of the citizens and provided for day to day administration. The Prytaneum (administrative offices) and Bouleuterion (council chamber) opened off the north-east corner of the Agora; generous stoas offered elegant surroundings and shelter for public ceremonies as well as informal meetings of citizens. A row of statues on imposing pedestals commemorated notable Prienians and an altar to Hermes, the messenger of the gods and the god of commerce, stood near the centre. In the early Hellenistic era the Agora covered only two insulae and a main road crossed its north side, but in the second century CE a benefactor commissioned an immensely long stoa, known as the Sacred Stoa, along the north side of the road, which was then closed to traffic. An arch spanned the entry to the Agora from the street.

When you stand in the middle of the Agora, you will see all along its

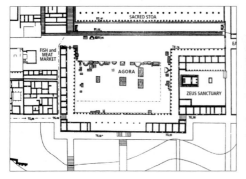

(L) Plan of Agora (R) The steps along the north side of the Agora

(L) Reconstructed view from the Agora to the Temple of Athena Polias
(R) The same view today. The Stoa built on the south side of the temple terrace in the second century obscured the view of the temple from the Agora. Today we can see the columns of the temple.

north side the remains of steps that rose to a promenade 116 m. long in front of the Sacred Stoa. Although designed in the Doric style, it embodied some Ionic elements. On the exterior, 49 Doric columns, fluted in the Ionic manner supported an entablature with an Ionic cornice above the traditional Doric frieze of triglyphs and metopes. Such eclecticism appeared occasionally in the Hellenistic era. Twenty-four Ionic columns divided the interior into two aisles and helped to support the wooden roof. A row of small rooms opening off the rear wall served civic purposes. Inscriptions carved into one of its walls stated that King Ariarathes VI of Cappadocia had donated this stoa to Priene. At the eastern end, two entrances led into the Bouleuterion, one at the lower level, the other via a flight of steps to the upper seats. Another doorway led into the court of the prytaneum. The stoas on the three other sides were in a more traditional Doric order. Only the one on the west side contained shops; directly behind it lay the market for foodstuffs, clothing and household goods. The central section of the South Stoa opened southwards to the view over the Lower Gymnasium, the Stadium and the valley beyond. Since the ground beneath it slopes downwards, it was raised up over a basement. The East Stoa backed onto the sanctuary of Zeus and separated that religious space from the civic Agora. While in most Greek cities the agoras were built with uniform architectural enclosures on level ground, this civic space in Priene stands out for its variations, with one stoa raised up as a stage for civic ceremonies, another acting as a belvedere with a prospect to the south.

Before the construction of the stoa on the southern side of the temple terrace, people looking diagonally north-west from the Agora could look up over the Sacred Stoa and see the Temple of Athena rising above it. From that vantage point, they would approach the temple indirectly. As they climbed the steps beside the retaining wall they would lose sight of it until they entered the temple precinct. With the richly ornamented altar in the foreground they would encounter it again, in its full glory, from a close viewpoint. Even today, with many buildings lost, and the site covered with pine trees, we can enjoy a rich sequence of experiences as we move from the Agora, to the temple.

The Temple of Olympian Zeus

The small Ionic temple of Olympian Zeus, stood in a precinct directly to the west of the Agora but was not connected to it; a roofed propylon made an entry from a street on the other side. Guided by an inscription, scholars first believed that this temple was dedicated to Asklepios, but recent evidence has confirmed that Zeus and Hera, whom the Prienians deeply revered, were worshipped here. Since the citizens gave priority to building their Temple of Athena, this one was only begun in the third century BCE; however, it was probably planned at the same time as the Agora. On its small west façade, two columns stood between antae ornamented with capitals. The details of the Ionic entablature appear similar to those of the Temple of Athena by Pytheos. The base of a pedestal in the cella is wide enough to have supported statues of both Zeus and Hera. The construction of a Byzantine fortress close to this temple, reusing much of its stone, made archaeological study difficult, but the restored stylobate indicates its size and position. A short section of the entablature displayed nearby, with lions' heads and a palmette motif, above the dentils, echo the design of the cornice of the Temple of Athena Polias.

Stylobate of the temple of Olympian Zeus

Part of the entablature with palmette and lion's head

The chapel of the Byzantine fortress, nave arcades and apse

The Prytaneum and the Bouleuterion

A sacred flame, dedicated to the goddess Hestia, burnt continuously in the hearth of the Prytaneum. This building, probably built at the same time as the Sacred Stoa, served as the official residence of the *prytaneis*, an elected committee of the boule that ran the city. Members of this group received free meals there. Arranged around a peristyle court, it possessed the character of a large Hellenistic house.

The *boule*, an elected city council, met in the Bouleuterion to make decisions for the day- to-day administration of Priene. This is one of the best-preserved buildings of its type; its "U" shaped seats convey an idea of a tightly packed assembly hall. Ten rows of seating on the east and west side, and sixteen rows on the north side rose from the central space

The Prytaneum

(L) The *bouleuterion*, interior restoration (R) The *bouleuterion* from the same viewpoint today

to accommodate 640 people. An altar at the centre, decorated with bulls' heads and garlands, signified the public duty to honour the gods. Pillars placed on the upper rows of seats supported a wooden roof. When the archaeologists first discovered the Bouleuterion, they found it beneath fire-damaged clay tiles that had protected it for centuries.

The Upper Gymnasium occupied one insula in a central position between the Bouleuterion and the eastern side of the theatre. In Hellenistic times it consisted of a palaestra and five rooms behind a stoa probably used for instruction of youths. The central one was open fronted, with two columns supporting its roof, like the better-preserved *ephebium* in the Lower Gymnasium. This complex changed substantially in the Roman period when a second palaestra and thermae were added. The heavy walls of the Roman thermae can be seen today, but little remains of the gymnasium.

The Church

The Christians of Priene built their church immediately south of the theatre, next to the Roman baths, on a site so constricted that its insertion caused a narrowing of the street. To make space for the apse, they cut into the massive west wall of the baths. Limited in funds, they reused materials from the temple precinct, including columns from the South Stoa, which had suffered earthquake damage. Eight pairs of columns, carrying arches, separated the nave from the aisles and supported a wooden roof. A later generation, perhaps with the intention of vaulting the interior, inserted rectangular piers between the columns; but no

(L) The nave of the church flanked by columns from Stoa south of the Temple of Athena Polias. (R) The ambo, decorated with vines, stands in the middle of the nave.

evidence of a collapsed vault exists. Since the ground to the west has not been excavated, we do not know whether the congregation entered in the customary way through a courtyard. From that side, two doors entered the narthex from which three openings gave access to the nave and aisles. At the east end of the nave, remains of the *synthronon*, the stepped stone seats for the clergy, can be seen in the apse. Part of the ambo, the raised pulpit for readings and sermons, still stands in the middle of the nave. On its sides, vine scrolls ornament the surfaces around niches; they recall Christ's words: "I am the vine; you are the branches". Fragments of posts and decorated panels of screens that separated the nave from the chancel also survive. It appears that plaster covered the walls and arches of the church; a few traces of frescoes have been found.

The Sanctuary of the Egyptian Gods

Only the base of an altar remains of the sanctuary of the Egyptian gods. However, inscriptions discovered there confirm that it marks a sacred place dedicated to Isis, Serapis and Anubis. They also assert that rites could not be performed there without a qualified Egyptian presiding. This pronouncement suggests that a group of Egyptian traders living in Priene worshipped here in an exclusive manner.

(T) The theatre set in the hillside (L) A marble seat for a dignitary

The Theatre

Priene possesses one of the best-preserved Hellenistic theatres in Turkey. Actors and musicians performed tragedies here, and before the construction of the Bouleuterion it served as venue for political meetings. A water clock, used to time speeches, still survives. Although only 15 of the original 47 rows of seating remain, the horseshoe-shaped cavea, carved into the hillside conveys the true character of a Greek theatre, beautifully related to its site. In the century after its construction, the performances took place in the orchestra; the proscenium, fronted with a row of Doric colums, and three doors provided a background. In the later Hellenistic period a stage was raised up, above the proscenium, so that the actors could play a more dominant role. The Romans widened the stage, moving back the Hellenistic wall behind it. The marble seats and thrones for dignitaries were not built until the second century BCE.

The Sanctuary of Demeter and Kore

An unmarked, indistinct path leads up the hillside to the northwest of the theatre. To find it, stand above the northwest corner of the church, facing the rocky cliff, and go up hill on a slight diagonal to the left. It passes between two piles of stones and continues among the trees to the

The sanctuary of Demeter

sanctuary of Demeter and Kore (her daughter Persephone). This was one of the first shrines in Priene; Demeter's early significance is shown in the emblem of an ear of wheat, celebrating her role in the harvest, on some of the city's earliest coins. Today, surrounded by pine trees and low walls, it is unlike the original site but, secluded from the rest of Priene, it possesses a haunting character. Like other places where these goddesses of agriculture and fertility were worshipped in the Hellenic world, this sanctuary differed from most temple sites. The entrance on the east side led into a long courtyard with an asymmetrical temple at the far end. Its Doric portico with widely spaced columns and no pediment opened into a cella of irregular shape with raised marble platforms along the walls on which offerings were placed. To the left of the portico a sunken pit with a wooden covering received libations of blood from sacrificed animals.

(L) The Lower Gymnasium and Stadium site from above
(R) The retaining walls for the Lower Gymnasium and Stadium from the road below

Today, a small pediment spans it at an odd angle. Just inside the entrance stood a stone altar on which the priestesses sacrificed animals as burnt offerings to the goddesses. Two statues of priestesses, one of marble, now in Istanbul, the other of bronze stood outside the gate; only their pedestals remain. Nearby on the slope below stood small houses for the priestesses; their walls are obscured by vegetation. In classical times this sanctuary offered an inspiring view of all Priene over its low south wall. Today you can just see the columns of the sanctuary of Athena. You can read a more detailed description of the ritual known as the *Thesmophoria* at a sanctuary of Demeter on p. 97 in the chapter on Pergamon.

The Lower Gymnasium

From the Agora, a path, partly in the form of stone steps, leads down the steep slope to the Lower Gymnasium. You will find a pile of soil from the excavations protruding from the southwestern corner of the Agora, whose flat top gives you a view over the lower part of the site. Immediately to the left you can make your way down. As you go, you will see the long, level area where athletes once competed in the Stadium. To the right, a spacious palaestra with rooms on two sides of it, provided for the education and exercise of Prienian youths. The lavish architecture of this facility, built in the late second century BCE demonstrates the prosperity of Priene at the time. An inscription states that a citizen named Moschion donated funds to help with its construction. Finely detailed Doric stoas not only surrounded the palaestra, but also stretched almost 200 m. on a level terrace above the stepped Stadium seating. To counter the steepness of the slope, buttressed retaining walls, holding back tons of fill made it possible to provide the flat ground needed for the palaestra and Stadium.

(L) Marble basins and a lion's head spout. (R) The floor of the ephebium with two column bases.

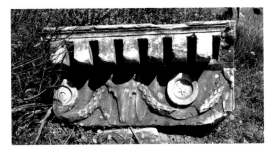

A piece of the bucranium frieze of a stoa.

Starting blocks in the Stadium

Part of the north wall of the gymnasium, hacked out of the cliff behind and faced with enormous blocks of stone, is still high enough to convey a sense of the space in the five rooms in front of it. At the left hand end, in the place where the athletes bathed, we can see marble basins in their original positions. One surviving lion's head spout reveals how the water flowed into the basins, while a channel carved into the stone paved floor, shows its disposal. Two lower basins served as footbaths. Athletes anointed their bodies with olive oil in one room and wrestlers coated themselves with sand in another. The largest room, fronted by two columns served as the *ephebium* where boys received their education. The bases of two columns still stand in its open front. A *bucranium* (bull's scull) and garland frieze ornamented the entablature of the stoas. At the western end of the Stadium, stone blocks mark the starting line for races.

Residential areas of Priene

Priene provides a well-known example of design taking advantage of passive solar energy. The principal rooms of virtually all the houses faced south through a columned portico onto a courtyard, so that the low winter sun would penetrate, while the overhanging roof shaded people from the summer sun. It seems that the planners of the city regulated the size of dwellings at an early stage. Houses were almost uniformly small, suggesting that the Prienians frowned on ostentation. Some of the houses still offer vignettes of courtyards from which columned porticoes led to secluded rooms. Walls are high enough to give an impression of their spaces, but few columns remain. Typically, eight two-story houses with three rooms on the ground floor fitted into each insula. On the main streets,

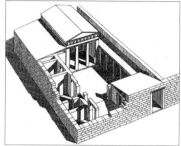

(L) The main residential street west of the Agora, looking eastwards
(R) A typical, south-facing courtyard house

small shops fronted some of them. Doors from side streets opened into the houses on the ends of the blocks, while passages between the shops led into the ones in the middle. When the houses were first built in the fourth century the rooms only occupied the north side of each court, but in time residents sacrificed courtyard space to add extra rooms on the opposite side. A few houses were enlarged in the late Hellenistic or Roman era. In one case a house in the northwestern residential area (designated as house 33) which originally conformed to the standard size went through two phases of enlargement finally filling an entire insula.

The houses generally included the *prostas*, an anteroom open to the court on one side, leading to the *oikos*, the principal living space. This was a lofty room about 4.5 meters square and 2.4 meters high, illuminated through the large doorway. It contained a hearth and opened to a windowless room on its north side. There is some evidence that this small, dark room often served as a weaving workshop where women at a loom must have strained their eyes, as they worked by the light of oil lamps. The *andron*, the reception room where men entertained their friends to banquets, opened off the north side of the *prostas*. This was large enough to hold three *klinai*, couches which could accommodate two people each. The foot of a staircase has been found in the *oikos* of some houses, leading to the assumption that most houses were two stories high. The second story may have provided women's accommodation. However, no houses with an upper floor have survived. The rooms on the southern side of the courts probably served as storerooms and in some cases as workshops for craftsmen or as shops. These opened directly to the streets. Although pipes distributed water

(L) A water distribution point near the east gate (R) Menorah flanked by two peacocks, Milet Museum

throughout the city, no evidence has been found of advanced sanitation; only one washbasin has been found in a house in Priene. Archaeologists have found no obvious bathrooms; they have assumed that the residents used pots that were carried away and emptied by slaves.

Near the end of the street running west of the Agora, a house has been identified as the one where Alexander stayed while visiting Priene in 334 BCE. A statue of him, now in Berlin, suggests that the house was turned into a place of worship in his honour. To its west, near the city wall, a large house (identified as House 22) appears to have served as a religious sanctuary. Its large court and spacious rooms, as well as a sacrificial table suggest its use as a shrine, but no clues have linked it to a particular deity. Nearby, just inside the west gate a small shrine, probably dedicated to the mother goddess Cybele, occupied a small irregularly shaped enclosure. It contained a bust now in the Istanbul Archaeological Museums.

A low relief carving of a menorah flanked by two peacocks and a palm leaf, found in House 24, suggested that this house was used as a Jewish place of worship. Recent archaeology has confirmed that the dwelling was converted into a synagogue in the late antique period. The series of changes made to the structure cannot be accurately dated, but it appears that final form was like a small basilica with a short nave and aisles, entered from a side street. It contained a bench along the north aisle and a rectangular niche for the Torah. Other crudely carved menorahs have also been found.

Ionic Stoa

MILETUS

During the Archaic Era, Miletus led the Hellenic world in both intellectual achievement and trade. As the Greeks of Western Anatolia contended with the Persian Empire, the Milesians played a pivotal role in events that affected all Ionia. Destroyed, rebuilt and finally abandoned, its ruins rise out of waterlogged ground or bare hillsides to haunt us.

Bronze Age Miletus

Miletus was the first city in Anatolia to be colonized by Greeks. In about 1700 BCE, in the Middle Bronze Age, Minoans from Crete were attracted by its ideal situation on a defensible peninsula with four natural harbours and good agricultural land. This place was known to Hittites as Millawanda. The surrounding area was sparsely populated, probably by a simple farming people of Anatolian origin. According to historians writing centuries later and basing their knowledge on legends, a Minoan named Miletus, who had fallen out with the powerful King Minos, fled there and gave his name to the city he founded. Since little archaeological evidence of Minoan occupation of the site was found, scholars tended to doubt that Minoans had settled there. A small amount of pottery could easily be explained by trade. But in the mid-1990s German archaeologists Barbara and Wolf-Dietrich Niemeier, excavating on Stadium Hill, found conclusive evidence of occupation by Cretans. This included walls built in a Minoan technique, pottery and kilns of a Minoan type as well as ritual objects, some examples of Linear A writing, and fragments of frescoes representing a lily and part of a griffin in the manner of those found in Cretan palaces. Another clue is that the Minoans chose, where possible, to build on promontories beside a good harbour, just like the site of Miletus. Furthermore the only other place named Miletus is on the island of Crete. It appears that archaeology has confirmed stories once dismissed as myths.

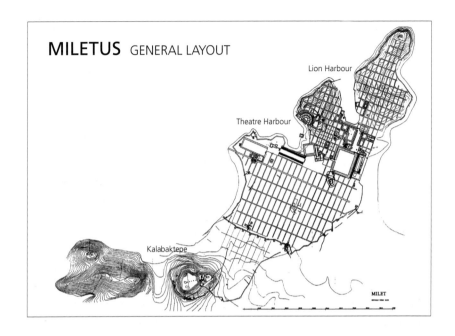

MILETUS GENERAL LAYOUT

Lion Harbour

Theatre Harbour

Kalabaktepe

MILET

The peninsula was almost a kilometer wide allowing plenty of space for urban growth. Since it was in a river valley, it also offered contact with the hinterland. For a few centuries it provided the Cretans with an important trading link between the Aegean and nearby Asian cities. But around 1470 BCE Minoan civilization went into rapid decline: Its palaces and its naval power were destroyed. Myceneans then occupied Minoan territory, including the city of Miletus. It is hard to determine the exact form of the Mycenean settlement; not even the foundations of a megaron (principal room of a palace) have been found. Later building on the same site has obliterated the evidence. However, pottery and other artifacts survive to convey the idea of a Mycenean city thriving for more than two centuries. Some examples can be seen in the Miletus Museum.

The success of this Mycenean foothold in Asia contributed to its downfall. Rulers of the powerful Hittite Kingdom, with its capital at Hattusha in central Anatolia, resented the Hellenic presence on the landmass they dominated, and they sacked Miletus in *ca.* 1317 BCE. However, the Myceneans built a citadel on nearby Kalabak Hill. It appears that in the fourteenth century possession of Miletus slipped back and forth between

Hittites and Myceneans. Around 1200 both the Hittite Empire and the Mycenean civilization collapsed, leaving this excellent site open for new settlers from Greece.

Emergence from the Dark Age and Milesian Colonization

The Greeks who migrated from Attica to the region of Miletus called themselves Ionians before they left the mainland. According to legends on which later historians based their stories, they were led by Neleus, the son of Kodros, King of Athens. They were said to have been guided across the Aegean by their patron god Apollo in the guise of a dolphin. Their first act would have been to build an open-air altar so that they could make sacrifice to him and give thanks for their safe arrival. These colonists, who named their new land Ionia, were probably joined by people from other parts of Greece, but a strong bond endured between Athenians and Milesians. The similarity between Athenian and Ionian dialects supports this idea. The area was previously occupied by a small population of Carians, a people speaking an Indo-European language, who had migrated there at about the same time as the Myceneans. The story told by Herodotus that the Ionians slaughtered the Carian men and married their wives is disputed by scholars today.

Of all the cities of the Hellenic world, Miletus founded the most colonies: Sparta was responsible for only one. Megara established colonies both in Sicily and on the Bosphorus, most notably Byzantium and Chalkedon. Athens founded about eight, but Miletus eclipsed all others by launching at least forty-five. The earliest of them, colonized no later than 756 BCE, were Sinope and Trapezous, now the major cities of Sinop and Trabzon on the south coast of the Black Sea.

Greek colonization did not generally begin with conquest, nor did it involve the subjugation and ruling of vassal states from the mainland. Colonies were independent and self-sufficient, with cultural ties to their mother cities. Miletus, a significant trading hub in the eastern Aegean, launched expeditions to search for ideal sites. They sought territory where the indigenous people, living nearby, welcomed trading partners and were not hostile to an influx of Greeks. In many cases the inhabitants were semi-nomadic people, who welcomed a market for wool, leather and meat from their flocks that they could trade for manufactured goods. The Milesians tended to select sites such as islands or peninsulas that could easily be fortified. Each colony was founded by an *oikist*, a leader who after consulting the oracle at Didyma searched for an ideal site with navigable water, a defensible position, and a potential for trade with friendly neighbors. He was responsible for planning the town and for organizing the city's government and administration. Connection with the metropolis, the mother city, was vital. Indeed this bond was often symbolized, at the founding of a colony, by the carrying of a sacred flame from the hearth of the metropolis. In many of the colonies, as in Miletus, the people revered Apollo as their patron god.

Most of the Milesian colonies lay to the north, on the Pontos Euxeinos (Black Sea) or on its approaches through the Hellespont and the Propontis (Sea of Marmara.) They peacefully coexisted with two powerful colonies of Megara, Chalkedon (founded 676 BCE) and Byzantium (founded 660 BCE), which exercised control of the Bosphorus. It is easy to imagine rivalry and occasional strife between the Milesian and Megaran colonies, particularly as Megara had Dorian origins, but mutual benefits probably prevailed over the urge to fight. Colonies became valuable trading partners for Miletus which imported flax, timber, metals and fruit as well as luxury goods, and traded pottery made from good local clay, furniture, olive oil and wine. The most valuable exports were textiles, particularly purple cloth coloured with Tyrian purple dyes made from rotting mollusks. In the later days of Milesian commerce, this cloth was particularly prized by the Byzantine court in Constantinople. The colonies also played another role in the fortunes of Miletus. After the city was destroyed by the Persians in 498, culturally linked citizens of her colonies were ready to repopulate and help rebuild their mother city.

The Archaic Period

In the Archaic period Miletus flourished as a centre of trade. With limited arable land, the Milesians were obliged to import grain and, as they became wealthy, they acquired goods from many distant places. Their trading partners were far flung and illustrious. They had close relationships with their Ionian neighbor Erythrai (Ildırı), 120 kilometers to the northwest, with the Cycladic island of Paros, Eritrea on the large island of Euboea, and the rich city of Sybaris in *Magna Graecia* (southern Italy).

Philosophy and Science

The far-flung trade enjoyed by Milesians exposed them to other cultures and ideas. Their traders returned from Egypt and Mesopotamia with better knowledge of astronomy and new inventions that could enrich their lives. The wealth of Miletus made it possible for some citizens to devote themselves to intellectual pursuits; indeed the city became the birthplace of Greek philosophy and the closely related discipline of natural science. The Milesian **Thales** (*ca.* 624 -*ca.* 546) has been called the "first philosopher" and the "father of science". While his predecessors looked for explanations to life's mysteries in mythology, he tried to understand natural phenomena through observation and reason. His use of the gnomon, an astronomical instrument invented in Babylonia that shows variations in the path of the sun, suggests the broad range of his inquiry. We know of his work only through Aristotle, who revered him; none of his original writings have survived.

Following in the footsteps of Thales, **Anaximander** (*ca.* 610-546 BCE) developed a theory that the earth, suspended at the centre of the universe, was a cylinder surrounded by the other heavenly bodies. He believed that it was originally mostly covered with water and that all life, including human life emerged from the sea. Anaximander travelled widely enough to make the first known map of the Mediterranean, and could be hailed as the world's first geographer. While in Egypt, he developed a mathematical method for calculating the height of a pyramid. He also explained the concept of infinity. **Anaximenes** (585-528 BCE), a student of Anaximander, continued the work of the older philosopher but arrived at different conclusions. He concluded that air, rather than water, was the essential material of the cosmos. He conceived of the earth as a thin disc floating on a cushion of air, with the heavenly bodies circling around it. **Hekataios**, writing in the late sixth century, was involved with mythology but also continued in the Milesian scientific tradition. He sailed to many parts of the Mediterranean, recording what he saw and making major improvements to Anaximander's maps. He was admired for his detailed descriptions of cities.

An enlightening BBC program by Michael Goldfarb sheds further light on Milesian philosophers and their place in the world. It has been archived at: https://soundcloud.com/michael-goldfarb-1/faith-without-god-prog1

Lydian and Persian Conquests

In the sixth century BCE, Miletus stood out as the leading city in the Greek world, surpassing Athens both in prosperity and intellectual achievement. However, it was threatened by powerful neighbors. Miletus possessed the military strength to resist an attack from King Gyges of Lydia and used diplomatic skill to make a peace treaty with his son Alyattes. However, in 585 BCE his successor, King Croesos, fabled for his richness in gold, took all of the Greek cities of Aeolis and Ionia into his Empire. In 547, when Croesus attacked the Persians and was defeated by them, Miletus, along with the other Greek cities of Ionia, fell under Persian rule.

The Milesians persuaded the Persians to let them practice their own religion and maintain their culture. However, they were a proud and independent people who resented the heavy taxation and the despotism of the satraps imposed by the Persians to govern them. In the late sixth century, Miletus became a pivotal source of opposition to Persian rule and suffered the consequences. The story of the Ionian Revolt which also affected other cities is told in the introduction. In 494/3 after the naval battle of Lade off the coast, which destroyed the Greek fleet, the Persians besieged Miletus by sea and from the land. By this time defensive walls entirely surrounded the city, so the Persians had to deploy sappers and siege engines to breach the fortifications. The length of the siege is unknown, but the attackers prevailed. The Persian King Darius, determined to avenge the Milesian insurrection, massacred all the men and enslaved the women and children. He forced a few survivors to march hundreds of miles to Susa and settled them near the Persian Gulf. He burnt the whole city, pulling down the defensive walls and any masonry that still stood. Only a few fragments of archaic Miletus remain, notably a marble lion now in Berlin. Vanessa Gorman, author of Miletus, the Ornament of Ionia, wrote that after the Persian destruction, Miletus was "reestablished by the same society that inhabited it immediately before the destruction." After studying all the available texts, as well as archaeological evidence, she concluded:

" ...everything we do know confirms the literary accounts. Miletus was a great commercial centre, a trading power, a mighty metropolis, swollen with inhabitants who shared in its remarkable opulence. From this height, the city fell into complete disaster, sufficient to wipe it from the face of the earth. But that was not to be. The Milesians returned and rebuilt, and characteristically they did so in a manner that demonstrated their progressive attitude and their confidence in the restoration of their previous prosperity" (Gorman 212-13)

Citizens of Milesian colonies, who held the values of their mother city, and some residents, who had been absent when their city was razed, returned to rebuild it from the ground up and to reestablish its civic life and trade.

The Classical Period

The plan of Miletus, as it was rebuilt after the city's destruction by the Persians in 494, is famous. Attributed to the Milesian architect, philosopher and city planner **Hippodamus**, it has been regarded as the archetype of rational city planning. Recent discoveries prove that the grid plan actually appeared earlier in several Greek cities. Even the archaic city of Miletus had been built on a grid, but Hippodamus received credit for this type of urban design because he wrote a treatise on it which convinced Aristotle to name him as the "father of city planning". It seems likely that as a young man he assisted in the design of Miletus and made his experience the basis of theories. Subsequently, in the mid-fifth century, when writings had made him famous, Pericles of Athens commissioned him to create a plan for Piraeus, the port of Athens. At the end of the century, according to Strabo, he planned the city of Rhodes.

Hippodamus believed that the ideal population for a city was about 50,000 including women, children and slaves. He divided the 10,000 adult men into three classes: artisans, farmers and soldiers. He recommended setting out an orthogonal grid of streets some of which were designated as wider principal thoroughfares. All buildings should be aligned with the streets. This pattern was to be interrupted by generous spaces for civic and religious buildings; residences would be placed in separate zones and oriented to the south to benefit from solar energy. As the plan shows, all the streets in Miletus except the Sacred Way and one leading south to the Sacred Gate were equal in width. In Priene, laid out after the publication of his treatise, a few principal streets are wider. In Miletus ample space was allowed for civic and religious use; indeed the South Agora, built after the northern one, was the largest in the Hellenic world. Hippodamus possessed other expertise: His study of weather conditions earned him credit as the first scientific meteorologist. He also argued that people should be rewarded for useful inventions, thus anticipating patent law.

Miletus, reviving phoenix-like after its ruin, must have been a splendid city--Herodotus characterized it as "the ornament of Ionia"--but it had lost the preeminence it enjoyed in the Archaic Era. The destruction in 510 BCE of Sybaris, where Milesian fabrics had been in high demand, reduced trade and piracy made the seas more dangerous. Furthermore, the rise of Athens created serious competition.

From the Persian Wars to the Peloponnesian War

The wars between Persia and Athens (490-466 BCE) and the formation in 478 BCE of the Delian League made a deep impact on the fortunes of Miletus (See Introduction p. 17-19). King Darius's desire for revenge against Athens for supporting Miletus in its revolt against his rule ended in failure. The subsequent union of Greek cities around the Aegean and Black Sea, under the leadership of Athens, led to the virtual collapse of Persian power. In 478 BC, with the help of the Milesians, the Athenians vanquished the Persians on the slopes of Mount Mycale near Miletus. In 470, after the Athenians destroyed two hundred Persian triremes at Eurymedon on the Mediterranean coast of Anatolia, the Greek cities regained their freedom from Persian domination. However, the disastrous Peloponnesian War between Athens and Sparta helped the Persians to regain their power.

When this war broke out in 431 BCE, Miletus supported Athens, but, before long, the Athenians demanded higher taxes on their trade, causing the Milesians to turn against them. To make matters worse, Alcibiades, the Athenian general who changed sides in the conflict, helped the Spartans to build up a navy and deployed it to prevent Milesian colonies from shipping grain to Athens. Alcibiades used Miletus as the Spartan naval base in Ionia, and when Athens was defeated in 404 BCE he betrayed the Milesians to the Persians. Once again they became subjects of the Persian Empire.

Alexander the Great and the Hellenistic Era

Sixty years later, Alexander the Great launched his campaign to vanquish the Persians and to create his own empire. After crossing the Hellespont in 334, winning the battle of Granicus and offering sacrifice at Troy, he moved rapidly south taking all the cities he encountered until he met opposition at Miletus. The Persians had rebuilt the fortifications and offered stiff resistance, but Alexander, blockading the harbour with his ships to prevent food and reinforcements from arriving, used siege engines to breach the walls. Few Persians survived the invasion, but he offered the Greek population clemency because of their past loyalty to Athens. Although forced to pay heavy taxes and to live under a Macedonian garrison, Miletus became a relatively free Greek city again.

In 323 BCE, when Alexander died, his generals, known as the Diadochi, vied for control of his empire and eventually divided it into three regions. At first, Western Anatolia was ruled by Antigonus, but after the battle of Issus it fell to Lysimachus and then to the Seleucids. During the Hellenistic era, fulfilling at least part of Alexander's goal, vast areas became Hellenized and, despite political conflict, Ionian cities enjoyed prosperity. Whoever was in power tended to flaunt success by spending the fruits of war booty on impressive architecture. Some of this survives in Miletus today. After the death of Lysimachus and Seleucus, Philetaerus the governor of Pergamon to the north established the Attalid dynasty which in 238 BCE succeeded in annexing all the Greek cities on the Aegean coast of Anatolia including Miletus. The Attalids were skillful rulers with great architectural achievements. When Attalos III died without an heir in 133 BCE he bequeathed his kingdom to Rome.

The Roman and Byzantine eras (133 BCE to the seventh century CE)

Thus Miletus passed without bloodshed from the benevolent century-long regime of Pergamon to Roman rule. The *Pax Romana*, a period of peace and good administration, ensured a further two hundred years of prosperity. During this time, many new buildings added to the architectural splendor of the city. In the middle of the first century CE Miletus played a role in the advent of Christianity to Roman Asia. It was one of the cities where St Paul preached, and he selected it as a meeting place for the bishops in Roman Asia. Under the Emperor Constantine, Christianity gained strength. In 325 CE, he summoned the Milesian Bishop Eusebius to the pivotal Council of Nicea to confer with bishops from all over the empire. The churches discovered by archaeologists in Miletus date from the Byzantine period. The most celebrated citizen of this time was Isidorus of Miletus who, with Anthemius of Tralles, designed the stupendous church of Hagia

Sophia in Constantinople for the Emperor Justinian in 532 CE. However, by this time the city was in decline. During the early centuries of the new millennium, inexorable natural forces changed the fortunes of Miletus. The River Maeander became clogged by silt, making access to the harbour difficult and impeding trade. The marshes of the river delta became malarial, posing a threat to the health of the diminishing population. In the eleventh century an earthquake toppled many buildings. Meanwhile Turkic invaders began to present a threat, compelling the Byzantine governor of Miletus to enclose a smaller area with walls and to build a fortress on the highest ground above the theatre. It still towers above the site symbolizing the doomed effort to defend a city and an empire.

Muslim Rule

After 1071, when the Seljuk Turks defeated the Byzantine army at Manzikert they captured Miletus, but in 1307 their empire collapsed. The Ottomans took over and the name of the city changed to Balat. A century later the Mongol conqueror Timur defeated the Ottomans and Miletus came under the control of the Beys of Menteshe, who built a fine mosque that still survives. But their possession was short lived; the Ottomans regained it two decades later.

Rediscovery and archaeology

A few European travelers as well as the eminent Turkish writer Evliya Chelebi visited Miletus in the seventeenth century, and noted its significance. Richard Chandler made some engravings of the site for the British Society of Dilettanti in 1764. In the late nineteenth century serious excavations under the direction of Theodor Wiegand were sponsored by the German Archaeological Institute; their work continues today with Turkish and international assistance. Their commitment to accurate recording of findings resulted in the publication of many large volumes of data and interpretation. Disruption of the water table by earthquakes imposed severe difficulties on the excavators, forcing them to pump water from their trenches as they worked and flooding important areas of the site. In the early days of archaeology at Miletus many important findings were carried off to Berlin to be displayed in the Pergamon Museum. The monumental Market Gate built in 120 CE and destroyed in an earthquake has been completely reassembled there. Today, however, no archaeological discoveries may leave Turkey.

VISITING MILETUS

As you approach from the ticket office, the massive Roman theatre rises tall before you, just as it did for mariners sailing in two thousand years ago. You are standing where the Theatre Harbour originally opened to the Gulf of Latmos. The Byzantine citadel still perches on the upper tiers of the theatre, the most dominant feature of the site. Since it is hard to make sense of the archaeological remains that lie beyond them, I advise you to climb to the topmost row of seating and emerge eastwards though the citadel walls to a place where the remnants of the ancient city lie before you. From there you can reconcile the site map with what you see on the ground.

Looking northeast (to your left) you will see an irregular patch of water at the original mouth of the lion harbour. This was a perfect natural harbour, visited by ships from all over the Mediterranean and Black Sea. It received prestigious visitors, from Greek sages to Roman Emperors. Triremes gathered here in times of war, and pirates lurked in its waters after the fall of the Byzantine Empire. Beyond it the Miletus

The Theatre and Byzantine Citadel

Mouth of Lion Harbour   residences

Panoramic view from the Byzantine fortress

Peninsula is no longer surrounded by water, but by agricultural land. The higher ground that was once covered with orderly blocks of houses stands out against the flat fields that were the sea. The inner part of the harbour is now dry, but, to the right, a pool of water (except in high summer) surrounds the Roman harbour monument that once stood on the paved wharf. A little further to the right, due east of your viewpoint, a neat rectangle still defines the sanctuary of Apollo, known since archaic times as the Delphinion. To the right of this sanctified place, the sacred way formed a broad ceremonial street, 100 m. long, between the Hellenistic North Agora, and a Roman stoa. It led south to the impressive Roman Market Gate (now in Berlin) – the formal entry to the vast, unexcavated South Agora that remains invisible beneath fields. Further to the right and closer to the theatre, the massive structure of the Baths of Faustina completes an initial view of Miletus from above. Beyond the Baths, no longer visible, was a large stadium, and further away in the same direction another agora and a Temple of Athena of which no trace can be seen. Residential quarters, laid out on a rigorous grid surrounded the urban core and stretched far to the north and south, but no vestiges of the streets or houses survive. Defensive walls of which scarcely a stone remains protected the entire perimeter of the city.

Harbour
monument   Delphinion   Ionic Stoa   Bouleuterion   South Agora

The central area encompassing the lion harbour, the Delphinion and the two main agoras was the urban heart of one of the greatest cities, most hallowed religious places and busiest trading centres of the Greco-Roman world. Processions for the annual Festival of Apollo Hebdomaios set off for the Temple of Apollo at Didyma, and commerce thrived in the shops behind the grand stoas. Today the Delphinion and sacred way are usually impassable under water; only fragments of the architecture remain. However, you will find clues that will help you bring Miletus to life. A few column bases of the Hellenistic Harbour Stoa still imply its form. A reconstructed section of the Roman Ionic Stoa gives a key to the elegance of the city. The Corinthian capitals of the Bouleuterion, standing close to its semicircular tiers of seating, proclaim the importance of this democratic institution. Scattered over the ground, broken pieces of column shafts, capitals, cornices and fragments of architectural ornament hint at the sumptuous nature of the buildings. The marshy terrain and mounds of vegetation-covered soil from the excavations make it difficult to follow a rational path through the ruins. I suggest that you explore the site in the progression explained below by following the numbers on the plan: they are arranged in a sequence beginning at the theatre that allows you to approach the buildings easily.

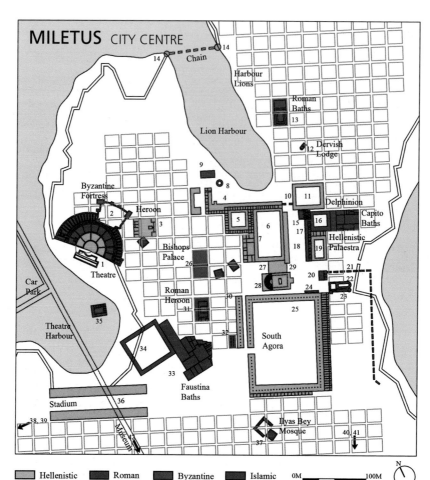

MILETUS CITY CENTRE

14 — Chain — 14

Harbour Lions

Roman Baths
13

Lion Harbour

Dervish Lodge
12

9

8

Byzantine Fortress

Heroon
2

3

Delphinion

Capito Baths

10   11

4

5

6

15
16

17

Bishops Palace
26

7

18

19

Hellenistic Palaestra

27   29

21

20

22

28

24

23

Car Park

Theatre
1

Roman Heroon
31

30

25

Theatre Harbour

35

32

34

South Agora

33

Faustina Baths

Stadium   36

38, 39

Ilyas Bey Mosque

37

40, 41

| ■ Hellenistic | ■ Roman | ■ Byzantine | ■ Islamic | 0M ——— 100M | N |

1. Theatre
2. Byzantine Fortress
3. Hellenistic Heroon
4. Harbour Stoa
5. Small Agora*
6. North Agora*
7. Agora temple*
8. Harbour Monument
9. Synagogue*
10. Gate to sacred way*
11. Delphinion
12. Dervish Lodge
13. Humaytepe Baths
14. Harbour lions

15. Hamam (Turkish baths)
16. Capito Baths
17. Ionic Stoa of Capito
18. Sacred way
19. Hellenistic gymnasium
20. Nymphaeum
21. Aqueduct
22. Great Church
23. Temple of Dionysus*
24. Market Gate (in Berlin)
25. South Agora*
26. Bishop's Palace & Church
27. Asklepion*
28. Bouleuterion

29. Temple of Imperial cult*
30. Storage Building
31. Roman Heroon
32. Temple of Serapis
33. Faustina Baths
34. Faustina Palaestra
35. Caravanserai
36. Stadium*
37. Mosque of Ilyas Bey
38. West Agora*
39. Temple of Athena*
40. Sacred Gate*
41. Sacred Way to Didyma*
42. Museum

* denotes buildings demolished or unexcavated

The Theatre (1)

The first theatre at Miletus was probably a grassy slope curving into the hillside. By the Late Classical period, in the fourth century BCE, it was built up with stone seats. In the Hellenistic era it was enlarged still further to seat 3,500 spectators, and the Romans increased the capacity to 15,000. On the surface, it is hard to see the changes between the Greek and Roman design. Even the lions' paws at the ends of the rows were replicated in each phase. However, the underlying structures differ. While, in the traditional way, the seats of the Greek lower tiers rest on the ground, the Romans built up walls and vaults to support the upper tiers. Large arches penetrate the two end walls of the theatre, allowing the audience to enter through passages that led up to the seats through 'vomitories' (small openings through which the public were disgorged into cavea). Today you can walk through some of those passages and imagine the excited populace jostling through them to emerge in the sunlight. Four columns rising from the centre of the lower part of the cavea supported a canopy to protect the audience from the sun. If the emperor visited Miletus he sat on a marble throne in the middle of the front row.

Originally the theatre rose a whole story higher than it does today; the upper tiers were used as a quarry in the Byzantine period to provide stone for the fortress that stands above it. A more significant change was caused by the collapse, in an earthquake, of the imposing stage building

The cavea and the orchestra of the Theatre. The Caravanserai (the walled compound in the background), the concession stands and the car park occupy the site of the Theatre Harbour. The Stadium was easily visible only 250 m. away, beyond the Harbour

(L) Vaults under the cavea of the theatre, leading to the upper seats (R) Vomitory, exit to the seating

that closed off the interior of the theatre from the outside view. Enough elements of it remain to enable the archaeologists to reconstruct it in drawings. Many carved blocks of stone lie on the ground as evidence of its architectural quality.

The Byzantine Citadel (2) was built on the highest point of Miletus when Turkic invaders began to threaten the city; it served as the palace of the governor. The remains of its eight towers give an idea of its design for defensive purposes, but it stands open to the sky and its rough walls give no hint of the former luxury of its interiors.

A few steps east of the citadel on the slope below it is the **Hellenistic Heroon (3)**. This was the tomb of an unidentified hero with a vaulted chamber under a mound of stone. It was entered through a courtyard with rooms opening off it. Today we can see five recesses in the lower wall for subsidiary burials, but the central sarcophagus, likely to have been placed under the vault, is missing.

Continuing down the hillside, you will see nothing but a few stone fragments of the **Small Agora (5)**, the **North Agora (6)** and the **Agora Temple (7)** which lay straight ahead of you, but if you walk a little to the left you will find a line of column shafts standing in water and a few Doric capitals near them. They belonged to the Hellenistic **Harbour Stoa (4)**. The sharply chiseled fluting of the shafts will help you to visualize the architectural effect of this Stoa. It turned ninety degrees and stretched 160 m. along the southern side of the **Lion Harbour**, bringing order to the chaotic scene of maritime commerce. Behind it, thirty small shops

The Hellenistic Heroon

plied their trade. Nearby, usually surrounded by water, is the circular, stepped plinth of the **Harbour Monument (8)** that commemorated the triumph of Octavian, the future Emperor Augustus, over Antony and Cleopatra at the decisive battle of Actium in 31 BCE. It was built to an original design in three vertical tiers. Three ships' prows projected from the triangular lower part and between them, continuing the marine theme, dolphins and tritons cavorted in low relief. Part of this scene has survived, and stands on the plinth. The next level consisted purely of inscriptions, while the upper tier, now in Berlin, was a large cauldron supported on a tripod.

In the marshy ground, a few steps northeast of the harbour monument you may be able to see a few stubs of columns that belonged to a

(L) The remaining columns of the Hellenistic Stoa with the remains of the Harbour Monument on the right (R) A block from the Harbour Monument, with a triton whose tail curves to the left

(L) Two marble lions, carved in the Hellenistic era and weighing about 23 tons each, marked the harbour entrance. (R) The Byzantine citadel above the theatre dominates the view from Humaytepe on the northern peninsula of Miletus.

basilican structure, which might have been the **synagogue (9)**. Epigraphic evidence shows the acceptance of Judaism in Roman Miletus.

If you want to see the **Harbour Lions (14)**, follow a track first east and then north. You will pass the walls of a **Dervish Lodge (12)** with a large pointed window, and the substantial remains of the **Humaytepe Baths (13)**, which served the residents of the northern peninsula. In addition to the usual *frigidarium, tepidarium, calidarium* and changing rooms, these Baths included a palaestra for exercise.

Two marble lions, carved in the Hellenistic era and weighing about 23 tons each, marked the harbour entrance. One is almost complete, but little remains of the other. Today, they are often half submerged in water, but they give an idea of the extremely narrow opening between the harbour and the gulf of Latmos. It was only just wide enough for a trireme to row through it; to keep out hostile vessels a chain could be stretched across it. Today, an earthen dyke closes the connection between the area of the Lion Harbour and the fields in the Maeander Valley.

If you are interested in exploring the peninsula, you will find no clear path, but it is easy to walk over the rough ground grazed by sheep. Nor will you see traces of the grid of streets or even recognizable remains of buildings, but you will clearly see the original shoreline and the present course of the river. Looking back to the south you will observe the dominant form of the theatre and citadel. To the northeast, on a clear day with the help on binoculars you may be able to see Priene.

Returning south, the path past the dervish lodge will take you to the **Delphinion (11)**. This probably occupies the site where the first Ionian

(L) The Delphinion with the Hellenistic Doric Stoa
(R) The partially submerged Delphinion today

migrants created an altar to Apollo when they landed close by. The Milesians never built a temple to Apollo in the city; this open-air altar served the purpose of honouring their patron god. However, they erected a magnificent temple at Didyma, the site of an oracle 15 km. to the south. Since there is evidence that Apollo evolved from an ancient Anatolian god, it is likely that the oracle existed before the arrival of Ionian Greeks at Miletus. The Festival of Apollo Hebdomaios, celebrated every year, began with rituals at the Delphinion, followed by a great procession on the sacred way. The throng of worshippers passed through the walls by the sacred gate and continued to Didyma. The priests made their sacrifices at a rectangular altar whose foundations still exist inside the central entrance of the Delphinion. Part of the cornice and a roof ornament, now in Berlin, have been dated to the sixth century BCE. During the Hellenistic era, the Delphinion was surrounded by double-aisled Doric stoas on three sides, providing shelter in an orderly architectural enclosure. These were replaced in the Roman era by taller Corinthian stoas with only one aisle. A few capitals have survived to show their ostentatious character. Curved bases for statues placed in the centre of the space are still visible when the water level is low.

If you stand near the original entrance to the Delphinion and face south, you will be looking down the **Sacred Way (18)**, a ceremonial street 28 m. wide and 100 m. long where many important events took place, and where statues were raised to honour important people. In the Hellenistic era it was lined on the west side by stoas with their backs to the **North Agora (6)**. A central entrance led into the Agora and faced the **Agora Temple (7)** opposite. On the east side, the sacred way was more open.

The flooded intersection of the lion harbour, the Delphinion (left) and the sacred way (right). The solid block in the centre is a Turkish bath. The Roman Ionic Stoa stands to its right. This vista was once closed by the Market Gate at the far end.

The principal buildings were the **Gymnasium (19)**, near the centre and the **Temple of Dionysus (23)** at the far end. The Romans added substantial buildings and gave it a greater sense of enclosure. At the entry from the Delphinion they placed a monumental eight columned **Harbour Gate (10)** and lined the east side with an Ionic Stoa, part of which has been reerected. At the south end they built the splendid **Market Gate (24)**, which closed the vista and made a grand entrance to the huge South Agora.

When the sacred way is impassable you will need to follow the paved walk all around the Delphinion. After you pass the solid block of the Turkish bath you will be able to explore the **Capito Baths (16)** donated to the city by Vergilius Capito, an important official for the Emperor Claudius. Capito also commissioned the **Ionic Stoa (17)**, which faces the sacred way. This is an excellent example of a Roman bath combined with a *palaestra*, a courtyard for exercise and athletic contests. It brought together the Greek belief in athletic pursuits for young men and the Roman obsession with bathing. Compared with the delicate post and lintel construction of the Capito Stoa, the architecture of the baths is muscular. Although the vault over the *tepidarium* collapsed long ago, the massive arches that supported it still stand. Most of the dome of the *laconium* (steam room) has fallen away, but we can still imagine the character of the space when it was in use. The rough stone we see today was lined with marble, up to the base of the dome.

(L) Capito Baths plan. The Hellenistic gymnasium is to the right (R) The arches supporting the vaults over the tepidarium and calidarium of the Capito Baths

Just south of the Capito Baths, the **Hellenistic Gymnasium (19)** consisted of the *palaestra*, an elegant courtyard surrounded by stoas, and, on its north side, a few rooms for teaching. Its position on the sacred way, close to the Delphinion, and the architectural quality of the fallen columns show the importance that the Greeks attached to education and athletic training for boys. The reconstructed back wall of the **Ionic Stoa (17)** faces the gymnasium; you can walk around to the other side to enjoy a close view of it. The four columns with their molded bases, finely chiseled fluting and exquisite capitals show the refinement of the Ionic order. They also offer a key to appreciating the architecture of the city. In an understated manner, such stoas, whether Doric or Ionic, gave order and continuity to the urban scene. The populace, sheltered from sun and rain, took advantage of them as meeting places for social, political and commercial purposes.

The Romans also added much more flamboyant architecture in the civic centre. To the south of the Ionic Stoa a mass of masonry, with a row of tall arches behind it, is all that remains of the Nymphaeum, a vivacious melding of architecture and sculpture. This was the place where water, flowing into Miletus on an aqueduct, was distributed throughout the city. But its unknown Roman architect transformed a mundane purpose into sheer delight. As in Rome, a city of many fountains, the Milesians were able to find relief from hot summers by reveling in the spectacle of

(L) The Roman Stoa of Vergilius Capito from the flooded site of the Agora
(R) The Market Gate, *ca.*120 CE, Pergamon Museum, Berlin

water flowing and splashing. Framed by columns and pediments, in a three-story marble structure, gods, goddesses and nymphs poured water from amphorae while it spurted from the mouths of fishes below. The first two stories were built in the second century CE by Marcus Ulpius, the father of Emperor Trajan; the third was added by the emperor Gordian III in the following century. The nymphaeum fell to the ground in an earthquake in the eleventh century, but the fallen debris enabled the archaeologists to visualize its form.

The **Market Gate (24)**, at the southern end of the Sacred Way, also showed the monumental scale and elaboration typical of Roman civic architecture. It was built in the reign of Hadrian in 120 CE. Seventeen meters tall, it dwarfed all other structures in the city except the nymphaeum. Similarly to the Library of Celsus, built 15 years later in Ephesus, its façade was brought to life with two tiers of columns standing forward, in front of its wall. A broken pediment added a flourish at the centre of its roofline. This gate opened through three arches into the **South Agora (25)**. The gate collapsed in the same earthquake as the nymphaeum. Theodor Wiegand retrieved the fallen pieces and reerected it in the Pergamon Museum in Berlin, where it still conveys its grandeur. The South Agora, the largest in the entire Hellenic world, lies buried beneath fields. Archaeologists have established its layout and dimensions, but it remains unexcavated.

The Byzantine **Great Church (22)**, built in the fifth century CE, stood between the nymphaeum and the market gate. Entered through an atrium, it followed a typical basilican plan with a nave flanked by aisles leading to an apse. Its creation on the site of the Greek **Temple of Dionysus (23)** represented the triumph of Christianity over the pagan cult of

The Great Church with the aqueduct and Ionic Stoa beyond

the god of wine and revelry. Ironically, for several centuries the faithful would have emerged from religious observances to the sight of gods and goddesses flaunting their nakedness on the adjoining Delphinion. Among the architectural elements of the great church you will see capitals of a distinctly Byzantine type. The most remarkable discovery made by the German archaeologists in recent years is a large floor mosaic showing flowers, plants and animals, including a lion attacking a deer, in beautiful colours against a white background. Half of this has been restored and placed in the museum; the remainder has been reburied for its protection until funds are available for restoration.

After exploring the east side of the sacred way, unless the ground is dry you will need to retrace your steps back to the Delphinion and across to the west side. Walk towards the red tiled roof that covers mosaics found in the **Bishop's Palace (26)** and then turn left. To your right you will see the sunken courtyard with a few Byzantine columns and capitals. It is believed that St Michael's church was also in this area. However, no foundations of it remain.

Continue south past a block-like Islamic building and turn left immediately on a path that leads to the Hellenistic **Bouleuterion (28)**, the place where the *boule* met to discuss the day-to-day running of the city. When you reach the top of the half-circle of seats you will have a view straight ahead into the courtyard between the council chamber and the sacred way; beyond it is the solid back wall of the Nymphaeum. To your right stood the Market Gate; to the left, the Ionic Stoa stretched 75 m. along the ceremonial street.

The entry to the Bouleuterion was through a fine Corinthian portico leading into the court. The symbols chosen to ornament the frieze were weapons, armor and shields carved in an intricate design; clearly, the Milesians knew from long experience that their independence depended on their strength. A few capitals, propped up on blocks, give an idea of the splendor of the architecture. The council chamber was covered by a wooden roof supported on four columns; its walls were adorned with an unusually ornamented version of the Doric order with an egg and dart motif on the capitals. The quality of legislation practiced in this architectural gem varied as Miletus changed back and forth from true democracy to oligarchy. In the centre of the court, the Romans erected a tomb to an unknown hero. Only its foundation remains on site, but archaeologists have been able to speculate on the design from a few surviving elements. The base was ornamented with lions' heads between garlands hanging from the horns of bulls' skulls; above it, free-standing Corinthian columns supporting an ornate cornice, framed scenes carved in low relief. Obviously those who commissioned it lavished great expense on this elaborate memorial.

From the court you can gain access to the site of the **Temple of the Imperial Cult (29)**, which appears to have shared a small site with the **Asklepion (27)**, the place of healing dedicated to the god Asklepios. Nothing significant can be seen of either structure.

(L) View across the Bouleuterion and its court to the Sacred Way and the Nymphaeum. A few column shafts of the Ionic Stoa can be seen on the far left (R) A Corinthian capital from the Bouleuterion

Storage Building   Pediment of the Serapis Temple

If you continue west and then south towards the massive structure of the Baths of Faustina you will encounter a walled enclosure containing the base of another unidentified hero's tomb, known as the **Roman Heroon (31)**. Further east, the foundations of a long, narrow structure are visible. This was the **Storage Building (32)** built in the second century BCE for use as a granary. It was over 160 m. long and stood next to the South Agora, to which it opened. Next to it was a latrine.

Close to the southwest end of the storage building you will reach the pediment of the **Temple of the Serapis (32)**. The Greco-Egyptian god Serapis was virtually invented by Ptolemy I, one of Alexander's Macedonian generals who succeeded him and ruled Egypt. He aimed to initiate a cult that would appeal both to Greeks and Egyptians in his realm. Serapis combined attributes of Osiris the sun god and Apis the bull, and respecting Greek tradition was represented in human form. His worship became popular in the Hellenistic world and this temple would have served Egyptian traders in Miletus. A circular symbol representing the sun with rays radiating outwards ornamented the centre of the pediment.

The **Thermae of Faustina (33)** are among the best-preserved baths in the Roman world. They were commissioned by M. Aurelius's wife Faustina in about 160 CE, a clear sign of imperial patronage in Miletus. They were entered from the adjacent palaestra by doors that led into the immensely long apodyterium, lined on its sides with 20 small, barrel-vaulted rooms for private changing and relaxation, rather like the rooms provided for the same purpose in Turkish baths today. For cultural and religious inspiration, citizens could turn left into the hall of the Muses, where fine marble statues of Apollo, Aphrodite, Asklepios and the nine muses were

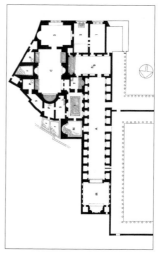

(L) The apodyterium with the Hall of the
Muses in foreground
(R) Baths of Faustina, plan

displayed. To the right, doors opened into the *frigidarium* and the *tepi-darium*. Unlike the Capito Baths, which were symmetrically planned on a central axis, the Baths of Faustina were organized in an irregular manner, conforming to the slope of the ground, not aligned with the city's grid. The three rooms of the *frigidarium,* two steam rooms *(sudatoria)* and the *calidarium* were fitted together in a complex manner. Although the vaults

Apollo, playing his lyre, and Terpsichore, muse
of dance, in the Hall of the Muses (Istanbul
Archaeological Museums)

over the principal spaces have collapsed, you can get the sense of the sequence of the spaces. The largest hall is the *calidarium* with an apse at the north end and vaulted niches and openings to other rooms in the sidewalls. Between these elements massive walls helped to resist the thrust of the vault over the wide space (See p. 31).

Under the floor of the *calidarium*, hot gases from three furnaces passed through a

(L) Reconstruction of the swimming pool in the frigidarium with sculptures of a river god and a lion, now in the Miletus Museum and replaced with replicas (R) The river god before removal to the museum

hypocaust under the floor and then rose through pipes in the walls to keep the surfaces warm. Marble panels on the walls and decorative mosaics on the floor added a sense of luxury. Next to the Faustina Baths stood a large *palaestra* for athletic training. Most of it is still buried beneath several meters of soil, but near the entrance to the hall of the Muses a line of column bases, a few Corinthian capitals and stones from the cornice hint at the splendor of the stoas surrounding it with 25 columns on each side.

Just to the southwest of the Baths of Faustina, the **Stadium (36)** stretched out 230 m. long by 74 m. wide. It was begun in Hellenistic times and enlarged by the Romans to seat 15,000. The archaeologists were able to determine its form, and even to make hypothetical drawings of an elaborate gateway through which athletes entered. However, no remains are

A piece of the Corinthian cornice, column bases and capital from a stoa of the palaestra by the Baths of Faustina

(L) Kalabaktepe in the distance to the south, with tamarisks flowering in the foreground.
(R) View from Kalabaktepe to Miletus, with the Theatre dominating. In classical times, the sea would have filled the left-hand side.

visible today. The road to the museum passes through the Stadium, but only changes of level in the ground reveal its former shape.

The West Agora (38) and the Temple of Athena (39) were sited southwest of the Stadium, but no trace can be seen of either. A level rectangular field planted with olive trees is probably the site of a fine Ionic Temple built there in the sixth century BCE and destroyed by the Persians.

Further to the south, the wooded slopes of Kalabaktepe (43) stand out against a background of higher hills. This is the site where Myceneans built a citadel after they had been driven from Miletus in the fourteenth century BCE. It is easy to understand why the Myceneans chose this easily defensible position, with level terraces close to the summit. It is hard to access it today. In the Byzantine era a cemetery church was built to the northwest of Kalabaktepe to serve a large graveyard. This was uncovered recently by German archaeologists who found the lower walls and mosaic floors. After recording their findings, they covered them again for protection.

The recently restored Ilyas Bey Mosque (37), reached from the road to the museum, is well worth visiting. It was built beneath a single dome in 1404 while Miletus was ruled by the Beys of Menteshe after Timur had defeated the Ottomans, with marble removed from Greek and Roman buildings; its entry is ornamented with finely carved capitals.

The Miletus Museum (42) just south of the archaeological site preserves important findings from the city. The museum has recently been

Ilyas Bey Mosque 1404. The subsidiary buildings in its complex have been protected with a freestanding roof

reinstalled with good lighting and explanations in English. The curators have presented a series of plans at different stages of the city's development, colour-coded to indicate the periods when the buildings were erected. In addition, chronological tables give key dates and photographs of a model showing a three dimensional reconstruction of the central area from the lion harbour to the Bouleuterion.

Displays of artifacts in well-lit cases are arranged by historic period

A high footed Mycenean cup

and thematically to shed light on the life of the city. The displays of Minoan and Mycenean artifacts help to verify that these people occupied Miletus in the Bronze Age as well as many from the later periods. Among the most intriguing are sphinxes and seated figures of Branchidae, the priests of Didyma, that lined the road from Miletus to Didyma. A sculpture garden includes some fine carved lions.

Column bases on the temple front

THE ORACLE AND TEMPLE
OF APOLLO AT DIDYMA

The oracle at Didyma, that issued many fateful pronouncements, dates back to the worship of a local Anatolian god in prehistoric times. When the first Greeks migrated to Ionia they perceived the sacred nature of the place and gave it new life by dedicating it to their own god Apollo. In the eighth century BCE they built an open-air altar there and in the seventh century enclosed it within a small temple. By this time it rivaled the more famous oracle at Delphi on the Greek mainland. In about 560 BCE King Croesus of Lydia, made fabulously wealthy by the gold produced in his city of Sardis, and an admirer of Greek culture, helped to finance the building of a vast new Ionic temple. The dipteral design displayed two rows of columns around the cella, 21 on the long north and south sides, 9 columns on the west end and 8 on the west making a total of a hundred and twelve. This number included two rows of four columns in the pronaos. The lower shafts of some of the columns on the east side were ornamented with sculpture in the manner of those at Ephesus. The cella was too broad to be roofed; open to the sky and planted as a grove of laurel trees it contained a naiskos, a small temple-like shrine that sheltered a bronze statue of Apollo holding a deer, by the sculptor Kanachos of Sikyon.

The temple and oracle were administered by the Branchidae, a priestly family who, according to legend, were descended from a handsome young man named Branchos to whom Apollo taught the gift of prophesy. Unlike those at Delphi who sought answers to their dilemmas verbally, supplicants at Didyma wrote their questions. In response, a priestess, after fasting and purification, sat over the sacred spring and uttered sounds that the Branchidae transformed into iambic pentameters. The pronouncements delivered by both oracles often appeared ambiguous; many of them led to momentous events. According to Herodotus, Croesus, the benefactor of this sacred site, gave equally valuable treasure to the oracle at Delphi. When considering whether to invade the rapidly expanding Persian Empire, he sent emissaries there as well as to Didyma. Ironically, he preferred the answer he received from Delphi that if he made war on the Persians, a great empire would fall. Croesus assumed that the Persian Empire would be the one to fall, but he lost both his own empire and his life. The Greek cities of Aegean Anatolia that he had annexed also succumbed to Persian Rule.

When the Persian King Xerxes defeated the Milesians in 479 BCE, the Branchidae, the hereditary guardians of the Didymaion, surrendered the temple and the contents of its rich treasury to him, and fled to Sogdiana beyond the River Oxus far to the east. Xerxes destroyed the temple and had the statue of Apollo carried away to Ecbatana in Persia. The sacred spring dried up and the oracle declined. The site remained dormant until Alexander the Great defeated the Persians at Miletus in 334 BCE and came to Didyma to pay his respects and assert his exalted status. He ordered the rebuilding of the temple on an even larger scale, making overwhelming demands of the stone masons. Archaeologists, studying records of expenditure, have calculated that the production of a single column required 20,000 hours of work. Since the design called for 220 columns, it is not surprising that the temple was not quite complete five hundred years later.

Alexander also resanctified the oracle, which affirmed that he was a son of Zeus and predicted his victory over Darius III of Persia at Gaugamela. The sacred spring soon flowed again as the prestige of the oracle revived. Remembering the perfidy of the Branchidae, he insisted that the oracle be administered by the city of Miletus under an annually elected priest. Alexander's final act concerning Didyma occurred in 329, after he had crossed the Oxus. Wreaking vengence on the innocent successors of the Branchidae, he massacred the entire male population of Sogdiana and sold the women into slavery. This volatile conqueror, understanding the outrage still felt by the Milesians over the betrayal by the Branchidae a hundred and fifty years earlier, believed it honourable to slaughter and defile their descendants and neighbors.

In about 300 BCE Seleucus Nicator, one of his three generals who took command of the empire after Alexander's death, recovered the stolen statue of Apollo and returned it to Didyma to stand in the *naiskos*. He also supported the continued construction of the temple. In Roman times, the Emperor Caligula (37-41 CE), who wished to be worshipped there as a god, demanded a surge in the construction work and it resumed again under Hadrian (117-138 CE). The oracle thrived under Roman rule until Christianity challenged its authority. While Christians preached against belief in oracles, the oracle at Didyma convinced the Emperor Diocletian in 302 CE that he should persecute them. This judgment led to a bloody oppression of Christians by Romans. The Emperor Theodosius finally closed it down in 385 CE and built a church within it. This was destroyed by an earthquake in the ninth century CE and partially rebuilt, but after the Seljuk and Mongol conquests it was deserted.

Rediscovery and archaeology

When the Italian merchant and humanist scholar Cyriacus of Ancona visited the site in 1443, he found the temple standing, with the cella transformed into a Byzantine fortress. However, an earthquake had destroyed it before an English traveller Dr. Pickering saw it in 1673. The following year, the Society Dilettantes of London sent an expedition led by Richard Chandler to investigate the site, and in 1812 they organized another headed by Sir William Gell, accompanied by the visionary artist J. P. Gandy, who made drawings of sculpture along the sacred way. Charles Newton transported ten of the statues they discovered to the British Museum in 1859. French experts began work there in 1873 and removed some sculpture for the Louvre in Paris. But they ceded the right to excavate to the German archaeologist Theodor Wiegand, who was directing the work at Miletus. Since then the German Archaeological Institute has run excavation and study.

The Sacred Way

The Festival of Apollo Hebdomaios, the most important celebration of the year for Milesians took place each year after the spring Equinox. It began with sacrifices to Apollo and Artemis at the Delphinion in Miletus, followed by a procession walking 16 km. along the sacred way to Didyma. The throng of citizens paused outside the city gate to pay homage at the tomb of their founder Neleus, and also stopped for ceremonies at other shrines placed along the road. At each stop a chorus sang paeans of praise. They passed many works of sculpture including statues of male and female members of the Branchidae family, prominent Milesians

A stretch of the sacred way that linked Miletus and Didyma, in the town of Didim. Emperor Trajan repaved it the in the first century CE. It runs parallel to the modern road, but is not easily accessible

and lions. One seated statue bears an inscription stating that it represents Chares, ruler of Teichoussia (a man remains unknown) and belongs to Apollo. Some participants in the festival travelled by boat from Miletus to the Panormos harbour and from there on foot to the temple. As they approached they were met by female seers. When the worshippers reached Didyma, they sacrificed animals at a circular altar directly in front of the temple. Athletes competed, in honour of Apollo, in the Stadium. This lay so close to the south side of the temple that its steps could serve as seats.

Sculpture from the sacred way: (L) Sphinx (Miletus Museum)
(C) Chares, ruler of Teichioussa, *ca.* 560 BCE (British Museum)
(R) Female figure (British Museum) (British Museum)

The architecture of the Didymaion

The Roman architect Vitruvius attributes the design of the Hellenistic Didymaion to Paeonius of Ephesus, and Daphnis of Miletus, who both also worked on the two largest temples in the Greek world, the Temple of Artemis at Ephesus and the Heraeum (or Heraion) at Samos. The Didymaion became the third largest. A significant discovery made by Lothar Haselberger in 1979, has shed some light on the architects' working methods. He found lines carefully incised on the left interior wall of the cella which are the oldest architectural drawings known. They include a detail of the entablature, profiles of moldings and a template for calculating the entasis of columns.

The Temple of Artemis at Ephesus, one of the seven wonders of the ancient world, has been reduced to a single column standing in a swamp; in stark contrast, enough of the Didymaion survives to allow us to visualize its splendor. The level stylobate, raised above seven steps, provides a generous platform; three columns standing, complete with their Ionic capitals and a short stretch of entablature, stand taller than those of any other Greek temple; the lower shafts of columns that surround the wall of the cella, in two rows, reveal the proportions of the peristyle, those in the pronaos convey the image of a dense forest of fluted marble; the refined column bases demonstrate remarkable workmanship and originality of design. On the ground nearby, fragments of the entablature show the intricate ornamental detail.

From the exterior, the temple appeared to be roofed; indeed the pronaos was covered. But the cella, planted with a grove of laurel trees, sacred emblems of Apollo, lay open to the sky. Within it, over the sacred spring,

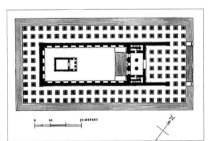 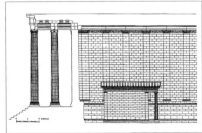

The Hellenistic Didymaion, plan and section, showing the naiskos in the adyton (A.W. Lawrence) The stylobate measures 51.13 x 109.34 m: The columns are 19.7 m. high.

(L)Temple of Apollo Didyma, frontal view from the northeast (R) South peristyle interior

stood the naiskos, a temple-within-a-temple. The public did not enter this court; it was only open to priests and officials taking part in ceremonies. While the cella walls of most temples in this region have served as stone quarries for Christian and Muslim builders, the enclosure at Didyma remains complete enough for us to experience the interior space.

In an unusual arrangement, a flight of 12 steps smaller than those that surround the rest of the temple provides an easy ascent to the front of the stylobate. In ancient times, visitors who climbed the steps and penetrated the pronaos between the serried ranks of columns were not confronted with the usual doorway in the inner wall, but with an opening, more like a window, above a threshold 1.4 m. high. This was clearly not an entrance, but most likely an elevated stage from which a priest declaimed oracles to the waiting supplicants. Behind this opening, a large room has been described as the *cresmographeion*, or "oracle room".

(L) The cella of the Didymaion looking west (R) The western end of the cella with the naiskos (Akurgal)

Griffins on the capital of one of the pilasters articulating a wall of the cella

The two Corinthian columns supporting its roof of this room are among the earliest known. Three doorways led from this important space into the court. Two sloping, barrel-vaulted tunnels, entered through arches in the pronaos, offer the only way into the court.

When you pass through them into the court and walk to the further end, you will find a board with a drawing showing the probable appearance of the Early Hellenistic *naiskos*, a miniature Ionic, temple-like structure, whose foundations are still visible. Turning back you will see the

Steps leading from the cella floor up to the chresmographeion   The oracle room window

monumental flight of steps almost 20 m. wide, leading up to a narrow platform in front of the three doors of the "oracle room". The walls rise high and the lower shafts of the eight pilasters that enlivened each side-wall remain. A few of their capitals representing griffins and plants can be seen near the entrance to the precinct.

The majestic ascent to the *cresmographeion* suggests that the priests and officials, privileged to enter the court, observed momentous rituals there in homage to Apollo. Outside the temple, the general public witnessed the sacrifices of animals at a circular altar directly in front of the temple. This altar probably consisted of a pile of ash and bones.

Ornamental details of the Didymaion

The copious remains of the Didymaion show in vivid detail the richness of Hellenistic design; the same spirit of innovation continued under the Roman architects. We are not absolutely sure exactly when the various parts of the temple were built, but elements in different styles convey the outline of their history. The corner capitals ornamented with the busts of gods and bulls' heads, project an almost Baroque character adopted in the Hellenistic era. Looking out from the frieze above the architrave, the faces of Medusa with venomous snakes for hair possess a similar verve; some of them appear uncharacteristically serene, others grimace. Playing the role of protectress she had the power to turn any who looked at her to stone. The most elaborate column bases on the east front were probably

(L) Column bases on the temple front, carved during the reign of Caligula (37-41 CE) the closest with a palmette motif, the second ornamented with a triton and nereid (R) Detail: the triton with a nereid riding on its tail

Symbolic elements from the entablature of the temple: (L) A head of Medusa, signifying protection, a benign version of the terrifying mythical creature who turned anyone who looked at her to stone C) Another, more frightening version of Medusa (R) A corner capital with bulls' heads and busts of gods. These elements may have been carved by sculptors from Aphrodisias in the second century CE

(L) A stone lion near the temple, probably from the sacred way (R) A chubby Eros tormenting a lion with a spear

commissioned by Caligula; others remain relatively plain. Some of the columns on the outer rows of the peristyle, particularly at the rear were never finished; the single column on the southwest side has not been fluted.

The Sacred Way

A short stretch of the sacred way still exists across the road from the temple and beyond the mosque, but it is hidden behind a wall. You can stand on a bench to look over this obstruction while imagining a procession passing between two rows of marble sculpture. I was able to fulfill my desire to stand on the stone paving of the Sacred Way by going behind the mosque and a small school, walking through long grass, negotiating a gap in a fence and a rocky slope. Another piece of the ancient road has been excavated between Didyma and Miletus, but is not announced by a sign.

Kapikiri village and ruins together

HERAKLEIA UNDER LATMOS

Sacred since prehistoric times, Mount Latmos, towers above Herakleia. The Turkish name for the mountain Beş Parmak ("five fingers") describes its jagged profile. The present village of Kapıkırı on a craggy bluff overlooking Bafa Lake clusters around the cube-like form of the Temple of Athena. The girdle of walls and towers that still surrounds the site of Hellenistic Herakleia proves that it was an extensive city. Herakleia flourished again in the Byzantine era as a centre of monasticism. Now surrounded by a national park and nature reserve, it offers many attractions

The mythical story of Endymion

Herakleia is associated with the legend of Endymion. Various versions of the story of Endymion have come down to us. Whether he was a youthful king of Elis, the region south of Olympia in the Peloponnese, or a shepherd tending flocks on the slopes of Latmos, he was a young man of beguiling beauty. In some versions he had an amorous encounter with Hera; in another, Zeus himself was enamored of him. When Zeus offered to give him anything he desired he chose everlasting youth and eternal sleep. The Herakleians believe that he slept forever in a cave on Mount Latmos, where the moon goddess Selene came down to him nightly in his dreams. She bore him fifty daughters. This legend exemplifies the Greek obsession with male beauty. It also inspired many works of classical sculpture and reverberated with poets and artists in the neoclassical and romantic eras of the nineteenth century. A marble figure by the Italian Antonio Canova, a painting by the French artist Anne-Louis Girodet and John Keats's poem Endymion are just a few examples that captured the public imagination.

History

Evidence of cave dwellers on Mount Latmos survives from as early as 6000s BCE. Astonishing red ochre paintings in certain caves points to their ceremonial and religious purpose. Unlike the cave paintings in other parts

Mount Latmos, the sacred mountain towering above Herakleia. The walls of the Temple of Athena can be seen in the centre right

of Europe that represented animals and hunting scenes, the prehistoric images discovered in this area depicted gods. The archaeologist Anneliese Peschlow, who was shown two of them by a farmer in 1994, has found 170 paintings or fragments of paintings. She believes that Mount Latmos was the throne of the weather god, who appears as the dominant figure with other gods in several scenes. The paintings also represented shamanistic rituals as well as scenes of marriage and mothers with children.

Also fascinating is the survival of an inscription in Hittite hieroglyphics on a cliff overhang close to Herakleia, displaying the royal cartouche of Prince Kupanta-Kuruntiya, the nephew of the Hittite King Mursilis II. This proves that the Hittites were here in about 1300 BCE, while they occupied nearby Miletus shortly before the collapse of their civilization. Although Herakleia is in Ionia, the inhabitants in the Archaic era were indigenous Anatolians, who became Hellenized by Greeks migrating into Caria and spreading north. In classical times Herakleia had a good harbour at the eastern end of the Latmian Gulf, but it could not compete with the great trading city of Miletus with its four harbours at the mouth of the gulf. In the fifth century BCE it was a member of the Delian League, but because of its relative poverty it only contributed one talent in comparison with the five or six of Miletus and Ephesus.

In the fourth century BCE Maussollos, King of Halikarnassos, 90 km. to the south, captured Herakleia by deceit. He professed friendship with the city, then marched his soldiers in through the open gates. The city prospered under his rule and he devoted much effort to improving its defense. He constructed high walls reinforced by 65 towers that seem not only to protect the town, but also to bolster the northern boundary of his territories. The walls were built up onto the slopes of the mountain and also down to the shore. They were probably completed by Lysimachus after the death of Alexander the Great. Despite the irregular terrain, the city plan followed a Hippodamian grid, stretching south and east of the Agora.

Over the centuries silt from the Maeander River gradually cut off the gulf from the sea as it turned the Latmian Gulf into an inland lake, now known as Bafa Lake. In the Byzantine era the rugged landscape riddled with caves attracted monks from Sinai in Egypt, who were fleeing Muslim conquerors. Some lived as hermits in caves; others founded monasteries. By a curious twist in the telling of myths, the story of Endymion, the beautiful young man with amorous dreams of his liaison with a pagan goddess evolved into a story of a Christian mystic named Endymion, who devoted his life to learning the name of God from the moon. When he finally learned it he died. The monks made a practice of opening his coffin every year and listening to a strange humming sound from the bones, hoping perhaps to discover the name of God. By the tenth century three monasteries were established in the area; 200 years later there were eleven.

As the water level of the lake rose, inundating the lower part of the city and the walls that surrounded it, two of the hillocks near the shore on which monasteries were built, became islands. To protect themselves the monks built towers, walls and battlements. The one on Kapıkırı Island close to Herakleia and the Seven Brothers (Yediler) Monastery about 2.5 km. to the east, above the village of Gölyaka, are fine examples of fortified monasteries. Both still include ruins of impressive churches. The castle to the southwest has been identified as a fortified bishop's palace

Rediscovery and archaeology

In 1765, Richard Chandler and Nicholas Revett, the first European antiquarians to visit Herakleia, wrote their names on the fresco in a hermit's cave. The site then appears to have been undisturbed until the German archaeologist Theodore Wiegand, the director of the excavations at Miletus, went there with Herbert Knackfuss in 1905. They mapped the area and located the monasteries in the mountains and on the shore.

Since then, the German Archaeological Institute has continued to work there. Dr. Anneliese Peschlow, the director of the project, has focused her attention recently on the prehistoric paintings.

Visiting Herakleia

Not long ago Herakleia could only be reached by boat. In 1953 Freya Stark in *Ionia a Quest* described her arrival in a small craft at a "pathless shore… [with] white sands unmarked by human feet." Today an asphalt road leads to the site from the highway and guests at pensions near the water's edge enjoy access to the pleasant beach. To the right of the road a little before the village you will get a good view of the city walls and three towers at the head of a picturesque valley. The village and agricultural activity have obscured much evidence of the ancient city. It does not take long to visit the temple and the nearby ruins, but if you want to climb up the mountainside to trace the walls you should allow several hours. Be prepared for rough ground.

The remains of monasteries both on islands and on the mountain, the caves where hermits lived, as well as those with prehistoric paintings are hard to visit or even locate without a guide. But the owners of the nearby pensions can give information on guided hikes, camping trips with donkeys and boat trips on the lake. A valuable nature reserve has been established in the area. With a landscape that ranges from marshland by the lake to dry rocky slopes, it attracts a huge variety of birds, animals and plants.

The Temple of Athena stands on a high position above the Agora. An inscription confirms its dedication to Athena, but its date is uncertain.

Temple of Athena

Market building below the Agora

Since its walls do not follow the planning grid, it seems likely that it predates the city layout. The temple, with no peristyle of columns around it appears austere. Four columns in antis, between projecting walls, opened to a pronaos almost as large as the cella.

Sanctuary of Endymion

The site of the **Agora** is partly occupied by the village school, but two story shops below its southern end are remarkably complete, though partially buried. To the east, against the mountain, recognizable remains of the **Bouleuterion** and the theatre can be found among houses. The theatre, which has lost most of its seats, serves today as an olive grove. From the western edge of the Agora you can enjoy a view of the lake with the **Byzantine castle** in the middle distance.

Down the slope, about 350 m. in the direction of the castle, the **Sanctuary of Endymion** nestles into the hillside. A row of five columns between two square piers stood at the entrance to a space partly carved out of the rock behind and the rest built of large blocks. Its curved back wall seems to replicate the character of a cave.

The **Necropolis** is unique. On strangely rounded rocks along the shore below the castle, the people of Herakleia showed their ancient Carian roots in the form of rock cut tombs. Unlike tombs in Lycia, carved into cliff faces, they are cut downwards into the stone. Some lie open today while others have stone lids still in place.

The **walls** stretch 6.5 km. over the rough Latmian terrain and rise almost 5 m. high; they are the most remarkable feature of Herakleia. Freya Stark wrote of her first view of them from a boat: "Round a bend, in the solitude, the fair Greek stones, the walls of Herakleia appeared. Grey like the mountains, they climb through the chaos of boulders high up the mountain shoulder; they lose themselves and reappear among rocks like swimmers in waves." In several places, where the walls have disappeared, you can see flights of steps carved out of the giant boulders as foundations for the wall. Some of the towers were large enough to garrison many soldiers.

Temple of Zeus, Euromos, second century CE

EUROMOS

The Roman Temple of Zeus at Euromos can be seen among olive trees from the main highway from Söke to Milas; the romantic setting in a small valley makes it a pleasant place to stop for a short visit. Since the road signs give little warning, you should be ready to turn off 10 km. north of Milas.

Euromos became a prosperous city in the Hellenistic era, receiving support from King Maussollos of Halikarnassos, and continued to thrive under the Romans. The temple, believed to have been built during the reign of Hadrian in the second century CE, seems like a smaller version of Hadrian's great temple at Pergamon, erected at about the same time. With six columns on the front and eleven on the sides it was approached by a flight of steps leading through a double row of columns to the pronaos. A cult statue of Zeus stood in the small cella.

This is one of the best-preserved Corinthian temples in Anatolia. Sixteen

Temple of Zeus, Euromos from the nearby hill to the south.

columns still stand; they carry an entablature on three sides, allowing us to appreciate the architectural volume more fully than is possible at most ruined temples. Since the hillside to the south is close to its peristyle, we can easily climb to a position that gives us a close view of the elegant capitals.

Inscriptions state that twelve of the columns were donated by leading citizens of Euromos. Since some of them remain unfluted, we can assume that the temple was never entirely finished.

Only a few fragments of other buildings survive. The front rows of the theatre were visible in recent years, but are now overgrown; a round tower connected to a short stretch of the city wall can be found about 100 m. north of the temple.

Rediscovery and archaeology

Euromos was visited in 1764 by Richard Chandler for the Society of Dilettanti, who found local people at work burning marble in kilns

Temple of Zeus, from *Voyage Pittoresque dans l'Empire Ottomane* by Choiseul-Gouffier (1842)

to make lime. The Comte de Choiseul-Gouffier, the French ambassador to Constantinople, stopped there in about 1776 on a tour of classical sites in Greece and Turkey. The drawings his artist made at Euromos and the engravings that he published in his book *Voyage pittoresque en Grèce* show both the passion for the picturesque and the meticulous recording of detail typical of antiquarians of his time. This successful work reprinted as *Voyage pittoresque dans l'Empire Ottomane* in 1842, include not only a plan, an elevation and a detail of the graceful Corinthian order but also a view of Euromos, with

Temple of Zeus, looking into the cella from the pronaos

Ottoman soldiers striking dramatic poses among the ruins.

Turkish archaeologists began to excavate there in 1969, discovering the front rows of seats in the theatre and some remains of an Agora.

Looking from Oikoi Building towards
Temple of Zeus and the Temple terrace

LABRAUNDA

Set in a striking landscape, it is easy to see why local people believed Labraunda to be an abode of Zeus. Unlike all the other sites covered in this book, except Didyma, Labraunda lacked the resident population and social institutions of a city; it served primarily as a religious sanctuary. Labraunda's inhabitants consisted mainly of priests and servants of the temple. But, at the time of festivals, the numbers swelled to thousands. Located in Caria, a region with its own language and customs, it was dedicated to Zeus in the sixth century BCE or perhaps much earlier. The name Labraunda refers to the labrys, the double headed axe carried by Zeus in effigies described by ancient authors, and preserved on coins.

According to Herodotus, a native of nearby Halikarnassos (modern Bodrum), Labraunda was the meeting place of the Carian League. When Darius, king of Persia invaded their territory in 497 BCE the Carians assembled a force and, aided by a contingent of Milesians, engaged them in battle at Labraunda. After heavy losses on both sides they were defeated and Caria became part of the Persian Empire. Darius, who rarely appointed local rulers as satraps to rule over the cities he had conquered, placed his trust in Hekatomnos of Mylasa, king of the Carians, and appointed him as satrap. Hekatomnos and his more famous son Maussollos gained a degree of autonomy for Caria and presided over a period of prosperity. They revered Labraunda as the most sacred place within their domain, and devoted considerable resources to the architecture there.

Archaeologists have found evidence of an earlier settlement, and an older temple, but almost all the buildings that we see today date from the time of Maussollos (377-352 BCE) and his brother Idrieus (351-344 BCE). They must also have built the sacred way from Mylasa (Milas), used both for religious processions and for hauling heavy blocks of marble from quarries beyond Mylasa. Maussollos, famous for the vast scale of his Mausoleum at Halikarnassos, became unpopular for the high taxes

The Temple of Zeus, with Andron B on the slope to the left

he levied to pay for his ambitious projects. The walls we see on the hillside today are of the local gneiss, but in the late fourth century, shining white marble adorned the most important buildings.

Little building took place during the Hellenistic and Roman eras. The only significant additions are the so-called Andron C, the South Baths and the Byzantine Church. Once the Roman Empire became exclusively Christian, Labraunda lost its purpose as a sacred place and soon declined.

Rediscovery and Excavation

While on a mission for the Society of Dilettanti in 1764, Richard Chandler, discovered the Temple of Zeus at Euromos, and mistakenly believed that he had found Labraunda. The presence of brigands, as well as bears and wolves, in the mountains may have deterred curious antiquarians for a while, but, sixty years later, a British military man, William Martin Leake, with Herodotus and Strabo as his guides, found traces of the sacred way, and concluded that they led to Labraunda. His report inspired the Austrian diplomat Anton Prokesch von Osten, in 1827, to follow stretches of the sacred way until he reached the ruins of Labraunda. The French archaeologist Philippe le Bas visited the site in 1844. He was the first to publish drawings of the site, signed by the architect Eugène Landron. No further progress was made until the French epigrapher, Alfred Laumonier, drew a plan of the site in 1933. He discovered an inscription on the base of a statue of Zeus that confirmed the dedication of the site with certainty. None of the early travelers had correctly identified the buildings at Labraunda; they all assumed that the structure now designated as Andron A was the Temple of Zeus. The first professional archaeology at Labraunda began in 1948 when Axel Persson, professor of classical archaeology at Uppsala University in Sweden began excavation there. He had devoted years of study to Bronze Age Greece, and was attempting to decipher the Minoan Linear B script of Minoan Crete. He theorized that the Carian people, who migrated from Crete in the Bronze Age, might have left examples of their writing at Labraunda. So, his primary purpose was to find ancient Carian inscriptions offering clues to help him in his challenging quest. Instead, he and his team found the Temple of Zeus that had eluded so many others before him. They also discovered inscriptions identifying two buildings previously thought to be temples as *andrones* (banqueting halls for men), which they called Andron A and B. After the sudden death of Axel Persson in 1951, Gösta Säflund directed the work. He continued to clear the temple terrace and revealed yet another banqueting hall, Andron C, in which he found a well-preserved marble sphinx that had fallen from the roof of Andron B. The next director, Alfred Westholm, discovered the Byzantine church and, after improving the landscape of site, handed it over in 1960 to the Turkish authorities. The Swedish archaeologists continued their study and issued several scholarly publications. As their work progressed they found questions calling for more investigation on site. Dr. Pontus Hellström of Uppsala University opened another campaign of excavations from 1987 to 1993 and published an excellent guide to the site in 2007. It offers fascinating detail, about the history, the architecture and the process of the archaeology. Dr. Lars Karlsson continued the work with support from the Swedish Research Institute of Istanbul. Since 2013 the excavations are directed by French archaeologist Olivier Henry as the head of an international, Swedish, French, American and Turkish team.

Visiting Labraunda

Until recently, Labraunda, 14 km. north of Milas, was only accessible to adventurous visitors with four wheel drive vehicles. Today it is reached on an asphalt road. Despite the nearby quarrying operation, it is a beautiful, secluded site with views over the valley below. From the car park a

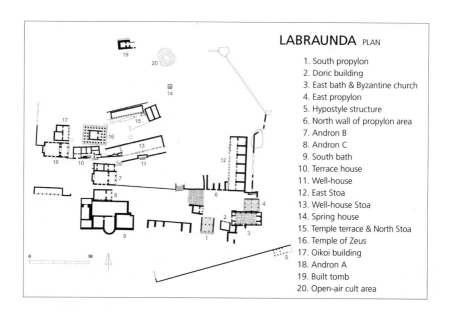

LABRAUNDA PLAN

1. South propylon
2. Doric building
3. East bath & Byzantine church
4. East propylon
5. Hypostyle structure
6. North wall of propylon area
7. Andron B
8. Andron C
9. South bath
10. Terrace house
11. Well-house
12. East Stoa
13. Well-house Stoa
14. Spring house
15. Temple terrace & North Stoa
16. Temple of Zeus
17. Oikoi building
18. Andron A
19. Built tomb
20. Open-air cult area

steep path leads up to the first terrace of the site. Hikers will be interested to know that Labraunda is a stop on the Carian Way, one of a network of hiking trails that are being developed in many areas of Turkey.

The architecture of Labraunda, arranged on five terraces, adapts to the landscape in an essentially Greek manner; the architects avoided symmetry, but created a subtle balance between volumes and spaces. As we move on a turning path, and climb from one level to the next, we experience the changing relationships between the buildings. The **South Propylon (1)**

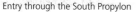

Entry through the South Propylon

The monumental staircase

serves its original purpose as the gateway to the sacred precinct at the end of the sacred way. We can pass through it into a spacious plaza and follow the path that pilgrims took in the late fourth century BCE.

A second gate, the **East Propylon (4)**, allowed people to come into the sanctuary from a road leading over the mountain pass from northeast. Between this gate and the south propylon is a handsome structure, known as the **Doric Building (2)**, probably well house. Four steps, stretching the whole width of the plaza, lead up a short way to the foot of a monumental staircase, which makes a ceremonial ascent to the next level. Straight ahead, is **Andron C (8)** built in the Roman era, but we will turn up a narrower flight of steps to the third terrace. The **East Stoa (12)**, which has not been excavated, closed the east end of the broad open space while **Andron B (7)** dominates the west end. This well-proportioned marble façade bore an inscription on its architrave that Axel Persson discovered: "Maussollos, son of Hekatomnos, gave the Andron and what is inside to Zeus Lambraundos." We can still read the inscription on broken pieces of the three long marble blocks laid out, facing south, in front of the andron. The elaborate capitals of the antae (the side walls of the portico) ornamented with delicate foliage are also displayed there. Since Maussollos died in 352 BCE, when the traditions of classical architecture were dutifully observed, it is surprising to find that the entablature of this otherwise Ionic façade is composed with a frieze of triglyphs and metopes which belong to the

Andron B (L) Reconstruction, showing the antae with elaborate capitals, the two Ionic capitals between them, the Doric frieze and the sphinxes at the ends of the pediment (R) View into the andron with the bases of the two columns in antis in the foreground. Andron A can be seen to the right.

Doric order. This originality predicts the freedom that developed in the Hellenistic era. The sphinx that adorned the pediment fell into Andron C, but remains unbroken. It is in the Bodrum Archaeological Museum.

The interiors of Androns A and B were furnished with couches around the walls on which the most important men attending sacrifices would recline at banquets. They would undoubtedly have received the juiciest cuts of meat while the crowds outside consumed the rest. The tradition of feasting at religious festivals probably continued on a smaller scale after the coming of Christianity. Pagan converts and their descendants would have climbed the hill at Easter to combine worship in the Byzantine church with enjoyment of the paschal lamb.

Such traditions endure today at many remote churches in Greece. On the Cycladic island of Amorgos, the whole community joins in celebrating the Assumption of the Virgin Mary at a church far above a mountain village. After the service they sit at long tables eating goat's meat stewed in great cauldrons. On the same island, an annual procession makes its way over a difficult mountain path to celebrate the feast of Stavro ("cross") at a church only used for that occasion. I have no doubt that these social rituals have roots going back to the Hellenistic era or earlier.

The Well House (11) between the East Stoa and Andron B is a simple structure set into the retaining wall of the temple terrace. It appears to be a later addition to the wall. But in fact the wall is later than the wellhouse. The wall was built to make the terrace behind rectangular, for the erection of a large Roman basilica. Today its basin is filled with water, making a welcome habitat for frogs.

The well-house on the third terrace near Andron B

Andron A, built by Maussollos's brother Idrieus, is the best-preserved building on the site. It is not surprising that it was first believed to be the Temple of Zeus. It is very similar in form to Andron B with a marble façade combining Doric and Ionic elements. Twenty couches around the walls greatly increased the number of men who could join the elite at banquets. Hellström suggests that the wide niche in the back wall, behind the couches, held a statue of Zeus, flanked by Idrieus and Ada, who was both his sister and his wife.

The original purpose of the **Oikoi Building (17)** next to Andron A is unknown. An inscription states that Idrieus dedicated the *oikoi* to Zeus Lambraundos, but does not specify its use: The word oikoi simply means "rooms." It seems likely that it was erected for the use of the priests and to provide extra banqueting space. The building consisted of a portico with four columns between antae and two doors in the back wall leading into rooms of different sizes. The archaeologists, noticing holes cut into the columns and antae to receive a bronze grill and a gate, concluded that one room was a treasury where precious gifts to Zeus would be safe.

The **Temple of Zeus (16)**, dedicated by King Idrieus, replaced a small archaic temple on the same site; it appears likely that the famous architect Pytheos designed it. He was at that that time working on the Mausoleum at Halikarnassos and had not yet started designing his masterpiece the Temple of Athena Polias at Priene. Similarities to the temple at Priene suggest his role at Labraunda. With six Ionic columns across the front and

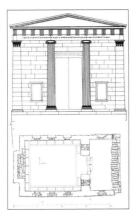

Andron A. View from the terrace below

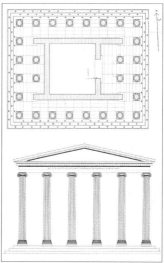

(L) View through the portico of the Oikoi Building to the Temple of Zeus
(R) Reconstruction of the temple

only eight on the sides, it was unusually short for such an important shrine. Hellström argues that it could not be made longer because an archaic altar, considered "sacred and inviolable," stood in the way. The small size of the temple allowed plenty of space for public participation in sacrifices on the same terrace. The squarish archaic altar about 3x3 m, immediately in front of the temple, probably served also in the fourth century BCE. The circular construction does not belong to the complex and will be removed. Except for cella walls, which were of gneiss, the temple was entirely of marble. Two columns in antis stood in the pronaos and also in the opisthodomos, enhancing the sense of depth Strabo wrote that the archaic cult figure of Zeus, carved of wood (presumably from the old temple) showed him with a spear in one hand and a two headed axe in the other.

Little remains of the **North Stoa (15)** that enclosed the north side of the temple terrace. A pre-Hellenistic Stoa probably stood here in the fourth century BCE, but a Roman one from the early second century CE replaced it. A clear inscription on its architrave shows that it was dedicated by Poleites, son of Aristeas, at the end of his priesthood to the emperor and the "to the greatest god Zeus and to the people." This inscription confirms that Labraunda was thriving three and a half centuries after the time of Maussollos and Idrieus.

A line of hereditary priests administered the sanctuary. We know little about them, but one of them may have been buried in the **Built Tomb (19)** which stands on the slope above the sanctuary close to the huge split rock that projects from the slope above the sanctuary. This structure with a corbelled vault, built of huge blocks of gneiss must have been intended for a very important person. You can climb up to it, and with the help of secure metal ladders, go into through a small court and an antechamber into the inner chamber, which contained shelves for three sarcophagi. Twenty-five m. east of the tomb is a place identified as an **Open Air Cult Area (20)**, but it has not been excavated. If you continue to scramble up the slope, you will come to the **Acropolis Fortress**, the upper fotress was built in Hekatomnid times, the largest part of wall probably in the early third century BCE. Eleven towers reinforced the walls, which stretched 280 m, enclosing an area where soldiers were garrisoned.

On the way down, you may pass the **Spring House (14)** from which pristine water has flowed for millennia, Finally, after descending the monumental stair, you can visit the **Byzantine Church (3)** dating from the fourth or fifth century CE. Partly constructed on space taken from the **East Baths**, it consisted only of a nave and apse and was covered with a wooden roof. Square rooms on either side of the entrance could have been the foundations of towers. Since the church appears to have been in use for about two hundred years, there must have been a populace at Labraunda and surrounding villages.

To the southeast of the church, a little way down the slope from the east propylon the shafts of seven columns rise out of the slope. They supported the roof of the **Hypostyle Structure (5)**, which is currently under excavation by a team from Brown University led by Felipe Rojas. Its purpose remains unknown but Hellström theorizes that it may have been a well house where eels mentioned by Aelian and Pliny were kept. He quotes Aelian who wrote: "In the shrine of Zeus at Labraunda there is a spring with clear water, where the fish have golden necklaces and ear-rings, also of gold."

Festivals in honour of Zeus would have included athletic contests as they did at most major religious sites. They took place in a Stadium a little over 200 m. west of the propylon. Lying partly under a cemetery and covered with prickly bushes, is not easy to reach, but the wall of its east end is visible from the road. The track was about 170 m. long and wide enough for 14 athletes. It is the only Greek stadium where starting blocks have been found at both ends.

St. Peter's Castle, now Museum of Underwater Archaeology

HALIKARNASSOS (BODRUM)

The great historian Herodotus, a native of Halikarnassos (modern Bodrum) in Caria, declared that Dorian colonists founded his city and that it became one of the six original members of the Dorian League. During the Archaic Era, the league held its meetings to organize the joint defense of their region in the Temple of Zeus at nearby Knidos (or Cnidus). Later, Halikarnassos shifted allegiance to the Ionian League. By the late sixth century BCE, unable to resist Persian might, Carian cities including Halikarnassos succumbed to the forces of Darius the Great. Apart from a short period of independence after the Athenians defeated the Persians in 470 BCE, the city remained under Persian rule for almost two centuries. In the mid-fourth century, the Persian King Artaxerxes II appointed the Carian leader Hekatomnos and his son Maussollos as satraps of Caria. But, taking advantage of a period of confusion in the Persian Empire, they gradually transformed it into their personal fiefdom. Maussollos, who ruled from 377 to 353 BCE established his capital in Halikarnassos and oversaw an age of prosperity. He built himself a lavish palace and began

  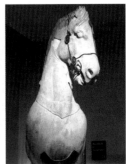

(L) Mausoleum of Halikarnassos, 353 BCE (British Museum)
(C) Statues of Artemisia and Maussollos (British Museum)
(R) Horse from the quadriga crowning the monument, attributed to the sculptor Skopas (British Museum)

The Amazonomachy from the frieze of the Mausoleum (BM)

erecting his own monumental tomb. Following the death of Maussollos in 353 CE, his wife Artemisia, who was also his sister, reigned for two years. She spared no expense in completing the Mausoleum (or Maussolleion, after his name) for her husband. She was succeeded by three sons, two of whom, in the odd family tradition married their sisters.

This monumental edifice, designed by the architect Pytheos, and adorned by the sculptors Skopas, Leochares, Bryaxis and Timotheus, achieved recognition as one of the "seven wonders of the world."

As designs for certain New York skyscrapers in the Beaux Arts style show, its unique form captured the imagination of individuals wanting to build on a grand scale. It also added the word Mausoleum to the lexicon. We do not know the exact composition of the Mausoleum, but surviving fragments and descriptions by Roman writers including Pliny the Elder have given credibility to several similar reconstructions. Pliny states that the Mausoleum possessed a pteron (colonnade) of 36 columns standing on a high base, surmounted by a 24-stepped pyramid, with a quadriga (a four horse chariot) at its peak. Imperial Roman architects, who employed

Site of the Mausoleum

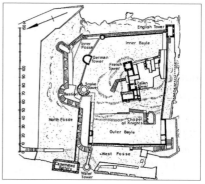
St Peter's Castle, Bodrum, Plan (A. Mauri and Müller-Wiener)

this dramatic device to crown Roman triumphal arches, may well have been inspired by Pytheos's design. The quadriga made triumphal appearances on the Brandenburg Gate in Berlin (1788), the Arc du Carousel in Paris (1806) and many other architectural symbols of

Theatre, Bodrum, with a distant view of the castle

imperial glory in the nineteenth century. Some of the sculpture, most notably statues of Maussollos and Artemisia and a horse from the quadriga, can be seen in the British Museum; a few fragments remain in Bodrum in the museum, but most of it was burned to make lime.

This vast monument collapsed in an earthquake. In 1402, the Knights Hospitaller of Rhodes took the stone including panels of sculpture to build a castle after they defeated the Ottomans at Bodrum and subsequently to enlarge it. A papal bull, issued in 1409, that offered absolution to those who contributed to the work, stimulated activity. The German architect Heinrich Schlegelholt designed the original walls, but as artillery became more destructive, it was reinforced. The addition of English, French and Italian towers demonstrates the international nature of the Knights of Rhodes.

St Peter's Castle withstood Ottoman sieges in 1453 and 1480 and finally fell in 1523. Dominating the harbour with its romantic silhouette, it is worth visiting as a "crusader castle." The castle's current role as the **Museum of Underwater Archaeology** offers fascinating insights for travelers. The evidence from sunken ships, going back to the Bronze Age, sheds valuable light on trading vessels, their routes and their cargoes, as well as advanced archaeological methods. The "Uluburun ship," which sank in the fourteenth century BCE, carried ten tons of copper and a ton of tin, as well as ceramics, ivory, glass, food and many other commodities; it is only one of the many astonishing exhibits to be enjoyed there.

Bodrum also possesses a well-preserved and restored Greco-Roman theatre, built in the second century CE. Set in the slope of a hill with a view of the castle and the bay, it is often used for performances in summertime.

Hierapolis, pool with thermal spring water and ancient columns in it

TRAVEL, ACCOMMODATION AND FOOD

Turkish people are generally friendly, helpful and honest. Hotel staff and people in travel agencies often speak English and they are eager to help. You can find a great deal of up-to-date information about travel in Turkey on www.turkeytravelplanner.com/ a website developed by Tom Brosnahan, the original author of the Lonely Planet guide to Turkey and a real expert on the country. It is always a good idea to learn a little of the language of countries you visit. The pocket sized *Rough Guide to Turkish: Dictionary Phrasebook* is well conceived and helpful.

Reaching the sites: The road system in Turkey is good and signage is helpful. Road works sometimes cause delays, and a few minor roads to more remote sites require extra care, but it is easy to drive to all the sites in this book unless otherwise noted. It is essential to have an up-to-date map. I recommend the *Reise Map of Turkey West/south* at a scale of 1:700,000 which marks all the archaeological sites. It covers European Turkey and the Aegean coast on one side and the Mediterranean coast on the other. It is convenient to drive between sites by car, but this is not essential, because Turkey provides excellent systems of public transportation that are safe, efficient and inexpensive. Having personally reached many of the sites by comfortable long distance buses and packed dolmuşes (shared minibuses serving a regular route,) I can say that it is possible to reach most of the larger sites without a car, but you need to allow plenty of time. Dolmuşes are more available in the high season than in the spring and autumn. It is possible to fly from Istanbul to Izmir and Bodrum or to take buses to many destinations and to combine public transportation and car rental.

Accommodation: Since new hotels are built and old ones change, no recommendations for hotels are included in this book. www.turkeytravelplanner.com/. provides current information and reviews by recent visitors.

Food: Turkish cuisine is excellent. From inexpensive fast food places and cafeterias displaying colourful and tasty dishes to high class restaurants, you will find many choices. You can make a whole meal out of *mezes* (appetizers). For a quick, cheap meal you can usually find a delicious, nourishing lentil soup with bread and a salad, or a serving of *börek*, but it is hard to resist the kebabs and grilled fish.

Picnicking and water: Since you may be on an archaeological site at lunchtime, it is a good idea to have food with you. I generally take a small container and fill it with *mezes* such as stuffed vine leaves and hummus at the restaurant where I eat the night before. Take a water container that you can fill from large bottles.

Footwear: Archaeological sites offer a challenge under foot. I am constantly grateful for my lightweight hiking shoes with Vibram soles and Goretex uppers.

Beaches and Resorts: Visiting archaeological sites can easily be combined with the enjoyment of beaches, seaside villages and resorts. It some areas, it is easy to spend evenings and early mornings by the sea and visit ancient cities in the daytime; in others this would involve more driving. Unfortunately several sections of the Aegean coast of Turkey have been spoilt by rapid and insensitive development, but attractive places with accommodation from simple pensions to luxury hotels can be found. The list below gives some suggestions which can be followed up by consulting www.turkeytravelplanner.com/. This site also includes information on camping. The village on the waterfront at Assos with historic buildings converted to hotels with limited beach access is charming but fairly expensive. Kadirga beach a little to the west offers an alternative with a bigger beach. Dalyan just north of Alexandria Troas is recommended. Foca is far enough north of Izmir to be relatively undeveloped. Its good, sandy beach, has one of the last colonies of the rare Mediterranean seals. The Cesme Peninsula is highly developed, but offers fine sandy beaches, natural hot springs and spas. The beaches include Ilica and Pirlanta on the north coast near Ceşme and Altinkum on the S. Adaland at Kusadasi is the biggest waterpark in Europe, Alanya has a smaller version.

GLOSSARY

Acanthus	A plant whose leaves inspired the ornament of Corinthian capitals and other decorative elements
Alabaster	A smooth, translucent stone, similar to marble.
Agora	The market place in a Greek city often also used for civic ceremonies and political events.
Acropolis	A high place in a Greek city, usually fortified and the site of a temple or sacred place.
Aedicule	A part of a façade framed by columns and an entablature sometimes capped with a pediment, often built to display sculpture
Amazonomachia	Conflict between Greeks and Amazons
Amphitheatre	A circular or oval arena with tiers of seats around a central performance space.
Anastylosis	The rebuilding of a collapsed structure, following archaeological evidence and using original elements
Andesite	An igneous stone
Anthemion	An ornament based on honeysuckle or palmette, common on Ionic architecture.
Anta	A pier or pilaster thickening the end of a wall, particularly the projecting walls on either side of the pronaos of a temple. Columns between antae are **in antis**.
Arcade	A row of arches
Arch	A rounded or pointed opening in a wall constructed with wedge shaped stones known as **voussoirs**
Apse	A semicircular space usually at the end of a church or a Roman basilica.

Asklepion	A sanctuary of Asklepios, the Greek god of healing.
Atlas	pl. Atlantes. A male figure in the place of a column supporting an entablature, based on the mythological Titan who was forced to support the heavens on his shoulders.
Atrium	A court surrounded by columns supporting a roof, in Greek or Roman houses, or at the entry to Byzantinee churches
Baptistery	The space added to a church for baptisms
Barrel vault	A vault in the form of a half cylinder usually supported on parallel walls.
Basilica	A Roman hall of justice, usually with a high nave with lower aisles on either side and an apse. Christians adopted the same form for churches.
Bouleuterion	The council house of a Greek city where the **Boule**, the legislative council of a city met
Calidarium	The hot room in a Roman bath
Capital	The top element of a column, making the transition to the entablature or an arch, usually decorated in the manner characteristic of the order (eg.. Doric, Ionic Corinthian)
Caryatid	A human figure carved in stone to serve as a column supporting an entablature
Cloaca	Roman sewer
Cavea	The tiered seating area of a theatre
Cella	The inner sanctuary or **naos** of a temple, usually containing the cult image of a god.
Colonnade	A row of columns for example at the front of s **Stoa**.
Corbel	A projecting stone in a wall supporting an element above it
Corbelled arch or vault	A structure in which stones project progressively further forward from a wall until they meet
Corinthian	(see **orders** p. 29)

Cornice	The projecting upper part of an entablature
Dentils	Small square blocks, like teeth, usually on the underside of a cornice.
Egg and dart, Egg and tongue	A decorative band in a moulding, often on a cornice in which ovoid forms alternate with narrow pointed or rounded shapes.
Dipteral	A type of temple design with two rows of columns around it (see temple types, p. 34, 215, 219)
Doric	(see **orders** p. 29)
Entablature	The horizontal, upper element, supported by columns, in classical architecture. It consisted of the **architrave**, (the structural beam) the frieze, and the overhanging **cornice**.
Ephebe	A young man between 18 and 20 years.
Ephebium	A room for education and training of young men in a **Gymnasium**.
Erotes	Figures of eros the Greek god of love often representes ac children
Flute	A vertical groove on a column.
Frieze	The horizontal band of an **entablature**, between the architrave and the cornice, ofter carved in low relief
Frigidarium	Cold room in a Roman Bath
Gigantomachy	In Greek mythology, the battle between the Olympeian gods and the giants, representing chaos, led by the giant Alcyoneus
Gymnasium	A place of education and physical training for young men
Heroon	A tomb or memorial where a hero was honoured or worshipped
Hypocaust	An under floor heating system in Roman **Thermae** and other buildings in which hot gases from a furnace passed between brick columns supporting the floor
Ionic	(see **orders** p. 29)

Metope	A square panel, often of low relief sculpture, between the **triglyphs** in a Doric frieze (see **orders** p. 29)
Mosaic	A decorative floor finish made by setting tesserae, small pieces of stone, glass or ceramic material into mortar.
Narthex	A vestibule at the entry to a church
Naos	The inner sanctuary or **cella** of a temple, usually containing the cult image of a god
Necropolis	A cemetery, usually outside the walls of Greek and Roman cities
Niche	A semicircular recess in a wall, usually with an arched top and covered with a half dome
Nymphaeum	A civic fountain often decorated with statues of nymphs.
Oculus	A circular opening in the crown of a dome, most famously in the Pantheon in Rome.
Oikos	The Greek home; principal room in the house; a room
Orchestra	The circular performance space in a Greek Theatre. In Roman theatres, it was reduced to a semicircle in front of a raised stage.
Order	A traditional system or style of building with columns and an entablature in Greek architecture. The Greek orders were the Doric, Ionic and Corinthian (see p. 29)
Palintonon	A siege engine, like a catapult for hurling large stones.
Palaestra	The court, usually surrounded by stoas in a gymnasium.
Pediment	The gable end of a temple roof, above the temple front
Peripteral	A type of temple design with a single row of columns around it (see temple types, p. 33)
Peristyle	A row of columns around a temple or a court.
Pier	A massive support, usually square, sometimes with a base and capital

Peristyle	A court surrounded by colonnades.
Portico	A covered space fronted with a colonnade, making a covered walk, as in a **stoa**.
Pronaos	The space between two walls in front of the **naos** or **cella** of a temple.
Propylon, propylaia	A formal, often monumental gateway to a sacred precinct.
Prostyle	A type of temple design with columns only at the front.
Prytaneum	A city hall or place to entertain guests in a Greek polis; the place where the perpetual sacred fire brought to the city by colonists from their mother city.
Pseudodipteral	A type of temple design with a single row of columns arranged far from the cella walls, creating the impression that it is dipteral (see p. 257)
Pteron	A row of columns surrounding a temple
Sarcophagus	A stone coffin
Scenae	frons the building behind the stage of a Roman theatre
Spolia	Remains of earlier buildings built into new structures.
Stoa	A portico fronted with a colonnade, providing a covered walk around an open space.
Sudatorium	Steam Room in a Roman bath
Stylobate	The stone platform, including its top step on which a temple is built
Synthronon	A semicircular arrangement of benches in the apse reserved for the clergy, with the bishop's throne in the centre
Temenos	A sacred precinct dedicated to a god or goddess.
Tepidarium	Room with tepid water in a Roman Bath
Thermae	Roman baths
Triglyph	An element of the frieze alternating with metopes in the Doric entablature

CREDITS

All photographs are by the author, except where noted below:
Bingöl, Orhan: 261B
Boratav, Ahmet: 74, 259T
DAI (German Archaeological Institute): 91TR, BL, 307L (Reconstruction dwg. of Delphinion), 309L (Plan of Capito Baths).
Glock, Wolfgang: 330
Greene, Rhonda: 106R, 107L,R
National Museums in Berlin: 82 (Head of Attalos I, by Johannes Laurentius), 86L (L. C. Humann and R. Bohn in the Sanctuary of Athena, from Antikensammlung SMB Archiv)
Laodicea Excavations Archive: 169BR
Osseman, Dick: 130L, 307R, 342L,R, 343
Rasmussen, Carl: 169R
Russo, Peter: 106L, 108R
Stevens, Gerald L.: 171L,R, 172L
Türkoğlu, İnci: 121TL,TR, 122B, 174, 186L,R, 187L,R, 226T, 251, 334, 337, 348, 352
Wilson, Mark: 83R, 287R
p.125: Lydian electrum trite c.600 BCE http://oldestcoins.reidgold.com/article.html
p.126: http://www.welcometohosanna.com/

Maps and drawings are taken from:
Migration map and map of central Miletus (p.302), drawn by Mike Derry.
p.6 Map showing the sites presented in the book: Ege Yayınları.

Introduction:
p.29 Orders of architecture, from the *Thames and Hudson Dictionary of Art Terms*, 1995, p.137.
p.33L: public domain
p.33R: The Temple Athena Polias at Priene (H. Schleif) from F. Rumscheid, *Priene, Pompeii of Asia Minor*, Ege Yayınları, Istanbul, 1998, p.118.
p.37 (Sardis, bath complex plan) fig. 264, 133 (Sardis, bath complex reconstruction) fig. 203, 314TR (Faustina plan) fig. 278, 315TL (reconstruction of frigidarium) fig. 283: from Fikret Yegül, Baths and Bathing in the Roman World, [courtesy of the Turkish edition by Homer, Istanbul, 2006]

Troy:
p.40, 50, 53BL: Troy II & VI reconstructions: Christopher Haußner.
p.47: The "Great Treasure" (H. Schliemann, *Ilios*, 1880, p.14); p.56 Map of Troy, from M. O. Korfmann, *Troia/Willusa, Guidebook*, Tübingen-Troia Foundation, Çanakkale, 2005.

Alexandria Troas:
p.61: Map, from E. Schwertheim, "Alexandria Troas", *Byzas* 3, Abb.1.

Chryse:
p.62, 64T,B, 65T,B: A. C. Özgünel, *Smintheion. Apollon Smintheus'un İzinde*, Ege Yayınları, Istanbul, 2013, p. 16, 35, 37, 56, 98.

Assos:
p.73: Map of Assos, from N. Arslan & B. Böhlendorf-Arslan, *Assos, An archaeological guide*, Homer, Istanbul, 2010 (Courtesy of Homer Publishers).
p.77: Reconstruction of Agora by J. T. Clarke, F. Bacon and R. Koldewey, *Report on the Investigations at Assos*, 1881.

Pergamon:
p.88: Map & p.106: plan of Asklepion, from Bayraktar, *Pergamon*, 1996, back cover and p.85 respectively.
p.96: The plan of the palace of Eumenes II: Renée Dreyfus ed., *Pergamon: The Telephos Frieze from the Great Altar*, vol 2, Fine Arts Museums San Francisco 1997, Dwg by Wolfram Hoepfner
p.103: Sanctuary of Egyptian gods from H. Koster, *Pergamon, Citadel of the Gods*, p.106: The Red Hall in Pergamon, fig. 1, K. Nohlen, University of Applied Science, Wiesbaden.

Teos:
p.120: Map, from M. Kadıoğlu, *Teos Guide Book*, 2012, p.2 (courtesy of M. Kadıoğlu).

Hierapolis:
From F. D'Andria, *Hierapolis of Phrygia (Pamukkale): An Archaeological Guide*, Ege Yayınları, Istanbul, 2010²: p.140: Map by P. Verzone and F. Baratti, p.44; p.145BL,BR: Reconstruction of the Agora and a detail of the Basilica, by R. Rachini, p.99, 100; p.147R: Reconstruction of the Nymphaeum of the Tritons by F. Ghio and L. Campagna, p.121; p.148T: Cathedral, plan and section, from Hierapolis 1987; p.149R: Reconstruction of the Temple Nymphaeum by D. De Bernardi Ferrero, p.133; p.153B: Italian Mission info board; p.154R: from p.186.

Laodicea on the Lycus:
p.166-167: Map by Laodicea excavation team, from C. Şimşek, *Laodikeia*, Ege Yayınları, Istanbul, pp.56-57.
p.158, 159, 164, 165, 168, 169L, 173TR, 173BR: C. Şimşek, Antik Kent Laodikeia, Denizli 2012; C. Şimşek, *Laodikeia (Laodicea ad Lycum)*, Laodikeia Çalışmaları 2, Ege Yayınları, Istanbul 2013 (with kind permission by C. Şimşek)

Aphrodisias:
p.180: Map & p.182 city centre, p.185R: Plan of the Sebasteion by New York University website, http://www.nyu.edu/projects/aphrodisias/
p.197L: Frons Scenae (Stage building) of the Bouleuterion restored, drawing by L. Bier, from *Aphrodisias Papers* 4 p.153 fig 13. fig. 6, with permission from *Journal of Roman Archaeology*.

Ephesus:
From P. Scherrer (ed.), *Ephesus, the New Guide*, Istanbul, 2000: pp.216-17: general map and pp. 220, 228, 242: detailed maps of districts; p.219T: Hellenistic temple of Artemis, p.53; p.221R: East Gymnasium and Baths (F. Miltner), p.71; p.229BR: Trajan's Fountain, reconstruction (Pellionis 1963), p.117; p.239R: reconstruction (Niemann), p.133.
p.215: The archaic temple of Artemis, plan A.E. Henderson, 1915.
p.219BL,BR: British Museum.

p.234: Plan of Terrace Houses, from S. Ladstätter, *Das Hanghaus 2 in Ephesos. Ein Archaeologischer Führer*, Ege Yayınları, 2012, fig. 51.

p.239L: Celsus Library Plan from Ward Perkins, *Roman Imperial Architecture*, Pelican History of Art, 1981, fig. 188.

p.240L: Hall of Nero and Circular Monument (drawing F. Huber) OAI (Austrian Archaeological Institute).

p.244L: Arcadian Street reconstruction by G. Niemann. OAI.

p.249: Vedius Gymnasium, reconstructed bird's eye view, from N. Zimmermann, S. Ladstätter, *Wall Painting in Ephesus*, Ege Yayınları, Istanbul, 2011, fig.44.

p.252: Church of St. John, from R. Krautheimer, *Early Christian and Byzantine Architecture*, Pelican History of Art 1965, fig.68.

Magnesia on the Meander:

p.257: Temple of Artemis Leucophryene, designed by Hermogenes, ca.150 BCE, elevation and plan, from M. Şahin, *Hermogenes*, Ege Yayınları, Istanbul, 2002, Çiz. 1 and Res. 1.

p.258: Site plan, from O. Bingöl, *Magnesia on the Meander, an archaeological guide*, Homer, Istanbul, 2007.

Priene:

From F. Rumscheid, *Priene: A Guide to the Pompeii of Asia Minor*, Ege Yayınları, Istanbul, 1998: p.266: Reconstruction of a fountain, fig.88; p.269: Reconstruction of Hellenistic Priene by A. Zippelius (1908), fig.20; p.270: Map, fig. 18; p.271: Plan of Athena Sanctuary (by W. Müller-Wiener) fig.90; p.274: Statue of Athena, fig.101; p.275: Altar, fig. 95; p.276L: Plan of Agora, fig.55; p.277L: reconstructed view, fig.56; p.280L: reconstruction of bouleuterion, fig.40; p.286R: courtyard house (Th. Wiegand), fig.130.

p.265: Coin minted in Priene c.290-250 BCE (www.asiaminorcoins.com).

Miletus:

p.290: Map of Miletus, from V. von Graeve, "Milet", *Byzas* 3, 2006, 257 Abb.8.

Didyma:

p.323: The Hellenistic Didymaion, plan and section, from A.W. Lawrence, *Greek Architecture*, revised by R. A. Tomlinson, Yale University Press 1996 p154 figs. 240-241.

p.324: E. Akurgal, *Ancient Civilizations and Ruins of Turkey*, Istanbul, 1990[7], fig. 85

Euromos:

p.336: Temple of Zeus, engraving from Choiseul-Gouffier, *Voyage pittoresque dans l'Empire Ottomane*, 1842.

Labraunda:

From P. Hellström, *Labraunda, A Guide to the Karian Sanctuary of Zeus Labraundos*, Ege Yayınları, Istanbul, 2007: p.342: Plan, p.48; p.343L: Reconstruction of Andron B, by T. Thieme and F. Lövenberg, p.86; p.345L: Plan and elevation of Andron A, by T. Thieme, p.126; p.346: plan and elevation of Temple of Zeus, by T. Thieme, p.112.

Halikarnassos:

p.349L: Mausoleum of Halicarnassus 353 BCE, Reconstruction British Museum, drawn by Susan Bird after G.B. Waywell.

p.350BR: Plan, St. Peter's Castle, by A. Mauri and W. Müller-Wiener.

Byzas 3: W. Radt (ed.), *Stadtgrabungen und Stadtforschung im westlichen Kleinasien*, DAI Istanbul, Istanbul 2006.

INDEX

363

Further Reading
Books for general topics

E. Akurgal, *Ancient Civilizations and Ruins of Turkey*, Istanbul 1970 revised 2002

G. Bean, *Aegean Turkey. An Archaeological Guide,* New York (out of print)

S. Lloyd, *Ancient Turkey: A Traveller's History*, Berkeley 1989

B. McDonagh, *Blue Guide, Turkey The Aegean and Mediterranean Coasts,* London 1989

J. Boardman, *The Greeks Overseas,* London 1973

J. M. Cook, *The Greeks in Ionia and the East,* London 1962

J. M. Cook, *The Persian Empire,* London 1983

A. M Greaves, *The Land of Ionia: Society and Economy in the Archaic Era,* Wiley Blackwell, 2010

Herodotus, *The Histories*

A. W. Lawrence, *Greek Architecture*, Pelican History of Art, revised by R. A. Tomlinson, 1996

R. Martienssen, *The Idea of Space in Greek Architecture,* Witwatersrand 1956

D. Parrish, ed. *Urbanism in Western Asia Minor: New Studies on Aphrodisias, Ephesos, etc.* Journal of Roman Archaeology, 2001

D. S. Robertson, *A Handbook of Greek and Roman Architecture,* Cambridge 1964

G. McLean Rogers, *Alexander: The Ambiguity of Greatness,* New York 2004

R. R. R. Smith, *Hellenistic Sculpture*, Thames and Hudson, 1991

F. Stark, *Ionia, A Quest,* London 1954

Strabo, *The Geography,* Book XIII

P. A. Webb, *Hellenistic Architectural Sculpture,* University of Wisconsin Press 1996

R. Wallace, *The Three Worlds of Paul of Tarsus,* New York 1998

R. E. Wycherley, *How the Greeks Built their Cities,* New York 1962

F. Yegül, *Baths and Bathing in Classical Antiquity,* MIT 1992

B. Strauss, *The Trojan War,* New York 2007

M. Wilson, *Biblical Turkey, A Guide to the Jewish and Christian Sites of Asia Minor*, Ege Yayınları, Istanbul 2010

Books on individual sites

Troy:
M. O. Korfmann, *Troia/Wilusa, Guidebook,* Tübingen-Troia Foundation, Çanakkale, 2005

Assos:
N. Arslan & B. Böhlendorf-Arslan, *Assos, An Archaeological Guide*, Homer, Istanbul, 2010

J. Th. Clarke, *Report on the Investigations at Assos,* Boston 1881

Pergamon:
R. Dreyfus, *Pergamon: The Telephos Frieze from the Great Altar,* Fine Arts Museum San Francisco 1996

H. Koester, *Pergamon, Citadel of the Gods,* Harrisburg 1998

Pergamon: Panaroma der Antiken Metropole, exhibition catalogue, Pergamonmuseum, Museumsinsel Berlin, 30.9.2011-30.9.2012, Imhof Petersberg, 2011 (www.smb.museum/pergamon-panorama_/)

Ch. Habicht, *Die Inschriften des Asklepions, Altertümer von Pergamon VIII.*

W. Radt, *Pergamon: Geschichte und Bauten einer antiken Metropole,* Darmstadt 1999

Teos:
M. Kadıoğlu, *Teos Guide Book,* 2012

Sardis:
G. M. A. Hanfmann, *Sardis from Prehistoric to Roman Times,* Harvard 1983

Hierapolis:
F. D'Andria, *Hierapolis of Phrygia (Pamukkale): An Archaeological Guide,* Ege Yayınları, Istanbul, 2010[2]

T. Ritti, *An Epigraphic Guide to Hierapolis of Phrygia (Pamukkale),* Ege Yayınları, Istanbul 2007

P. Arthur, *Byzantine and Turkish Hierapolis (Pamukkale),* Ege Yayınları, Istanbul 2006

Hierapolis di Frigia, 5 volumes by the excavation team covering excavations and results

Laodicea on the Lycus:
C. Şimşek, Laodikeia (Laodikeia ad Lycum), Ege Yayınları, Istanbul 2007

C. Şimşek, Antik Kent Laodikeia, Denizli 2012

C. Şimşek, Laodikeia (Laodicea ad Lycum), Laodikeia Çalışmaları 2, Ege Yayınları, Istanbul 2013

Aphrodisias:
K. T. Erim, *Aphrodisias: City of Venus Aphrodite,* London 1986

R. R. R Smith and Christopher Ratté, *Aphrodisias Papers 4,* Journal of Roman Archaeology, 2008

Ephesus:
N. Zimmermann, S. Ladstätter, *Wall Painting in Ephesus,* Ege Yayınları, Istanbul, 2011

P. Scherrer, *Ephesus, The New Guide,* Ege Yayınları Istanbul 2000

S. Ladstätter, *Ephesos Yamaç Ev 2,* Ege Yayınları, 2012

Forschungen in Ephesos, 12 volumes, covering excavations over several decades, many authors

Magnesia on the Meander:
O. Bingöl, *Magnesia on the Maeander,* Homer Kitabevi, 2007

Priene:
F. Rumscheid, *Priene, Pompeii of Asia Minor,* Ege Yayınları, Istanbul, 1998

J. C. Carter, *The Sculpture of the Sanctuary of Athena Polias, Priene,* Society of Antiquaries, 1983

K. Ferla, ed. *Priene,* Foundation for the Hellenic World, 2005

Miletus & Didyma:
V. B. Gorman, *Miletus. The Ornament of Ionia,* Michigan 2001

A. Greaves, *Miletos. A History,* London 2002

Th. Wiegand, ed., 14 volumes on Miletus, including: Hubert Knackfuss, *Das Rathaus von Milet,* 1908; A. Rehm, *Das Delphinion in Milet,* 1914, Reinhard Köster, *Die Bauornamentik von Milet,* 2004

Labraunda:
P. Hellström, *Labraunda, A Guide to the Karian Sanctuary of Zeus Labraundos,* Ege Yayınları, Istanbul, 2007

Ann C. Gunter, *Labraunda: Marble Sculpture,* Stockholm 1995

Pontus Hellström and Thomas Thieme, *Labraunda: The Temple of Zeus,* Stockholm 1982

Alfred Westholm, *Labraunda, The Architecture of the Hieron,* Lund 1963

About the Author

Henry Matthews, born in England and educated at Cambridge University, is an architectural historian. He has practiced architecture and taught at universities on both sides of the Atlantic. His numerous books and articles cover topics from Islamic design in Turkey to the Modern Movement in America. A passionate traveler, he has led cultural tours in several countries. His recent publication *Mosques of Istanbul* (Scala 2010) reveals his interest in placing buildings in their social and historical context and bringing them to life for tourists. Readers are invited to enter his website where they will find additional photographs and information as well as recent discoveries in Aegean Turkey. http://henrymatthews.com

Prehistoric era
c. 6500 Çukuriçi Höyük, Ephesus

c. 6500 Cave paintings, Mount Latmos
• Indigenous people living in western
Anatolia

Bronze Age 3000-1100
2920-2550 Troy I
• Ancient settlement in Smyrna

2550-2250 Troy II
22250-1740 Troy III IV & V

1740-1300 Troy VI
c.1700 Minoan colony founded at Miletus
c.1450 Myceneans occupy Miletus
c.1400 Uluburun wreck

c. 1317 Mycenaean Miletus sacked by
Hittites c.
1300-1180 Troy VI i
• Priam King of Troy
c. 1180 Destruction of Troy

1100-1000 Migration of Greeks to Aegean
coast

Archaic Era 800-500 BCE
c. 756 Milesians found colonies at Sinope
and Trapezous

c.700 Cimmerians attack Greek cities in
Anatolia
c.700 first temple of Artemis at Ephesus
(*naiskos*)
c.675 Miletus attacked by Lydians and
Cimmerians
• Miletus the most prosperous city in the
Hellenic world
c. 651 King Ardys of Lydia conquers Priene
c.650 Ionian and Aeolian Leagues founded
Beginning of science and philosophy in
Miletus

585 King Croesus of Lydia annexes Greek
cities of Ionia and Aeolis
570 Archaic Temple of Artemis at Ephesus
547 Croesus invades the Persian Empire
546 Persians conquer Greek cities in Anatolia
• Temple, Neandria with Aeolic capitals
c. 530 Temple of Athena, Assos

THE HELLENIC WORLD
& BEYOND

c. 6500 Çatal Höyük, Central
Anatolia, earliest known religious
shrines, pottery, frescoes

• Invention of plough and writing Mesopotamia

c.3000 All Egypt united by king Narmer
c. 2667-2648 Tomb of Pharoah Djoser,
Egypt.
c. 2500 Great Pyramid of Giza, Egypt
c.2100 Ziggurat of Ur, Mesopotamia
1792 The Code of Hammurabi, Babylon
c. 1700 Epic of Gilgamesh, Mesopotamia
c.1700-1470 Palace of Minos, Knossos, Crete
1470 Minoan civilization collapses
c.1400 Lion Gate, Hittite capital Hattusha
1375 Cretan palaces destroyed
1378-58 Tomb of Queen Hatshepsut, Egypt

c. 1350 Hittite empire at its height
c.1250 Lion Gate Mycenae
c. 1180 Destruction of Hittite capital
Hattusha

c.1100 Dorian 'invasion' of Greek mainland
c.1100 collapse of Mycenean civilization

c.850 Palace of Asurbanipal II Nimrud

776 Olympic Games founded

750 Greek alphabet established
c.700 Homer born in Smyrna

• Homer, the *Illiad* and the *Oddysey*

640 first coins minted in Sardis

595 Solon's laws enacted in Athens
575 Ishtar Gate, Babylon

550 Achaemeanid Persian Empire founded

522 Darius becomes King of Persia

Classical Era 500-330 BCE
499 Aristagoras leads revolt against Persia

498 Ionians capture and burn Sardis
494 Persia conquers and destroys Miletos
494 Greek fleet destroyed at Lade

479 Defeat of Persians at Battle of Mycale

478 Delian League founded

440 Miletos at war with Samos over Prien

412 Milesians rebel against Athenian
hegemony
• Priene moves to new site

386 Greek cities under Persian rule again
359-351 Mausoleum of King Mausollus
Halicarnassus
356 Archaic temple of Artemis at Ephesus
burned and new temple of Artemis begun
348-345 Aristotle in Assos

341 Persians invade Assos

334 Alexander starts fighting the Persian
Empire, Battla of Granicus
333 Battle of Issus

Hellenistic Kingdoms 330 -133 BCE
• Temple of Athena Polias Priene
• Temple of Apollo Didyma
323 Alexander dies. Empire divided
318-17 Antigonus (one of Diodachi) rules
Ionian and Aeolian cities

310 Antigonus founds Alexandria Troas

c.300 -150 Temple of Artemis Sardis

282 Philetaerus gains control of Pergamon
263 Eumenes I succeeds Philetaerus in
Pergamon.
253 Antiochus II moves 2000 Jews to Phry
238 Attalus I of Pergamon conquers Milet
c.220-190 Temple of Dionysus, Teos

THE HELLENIC WORLD
& BEYOND

518-460 Palace of Darius and Xerxes
Persepolis
510-44 Roman Republic

490 Persia's invasion of Greece fails
486 Darius, king of Persia dies
480 Persians defeat Spartans at Thermopylae
and sack the Athenian Acropolis
462 democratic reforms in Athens
457 Pericles initiates the Golden Age of
Athens
448-432 Parthenon begun in Athens by Icti-
nus & Callicrates Architects, Phidias Sculptor
441 Euripides wins prize for drama in Athens
431 Peloponnesian War Athens vs. Sparta
begins
404 End of Peloponnesian War

406 Erechtheion completed on Athens
Acropolis
399 Trial and execution of Socrates

356 Birth of Alexander the Great

c.350 Theatre at sanctuary of Asklepius,
Epidaurus
342 Aristotle begins as tutor to Alexander
338 Philip II of Macedon defeats Athens
and Thebes
336 Alexander the Great becomes king of
Macedon
332 Alexander Conquers Egypt, founds
Alexandria
331 Final Collapse of Persian Empire
330 Alexander in Persepolis

322 End of Athenian Democracy
320-310 Hermes of Praxitiles, Olympia,
Greece
312-15 Arch of Constantine, Rome
307 Epicurus founds school of Philosophy
in Athens
301 Battle of Ipsus. Lysimachus defeats
Antigonus

ia

c.220 Epigonus creates *The dying Gaul* for
Pergamon

HISTORICAL EVENTS IN
W. ANATOLIA

188 Romans defeat Antiochus III at
Magnesia
c. 175 Altar of Zeus built in Pergamon

Roman Rule 133 BCE – 306 CE
133 Attalus III bequeaths his empire to Rome
85 Aphrodisias sides with Rome against
Mithridates
41 Mark Antony & Cleopatra in Ephesus
31 Harbour Monument Miletus commem-
morates Octavian's defeat of Mark Antony
at Actium

Dates CE
17 Sardis damaged by earthquake
20 Sebasteion in Aphrodisias begun
22 Major earthquake in Ephesus
57 CE St. Paul visits Miletus
53/4 St. Paul lives in Ephesus

• The *Revelation* sent to the seven churches
of Asia

84 CE Frontinus Gate and Street Hierapolis
100 Population of Ephesus 200,000
117 Library of Celsus Ephesus
124 Hadrian visits Anatolia, Temple of
Aphrodite, Aphrodisias
125 Herodes Atticus
129-161 Galen, physician Pergamon
c. 160 Baths of Faustina Ephesus
160 The Market Gate, Miletus
c. 200 Synagogue created in Sardis baths,
Temple of Apollo Hierapolis
262 Temple of Artemis, Ephesus destroyed
by earthquake

Byzantine Empire 330-1453 CE

Church in Laodicea

431 Ecumenical Council, Ephesus; Martyrium of St. Philip Hierapolis
565 Church of St John Ephesus finished

Cathedral of Hierapolis

THE HELLENIC WORLD
& BEYOND

c. 190 Nike of Samothrace

Eumenes II builds Stoa of Attalos in Athens
146 Greece comes under Roman Rule

44-476 CE Roman Empire

27 BCE – 180 CE Pax Romana

c.15 Augustus Primaporta (statue). 13-9 Ara
Pacis Rome

Birth of Christ

63/64 Romans conquer Judea and Syria
79 Destruction of Pompeii by Mount
Vesuvius
c. 70/90 St. John writes the *Revelation* on
Patmos
72-80 The Colosseum in Rome
81 Arch of Titus, Rome
106-13 Forum and column of Trajan, Rome
118 The Pantheon, Rome built by Hadrian

160 Theatre of Herodes Atticus, Athens

302 Diocletian consults oracle, persecutes
Christians
313 Edict of Milan. Constantine legalizes
Christianity

324-330 Foundation of Constantinople
325 Council of Nicea
395 Partition of Roman Empire, Byzantine
Emperor Theodosius forbids non-Christian
worship

525-565 Justinian Emperor in Constantinople
532-537 Hagia Sophia built in Constantinople